FROM BAROQUE TO STORM AND STRESS
1720–1775

FROM BAROQUE TO STORM AND STRESS 1720-1775

FRIEDHELM RADANDT

CROOM HELM LONDON

BARNES & NOBLE BOOKS · NEW YORK
(a division of Harper & Row Publishers, Inc.)

© 1977 Friedhelm Radandt
Croom Helm Ltd, 2–10 St John's Road, London SW11

ISBN 0-85664-351-3

Published in the U.S.A. 1977 by
HARPER & ROW PUBLISHERS, INC.
BARNES & NOBLE IMPORT DIVISION
ISBN 0-06-495760-8
LC 76-42159

Printed in Great Britain by Biddles Ltd, Guildford, Surrey

CONTENTS

Acknowledgements

Abbreviations

1 The Philosophical Features of the Age of Enlightenment in   12
  Germany

    I The Determining Factors: A Diversity of Approaches   12
    II A New Reading Public   13
    III The Philosophical Assumptions   16
    IV The Historical Background   19

2 Rationalism and Classicism   24

    I New Approaches   24
    II New Norms: Gottsched   41

3 Sentimentalism and the Spirit of Rococo   50

    I The Challenge from Switzerland: Bodmer and Breitinger   50
    II The Challenge from Germany   54
    III Diversity in Drama: Krüger and Weisse   69
    IV Diversity in Poetry   72
    V The Use of Satire: Liscow, Rabner and Zachariae   83

4 New Standards   88

    I Klopstock and the Development of Lyric Poetry   88
    II Wieland and the Development of the Novel   96
    III Lessing and the Development of Drama   106

5 Sturm und Drang   126

    I A Change in Direction   126
    II Young Goethe   140
    III Fascination with the Stage   155
    IV Drawn to Nature: the 'Göttinger Hain'   173
    V A Critical Look at the Period: Lichtenburg   181

Bibliography   186

Index   203

ACKNOWLEDGEMENTS

I should like to thank here Dr George J. Metcalf, University of Chicago, and Professor Vincent R. Kling, Lake Forest College, for their careful reading of the manuscript in its early stages. Their thoughtful and detailed suggestions brought about many improvements in the text and in the presentation of the material. I am grateful too to the general editors of the series, Dr R. T. Llewellyn, Christ's College, Cambridge, and Professor Kenneth J. Northcott, University of Chicago, for their critical comments from the perspective of the entire series. Several revisions and additions, most of them completed early in 1976, go back to their questions and comments.

Lake Forest, Illinois   F. K. Radandt
April 1976

ABBREVIATIONS

DLE   Deutsche Literatur in Entwicklungsreihen
DNL   Deutsche National-Literatur
DU   Deutschunterricht
DVLG   Deutsche Vierteljahresschrift für Literatur- und
               Geistesgeschichte
EdL   Epochen der deutschen Lyrik
GLL   German Life and Letters
GQ   German Quarterly
GR   Germanic Review
GRM   Germanisch-Romanische Monatsschrift
JEGP   Journal of English and Germanic Philology
LY   Lessing Yearbook
MLN   Modern Language Notes
MLQ   Modern Language Quarterly
MLR   Modern Language Review
PMLA   Periodical of the Modern Language Association
ZDP   Zeitschrift für deutsche Philologie
ZfdA   Zeitschrift für deutsches Altertum

1 THE PHILOSOPHICAL FEATURES OF THE AGE OF ENLIGHTENMENT IN GERMANY

I The Determining Factors: A Diversity of Approaches

Despite the ambiguity of the terms 'Enlightenment' and *Aufklärung* as labels designating a cultural epoch of the eighteenth century, their widespread use suggests that they are still serviceable. Cultural historians have used these words to describe the period that began with the lawyer, philosopher and pedagogue Christian Thomasius in the 1680s and which reached its peak with the popularity of Christian Wolff in the 1730s and 1740s. The literary Enlightenment in Germany produced its first works in the 1720s, when Brockes published his collection of poems entitled *Irdisches Vergnügen in GOtt*, and achieved its greatest impact by the dominance of such influential authors as Wieland and Lessing from the 1750s to the 1770s. In a narrow sense, the Enlightenment encompasses those figures in the eighteenth century who acknowledged the autonomy of reason, and hence of the individual, and who sought to apply reason to all areas of human existence by using literature didactically, with a view to educating as many people as possible. But 'Enlightenment' is also a designation for the entire age, an age which was as little uniform in its goals and beliefs as any other.

The term 'Enlightenment' is frequently equated with a strict and exclusive rationalism. Yet it is well to remember that Pietism, so often presented merely as fervent religious enthusiasm, was indeed a significant and representative cultural force throughout the period and an integral part of the philosophical age. Philip Jakob Spener (1635–1705) had started the Pietistic movement just before the turn of the century, and August Hermann Francke (1662–1727) developed its social and educational institutions in Halle. But it was Count Nikolaus von Zinzendorf (1700–1760) – he offered the Moravian Brethren refuge on his estate near Leipzig and thus founded the *Herrenhuter Brüdergemeinde* – whose brand of Pietism had the strongest and most lasting effect on the eighteenth century, ethically, psychologically, and aesthetically.[1] To a degree Enlightenment philosophy and Pietism pursue similar aims. Both have a strong desire to educate; both provide an important impetus to the emergence of an intellectually independent middle-class society; both are essentially Protestant in nature and allegiance and therefore particularly strong in the northern parts of Germany as well as in

German-speaking Switzerland; both disagree with theologically orthodox dogmatism; both strive for clarity in the German language and both accentuate the absoluteness of strict moral and ethical codes. Thought and feeling are not such mutually exclusive regions in the eighteenth century as they are often said to be. Thomasius, referred to by many as the father of the German Enlightenment, was not only a rationalistic philosopher, but, at least at times, also a devout Pietist. This same blend of rationalistic and sentimental tendencies is noticeable in a number of writers of the age, in Brockes, Haller, Gellert, and Wieland, to name only a few.

Enlightenment does not only pertain to a historical period in the eighteenth century; its practitioners viewed it above all as a mental attitude or outlook on life. The influential bookseller and philosophical author Friedrich Nicolai (1733–1811), who helped make Berlin a center of Enlightenment culture, talks about this attitude in his novel *Das Leben und die Meinungen des Herrn Magister Sebaldus Nothanker* (1773–1776). The Leipzig bookdealer Hieronymus, one of the novel's minor characters, finds confirmation of the spread of Enlightenment attitudes in the fact that fewer worthless books were sold: 'Ich liebe die Aufklärung des menschlichen Geschlechts; sie fängt auch an, sich bei uns zu zeigen. . . . Ich merke seit einiger Zeit, dass in meiner Vaterstadt verschiedene schlechte Bücher, die ich sonst oft verkauft habe, liegenbleiben, und freue mich darüber.'[2] Hieronymus lives his philosophy by placing his desire to educate the public above his financial interests. When Immanuel Kant (1724–1804) looked back on the century in 1784 and defined the meaning of Enlightenment he summarized the effect which the 'enlightened' age had had on its cultural and social structures. Changes had taken place because the idealistic tenets of the movement had provided the intellectual base upon which man could feel free to use reason as his highest mental asset: 'Aufklärung ist der Ausgang des Menschen aus seiner selbstverschuldeten Unmündigkeit . . . . Sapere aude! Habe Mut, dich deines eigenen Verstandes zu bedienen! ist also der Wahlspruch der Aufklärung.'[3] Only three years before, in 1781, the philosopher from Königsberg in East Prussia had published his important treatise on human reason, *Von der Kritik der reinen Vernunft*. That, incidentally, was the same year in which Lessing died, who as dramatist and critic *par excellence* had attracted a great deal of attention because it was felt that he had lived by Kant's dictum. Nor is it surprising to discover that if reason was a watchword in the eighteenth century it was important not only to the so-called rationalists, but also to the Pietists.

Their point was, of course, that the fall of man had thrust human reason into darkness and that only divine illumination could renew its power and reliability. The term 'Aufklärung' was coined to express the period's faith in the clarifying effect of the light of reason; 'Erleuchtung' was used by the mystics and religious enthusiasts to stress that God is the source of the light of knowledge. To them the value of human reason was confirmed by its ability to test and certify feelings. Count Zinzendorf argued that intuition and religious enthusiasm must be checked against rational probing, for the process of reasoning must determine the value and appropriateness of any insight gained intuitively: 'Fühlen wird durch Prüfen *just*.'[4] In another context the Count states this principle again: 'Ein jeglicher Satz, der zugleich einer freyen und unbenebelten Überlegung natürlich und klar ist, von einem unaffectirten Verstande gebilliget, und von einer freyen und ungebundenen Einbildungs-Kraft gefühlet wird, der ist wahr.'[5] Such a viewpoint underscores the fact that rationalists and Pietists were, indeed, contemporaries, but ones with very different values and priorities, which often enough caused tension between them.

The Pietists did not acknowledge the autonomy of reason, and that issue prompted them to force Wolff's expulsion as a university professor from Halle in 1723, when the dominance of Pietism in that city was strongest. This action pointed up the irreconcilable nature of the conflict between the German Enlightenment philosophy with its deistic trends on the one hand, and the Pietistic movement with its emphasis on personal divine illumination on the other, in spite of any aims which they had in common. The most pronounced feature of the German Enlightenment philosophically was its preoccupation with theological issues, especially its attempt to formulate its concept of God.[6] The desire to prove the greatness of God was a dominating motif in Leibniz's and Wolff's philosophy. The correlative to this theological concern is their avowed aim to instill in the individual person a sense of moral responsibility. As rationalists they relied on reason to formulate moral principles, whereas the Pietists derived those principles from divine revelation.

II A New Reading Public

The Enlightenment was an intensely pragmatic age in its belief that truths arrived at by reason could be applied to govern all aspects of human existence, down to the smallest detail of everyday life. It was an axiom of this period that sufficient rational insight would enable man to develop reasonable forms of government; to engage in reasonable

religious activity; to formulate reasonable ethical standards; to learn to
refrain from vice through reasonable teachings; to instill artistic taste
through reasonable aesthetic formulations; and even to learn to write
poetry by following reasonable rules. The self-confidence implied in
this willingness to subject existing knowledge and traditions to the
scrutiny of rational criteria also implies a willingness to change. And
the changes that did in fact occur in the intellectual sphere were
mirrored by changes that the social structure was undergoing. The
emerging middle class was rapidly acquiring a sophistication that
enabled it to appreciate new ideas and new literary directions. The
message of the Enlightenment addressed chiefly this new middle class,
particularly in Protestant northern Germany and German-speaking
Switzerland, where there were fewer potential conflicts between
inherited religion and the new philosophical concept than in Catholic
regions.[7]

The Enlightenment was accepted relatively quickly because its
optimism and stress on independence provided the Protestant middle
class with a high degree of needed self-assurance. The concerns of the
overtly philosophical age included the intellectual and moral life of the
individual, the question of the role of knowledge and problems of
aesthetic values. While the new literature was both partially a sign and
partially a cause of social change, it did not directly advocate alterations
in the structure of society. Nor was it basically political. Rather, it
addressed social and political questions chiefly from the standpoint of
their applicability to aspects of middle-class life. Abstract political
theorizing would have seemed beside the point because political power
was concentrated in the hands of the nobility at the courts and was
thus not subject to change by discussion from the outside. Literature
was seen as the major vehicle for acquainting the middle class with the
new ideas, because literature, it was argued, relies on images for con-
veying meaning, and images are understood more easily than abstract
thought. Inherent in the Enlightenment belief in universal improvability
was the impetus to find a means whereby the new truths would be
most tellingly presented to a public which could not be assumed to have
had a systematic university education. A vital new form of publication,
modified from English models, was devised to interest readers in
literature and to instruct them in understanding and judging it. Weekly
periodicals, known as 'moralische Wochenschriften', achieved great
popularity as soon as they began to appear. Almost all important poets
and playwrights of the period made use of the opportunity to popularize
their ideas through the medium of the moral weekly.[8]

The first moral weekly which appeared in Germany was billed as offering excerpts from its two famous English predecessors, *The Tatler* (1709–11), and *The Spectator* (1711–12; 1714). Johann Mattheson (1681–1764) began his literary career with the publication of *Der Vernünftler* (1713–1714) in Hamburg. *Der Vernünftler* found followers in the Zurich publication *Die Discourse der Mahlern* (1721–1723), edited by Bodmer and Breitinger, and in the important journal *Der Patriot* (1724–1726), also appearing in Hamburg, and written by Brockes. The genre quickly became popular. Martens estimates that some 110 different moral weeklies were published in eighteenth-century Germany.[9] Like their English predecessors, most German moral weeklies were in existence for only a short time, about two or three years on average. Those writers who put out a moral weekly usually contributed all the articles themselves. They wrote about religious, philosophical and literary topics, but did not publish their creative literary works in them. The definition of a moral weekly did not permit that. However, moral weeklies could and did make value judgements about literature, for instance, often enough warning their readers against novels, which were thought to engage the imagination in idle speculation. Only gradually did the novel become an accepted form of literature in the eighteenth century. Moral weeklies also told the reader how to watch plays performed, and what to learn from them. There was general agreement that one of the theater's functions was to teach about virtue and vice. The relative importance of the ethical objectives and purely aesthetic issues was a matter of continual debate throughout the period. The major theater reforms that were accomplished during the thirties and forties were prompted by the desire to utilize the didactic opportunities inherent in theater. The theater which these reforms had in mind was based on the French drama with its emphasis on classicistic regularity.

The moral weeklies not only increased the number of middle-class readers, but also refined their sensibility through the discussion of taste in literary matters. Dramatists now began portraying in their plays middle-class characters who were readers of literature and who were knowledgeable about literary trends. The author's sympathy lay with these figures, who were usually young, and often women. To a large degree, the moral weeklies made the particular development of German literature in the eighteenth century possible, and their appearance demonstrates that this literature was written for a new public, one which was open to moralizing and didacticism. Their contributions were most significant during the first three decades of Enlightenment literature, from about 1720 to 1750.

III The Philosophical Assumptions

The university professor Christian Thomasius (1655–1728) broke with tradition when he announced in 1687 that he would lecture in German instead of the usual Latin. This decision was his way of putting into practice the belief that knowledge should be made available to a larger audience, and that the vernacular would be useful in disseminating it. The French with their pride in their language had inspired Thomasius to take such a daring step.[10] The implied patriotism to which Thomasius was thereby appealing was cultural rather than political, since Germany was merely a collection of many small states and not a political entity. He reinforced his convinctions about the value of German culture when he published, also in German, the journal *Monatsgespräche* (1688–1690), in which he reviewed current books and discussed philosophical topics. Thomasius' efforts to increase the use of German at the university were not immediately successful. It took two decades before others started publishing periodicals in German, or before Christian Wolff prepared his glossary of German technical philosophical terms. There were other ways in which Thomasius paved the road for Enlightenment culture in Germany. In Leipzig, where he was giving the German lecture series and publishing the *Monatsgespräche*, he came to the legal defense of the Pietists. When they were ordered to leave the city he too was expelled and went with them to Halle. The exodus of the Pietist Francke and his followers from Leipzig, in 1690, had consequences which were to affect the cultural scene of Germany during the Enlightenment significantly. The Pietists relocated in Halle, Prussia — a state that was just beginning its rise to political prominence. Soon after their arrival Halle became a university town (1694), and thus a major academic center in Prussia, a fact all the more significant because Berlin, the capital of Prussia and a center of Enlightenment culture in Germany, had no university. It was ironic that Thomasius, who had aided the Pietists in Leipzig, began moving in a different direction and finally broke with them in Halle. Around the turn of the century he read the works of John Locke, especially his *An Essay Concerning Human Understanding*, in French translation. Locke, a champion of empirical observation, had insisted on the sufficiency of practical reason, and put less emphasis on the need for so-called speculative philosophy. He had argued also against religious enthusiasm (in the fourth edition of his *Essay* in 1699) because it tends to ignore common sense and empirical knowledge. After his encounter with Locke,

Thomasius laid increasingly greater stress on rationalistic tenets in his writings. He exemplified the use of 'practical reason' in his convincing and effective attacks on witch-hunts and the use of torture, and when he refuted the common belief in apparitions of the devil.[11]

The pragmatism of the age was a direct reflection of a posture that sought to transfer philosophical assumptions to everyday life. In the process philosophy gained a position of considerable popularity, if by popularity we mean a growing general interest in the ideas of Rationalism and its proponents. Gottfried Wilhelm Leibniz (1646–1716), demonstrating Baroque mentality when he chose the life-long career of councilor, philosopher and librarian in the service of the princes of Brunswick-Lüneburg, at their court in Hanover, was to become the first and foremost representative of German Enlightenment philosophy. His goal was to examine and explain the relationship between physics and metaphysics. Rationalism as a mode of philosophical thinking had grown out of an appreciation for the clarity that marked scientific thought, particularly mathematics and physics. That clarity had prompted Descartes, the 'father of modern philosophy', to construct a philosophical system on the assumption that our world was created as a rational order. Philosophy then no longer was to serve theology, but rather to bring into harmony the scientific understanding of the world with the theological interpretation of human life. Leibniz made this his major task. The Dutch biographer van Peursen speaks of Leibniz's 'attempt to make transparent . . . the perplexities of human knowledge and the incongruencies of reality, with the question it poses regarding infinitesimal elements, the source of truth and the significance of evil, within a grand *"ars combinatoria"*.'[12] Leibniz was singularly qualified to undertake such a gigantic task because of his thorough knowledge of theology, but even more so because as a youth he had made a conscious decision to study mathematics, in which he excelled, formulating the basis for calculus. The mathematician Leibniz, however, had found that ultimately the laws of mathematics could be explained only by having recourse to metaphysical speculation.[13]

Leibniz desired to harmonize the mechanistic world view with a theological concept of God as a personal God. As a rationalist he postulated the fact of such harmony, but he also knew that he needed to be able to explain it. Before he could do so he had to provide an answer to the question of the existence of evil in a deterministic world. Leibniz did not accept the deistic point of view which saw in God the kind creator — with that part he agreed — yet rejected a God who would punish man. The problem of theodicy had to be solved as part of

Leibniz's task. Creation to him was the result of God's free choice. The created world, therefore, was one of many designs from which God had chosen the best of all possible worlds, not the perfect one. In this world man too has freedom of choice and is not simply determined by mechanistic laws to do evil. Leibniz deals with this subject in his famous *Essais de Theodicée* (1710), written, as the title suggests, in French.[14]

Leibniz based his mechanistic world view on the concept of monads, an expression of the philosopher's firm faith in the individuality of being. Monads were to define that unit which was truly indivisible, like the human soul to which he compared it. He chose the term 'monad' in preference to 'atom' because the latter does not constitute the truly indivisible unit, whereas the word 'monad' suggests just that. Leibniz's monads are material as well as spiritual in substance, for both matter and spirit ultimately were created by God, the first monad. The theory of monads thus reinforces and reiterates indirectly Leibniz's conviction that all mechanistic laws must be traced to their metaphysical origin. Since all monads derive their existence from God, they also have received their individual laws from God, and their development occurs according to these laws. Together, these individual laws of all monads are parts of the total harmony which Leibniz postulated. The theory of monads and the theodicy as he had formulated it led to the often quoted principle of a pre-established harmony between body and soul, used to disprove any direct influence of the spiritual on the material, yet acknowledging a relationship between the two.

Christian Wolff (1679–1754), like Thomasius, had embarked on his professorial career in Leipzig and then moved on to Halle. He took over many of the ideas of Gottfried Wilhelm Leibniz, and, what is more significant for the growth of German literature, organized the totality of Enlightenment thought into a system of philosophical knowledge which covered all aspects of human existence. The question of the arts and their function was part of the system. Thus, Wolff's complex work offered itself to the literary critics as a base on which they could construct their views about content, forms and genres. From the standpoint of the development of literature, Wolff's contributions came mainly as a result of his own philosophical system, and only in part because of his role as interpreter of Leibniz's ideas. It is true that Leibniz's theory of a pre-established harmony between body and soul has become so well known largely because Wolff propagated it. The illustration Leibniz used to prove the theory, more than the theory as such, accounts for its enormous popularity with Wolff and his contemporaries. The example of two clocks that run exactly alike because a talented clockmaker constructed them with perfect precision, seemed to attach particular importance and praise to the clockmaker – God. In that way the theory strengthened the theological interest that was characteristic of the German *Aufklärung*. In Wolff's rational world order God is explained as the purest and most perfect form of reason. Wolff's major treatise, *Vernünftige Gedanken von Gott, der Welt und der Seele des Menschen* (1719), contains his metaphysical thought. It is a defense of the creative power of reason, a concept which was fundamental to much of Enlightenment literature. Just as God had 'thought out' the best of all possible worlds, so must the artist construct a world that is based on reason. The delight the reader takes in such literary works results from the realization that their rational order and logical sequence of events reflect the same order that underlies all human existence.

Wolff's expulsion from Halle, during the rule of Frederick William I, came at the instigation of the Pietists there. They resented his assertion of the complete reliability of human reason in matters of ethics, because this tenet ignored the need for divine revelation in determining what is morally right and wrong. Frederick the Great, soon after his ascension to the Prussian throne in 1740, reinstated Wolff in Halle. The action was as much a tribute to Wolff's popularity as a demonstration of tolerance and 'enlightened' attitudes on the part of a king who enjoyed the company of philosophers and scientists. What Thomasius had hoped philosophy would do, namely help young people become polished citizens, had in large measure come about. Philosophy had become a pervasive force in shaping the cultural life of the century.

IV The Historical Background

Eighteenth-century culture in Germany is a result of a number of conflicting circumstances: on the one hand the continuance of a system of political fragmentation, highlighted in the existence of many, usually very small states with a desire for displaying power in Baroque splendor; the predominance of Baroque features in architecture and music; the presence of a powerful orthodox clergy, in habit, dress, language and general philosophy oriented towards the Baroque. This was compounded by the emergence of a strong and self-confident middle class, a fact which is underscored by the establishment of theater in such cities as Hamburg, Mannheim, Berlin; the defining and proclaiming of Enlightenment ideals in literary endeavors; the fast growth of Pietistic groups – often outside of the regular orthodox churches – with their emphasis on feeling, and the growing number of heterodox theologians inside the official church, sympathizing with the rationalists' philosophy. Because the Enlightenment is an age of transition, the cultural topography of Germany at this time appears as a mixed landscape in which Baroque mentality and Enlightenment attitude live side by side, although more and more in conflict with each other. The Enlightenment gains its self-image out of such conflict.

Enlightenment authors have captured the phenomena of transition and conflict most effectively through careful use of language, for example, pompous and involved Baroque sentence structure when orthodox ministers are portrayed. Numerous authors enjoy imitating this stilted language. Nicolai's *Nothanker* may once again serve as an example. The pastor who is to take over the demoted Nothanker's house explains his sense of urgency: ' . . . sintemal ich in dem Herrn entschlossen bin, mein Amt unverzüglich anzutreten, und zu dem Ende noch anheute auf meine nächstens zu haltende Antrittspredigt zu studieren.'[15] The same authors employ relatively limpid speech patterns when the representatives of the new age state their views. The period was conscious of such linguistic achievements, so much so that Count Zinzendorf, who as a young man edited the moral weekly *Der Teutsche Sokrates* in Dresden, said with some pride about Pietism's contribution to the period: 'Wir haben es in Europa so weit gebracht, dass wir eine ganz neue Sprache haben.'[16] He meant that the new language was capable of describing accurately the nuances of feelings and emotions, and that it avoided what by now were considered the clichés of Baroque poetry. Enlightenment literature in general strove for clarity and simplicity in language because it wanted to disassociate itself from the Baroque era, its society and its political complacency at the courts. Architecture and music, especially the opera, were much more dependent on financial support from a court than was literature. The literary artist could afford to be independent of the court where he desired to be so.

Literature more than any other form of art spread the ideals of the new age. Friedrich Nicolai's novel is a textbook of these ideals, and for that reason is of considerable interest to the student of the social and cultural history of eighteenth-century Germany. Set during and immediately following the Seven Years' War (1756–1763), the novel portrays quite comprehensively and perceptively the cultural and social forces of the time, critically judging the much-heralded achievements of the Enlightenment. By building the plot around the experiences of a heterodox theologian who is removed from his parish ministry by his orthodox and cold superior, and who spends the remainder of his life journeying through Germany defending and articulating his theological views, Nicolai has ample opportunity to describe culture and society in such leading cities as Leipzig and Berlin, as well as in small towns and villages. In the course of events the reader is introduced to the life of the small court nobility, which is faulted for its exclusive devotion to good food, in this case German delicacies which are praised at the expense of French cooking. Nicolai supports things German and deplores the dependence of French models, a posture which had become the norm by the early 1770s. While at first the German Enlightenment pointed to and even imitated French achievements in literature and general culture, the movement grew increasingly patriotic and developed its own distinct characteristics and themes. The novel describes in some detail the society of Berlin, the German city with a reputation for tolerance and enlightened views. Berlin's citizens, under the immediate influence of the Prussian court, practiced religious tolerance, but only in response to Frederick the Great's orders. Nicolai, himself one of Berlin's famous citizens of the period, finds it difficult to refrain from a slightly ironic depiction of the society in that city. In describing the Sunday afternoon peripatetic middle class — the emphasis on middle and lower-middle class is easily noticeable and is in itself a significant expression of a new emphasis — he criticizes their rather bourgeois values and limitations. Sebaldus discovers how virtually impossible it is for a teacher of philosophy to earn his livelihood in Berlin.[17] Nicolai concludes that Berlin's reputation as a successful center of Enlightenment culture and ideals is justified only to a degree and only by comparison with other cities or areas in Germany.

The image of the Prussian court throughout Europe was not merely one of political and military strength. It was one also of moral strength and high ideals, where reason rather than tradition ruled and where the court did not exist for its own glory. Yet the Prussian court under Frederick the Great, its ablest representative, looked toward France for formulating Enlightenment philosophy and for producing Enlightenment works of literature. Frederick even brought Voltaire to Berlin for a while. Thus it was an irony that the court which was hailed most in Germany for its enlightened stance displayed little interest in the development of German literature. Frederick the Great's general contempt for the accomplishments of German authors and poets is well known.[18] Nevertheless, it was the remarkable personality of this Prussian king that inspired many a poet in Prussia and throughout Germany. Young Goethe's assertion that Frederick the Great was a unifying figure, especially in the eyes of young writers, helps us understand the influential role of the most progressive Enlightenment ruler in Germany. The king who worked hard and who saw himself as the first servant of his state came to stand for Germany as a whole. The contrast between the majority of the German courts, where the rulers lived primarily to enjoy a good life with little interest in their subjects,[19] and Prussia, where under Frederick the Great's father, Frederick William I, who ruled from 1713–1740, luxury was unknown, is unmistakable. In Maria Theresa's Austria, reforms were not introduced until after 1750.

However, the courts were also centers of culture. Many continued to devote a good portion of their resources to the arts — in Baroque fashion staging elaborate operas and accumulating impressive art collections — often motivated by a sense of competition. Since the majority of principalities were too small to have their own industry, the cost of maintaining a lavish court life left many states poor. The annals of the period are not without social criticism of these aspects of the system of political absolutism. When Gottsched spoke out against the opera he criticized, at least indirectly, the extravagances at the courts. Such criticism became more vocal in the writings of the *Sturm und Drang*. The praise for Frederick the Great's personal interest in the industrial and agricultural well-being of Prussia and its people — he was successful, too, in building a strong general educational system — was, as well, a form of criticism of other rulers.

From this perspective it is not difficult to see why Enlightenment culture, especially literature, developed independently of and separately from the cultural life at the courts. Its centers were Hamburg, the wealthy merchants' town, Berlin, a growing city with a sizable population of Protestant immigrants from France, Leipzig, so often referred to as the German Paris, and Zurich, the intellectually active Swiss city. Königsberg in East Prussia was to play an increasingly important role, especially during the beginning *Sturm und Drang*, as were Frankfort and Strasbourg, and also the small university town of Göttingen.

Notes

1.   Marianne Beyer-Fröhlich summarizes her impressions of Zinzendorf's contributions to the age in *DLE, Reihe: Deutsche Selbstzeugnisse*, I, 161: 'Am stärksten von allen hat Zinzendorf auf das spätere 18. Jahrhundert gewirkt: ethisch hinsichtlich des Toleranzgedankens . . . psychologisch in der Seelenanalyse . . . ästhetisch in einer neuen . . . Sprache, deren Wortschatz dem Schrifttum der sentimentalischen Epoche zugute gekommen ist.'
2.   *DLE, Reihe: Aufklärung*, XV, 71.

3.   Immanuel Kant, *Werke*, ed. Ernst Cassirer (Berlin, 1922), IV, 169. It should be noted that the exhortation to rely on one's own powers of reason was taken from an inscription that appeared on a coin in 1736, a special coin of the Societas Aletophilorum struck in honor of Leibniz and Wolff whose portraits were printed on it.

4.   Quoted after K. A. Varnhagen von Ense, *Leben des Grafen von Zinzendorf* (Berlin, 1830), p. 467.

5.   *Der Teutsche Sokrates*, 2nd ed. (Leipzig, 1732), pp. 293–94, in Zinzendorf, *Hauptschriften*, ed. E. Beyreuther and G. Meyer (Hildesheim, 1962), I.

6.   See Fritz Brüggemann, *DLE, Reihe: Aufklärung*, II, 7; and XV, 8–10; and John Herman Randall, *The Career of Philosophy* (New York, 1962), II, 52: 'As the chief intellectual concern in Germany remained religion and theology . . . .'

7.   Only after Maria Theresa had lost in war against Prussia, in the early 1740s, did the principles of enlightened absolutism, as they were practiced in Berlin, find growing acceptance in Vienna. See Adam Wandruszka, in Emil Ermatinger, *Deutsche Kultur im Zeitalter der Aufklärung*, Handbuch der Kulturgeschichte (Frankfort, 1969), p. 11.

8.   Wolfgang Martens, *Die Botschaft der Tugend: Die Aufklärung im Spiegel der deutschen Wochenschriften* (Stuttgart, 1971), has analyzed in detail the significant contribution of the moral weeklies in helping the philosophical Enlightenment gain acceptance in Germany, and in preparing the middle class for Enlightenment literature.

9.   Martens, p. 162. This valuable treatise on the phenomenon of the moral weeklies in Germany provided much of the information here reported.

10.   See Isaiah Berlin, *The Age of Enlightenment* (Boston, 1957), pp. 30–112; also *DLE, Reihe: Aufklärung*, I, 109–21.

11.   See Robert Spaethling, 'On Christian Thomasius and his Alleged Offspring', *LY*, IV, 194–213.

12.   C. A. van Peursen, *Leibniz* (New York, 1970), pp. 12–13. The phrase *ars combinatoria* was the title of Leibniz's Master's degree thesis.

13.   Van Peursen, ibid., p. 17, quotes Leibniz as saying that it proved impossible for him to ground the foundations of mechanics and of the laws of motion in mathematics, and that he had to revert to metaphysics.

14.   In 1679 Leibniz published his *Ermahnung an die Deutschen*, and in 1697 his *Unvorgreifliche Gedanken betreffend die Ausübung und Verbesserung der deutschen Sprache*. There was a discrepancy in the fact that he had called upon the Germans to use their intellect and their language more carefully, yet he himself wrote mainly in French. As a consequence, his ideas became known only gradually in Germany, mainly through interpretation by others. They proved to be no less effective.

15.   *DLE, Reihe: Aufklärung*, XV, 40.

16.   Quoted after Erich Beyreuther, *Studien zur Theologie Zinzendorfs*, (Neukirchen, 1962), p. 73.

17.   See book four of the novel.

18.   See his account of the contemporary literary scene in his *De la littérature allemande*, 1790. He expressed his belief that German literature would have a great future, but he did not acknowledge its achievements in the present.

19.   See the full account in W. H. Bruford, *Germany in the Eighteenth Century: The Social Background of the Literary Revival* (Cambridge, 1935), part I.

2 RATIONALISM AND CLASSICISM

I New Approaches

1 *Brockes*

Whereas the Hamburg poet Barthold Heinrich Brockes (1680–1747) appears to some a precursor of the Enlightenment, we see in him the first major literary figure of that movement and of the eighteenth century. If, as has often been asserted, the beginnings of modernity lie in the eighteenth century, Brockes was more modern than Johann Günther.[1] Even though he was fifteen years older than Günther, he removed himself more from the previous Baroque era sensibility. Brockes, who except for his student days spent his entire life in or near his native Hamburg, began his literary career around 1708, or probably somewhat earlier, writing a few original pieces in French and Italian, but mainly translating poems from these languages into German.[2] The philosopher Thomasius had been his teacher in Halle (1700–1702) at a time when Thomasius was leaning strongly towards Pietism, a fact which may have decisively shaped Brockes's development. The young student also took the usual, more or less required, 'educational tour' of Europe (Italy, Switzerland, France, the Netherlands), and obtained a law degree in 1704 at the University of Leyden before embarking on a career as poet and civil servant. His government service included positions as senator in Hamburg (1720), ambassador to Vienna and Copenhagen, magistrate of the small town of Ritzebüttel on the Elbe river, and even what we would now term superintendent of schools in that town. Basically, however, he devoted himself to literary matters. His financial independence made this possible, but his deeper motivation arose from his belief that a life of contemplation of the beautiful in nature was the best road to virtue and superior to a life of constant activity and striving.[3] Following the model of the seventeenth-century 'Sprachgesellschaften' Brockes founded a literary society in 1715, which was aimed at raising the general level of culture by improving the quality of literary works in German and by consciously developing German as a literary language. Accordingly, the members of this society, appropriately named *Teutschübende Gesellschaft*, met to read to each other from their own works. Brockes himself published in the same year his *Verdeutschter Bethlehemitischer Kindermord*, an adaptation of

the Italian Marino's *Strage degl'Innocenti* of 1620, an indication how
much the young Brockes still was part of the Baroque. In the Baroque
tradition is also the passion-oratorio *Der für die Sünden der Welt
gemarterte und sterbende Jesu* (1712), which was set to music several
times, including by Telemann in 1716, and by Handel in 1717. And it
was just as characteristic of the Baroque tendency to glorify one's own
ego that Brockes had this oratorio performed in his house before five
hundred guests, with the expressed intention of wanting to impress.

From the point of view of German literary history Georg Philip
Telemann's (1681–1767) setting of Brockes's passion-oratorio proved
to be of considerable import. This famous and prolific eighteenth-
century composer would continue to set Brockes's verse to music,
especially after his move to Hamburg, in 1721, as director of church
music of that city. Here he met the first two representatives of German
Enlightenment literature, Brockes and Hagedorn. As Brockes achieved
changes in the style and content of his poetry that removed him from
other Baroque poets, so did Telemann leave behind the world of
Baroque formalism. It may not be possible to determine whether his
living in Hamburg and his acquaintance with Brockes had anything to
do with that change. His trip to Paris certainly influenced him greatly.
Nevertheless, the fact that these changes in poetry and music did take
place almost simultaneously in Hamburg is noteworthy.

Just before 1720 Brockes's poetry underwent an abrupt change. We
can assume that it was the general shift toward a new religious and
philosophical climate in the early seventeen hundreds that determined
Brockes's view of man and nature and caused him to abandon the
affected and outmoded Baroque style in favor of a lucid and rational
presentation. At any rate, when Brockes began publishing his most
famous work in 1721, *Irdisches Vergnügen in GOtt bestehend in
verschiedenen aus der Natur und Sitten-Lehre hergenommenen
Gedichten* — in later editions the title was changed slightly to the more
abstract and modern sounding *Irdisches Vergnügen in Gott, bestehend
in Physikalisch-und Moralischen Gedichten* — his chief aims appear to
have been close observation of natural phenomena and deduction from
these phenomena, through analogy, of a set of guidelines suitable for
explaining man's existence and for governing his behavior. These poems
were published in nine volumes between 1721 and 1748. With the title
Irdisches Vergnügen in Gott, Brockes seems to be pointing up a sort of
intellectual delight which results from the realization that nature is our
'Weltbuch ABC', telling us about God. The detailed and very accurate
description of what the poet actually sees in his garden, be it the garden

as a whole, or a specific flower, or an insect on the flower, or the wing
of an insect, or a view of the garden at night, invariably leads to a
feeling of contentment with one's lot in life, because that lot is
assigned by a God, whose ordering spirit is evident everywhere. Nature
is not merely the setting for extrapolated moral teaching, but is the
teacher itself. Hence we usually find in these poems first an exact,
albeit for the most not very vivid, description of nature, stressing both
its beauty and the divine wisdom manifest in the way nature works,
followed by an exhortation to delight in God's wisdom and be
satisfied with one's earthly existence. Analogy is the vehicle for
learning from nature that the discovery of beauty in God's creation
cannot compare to any other human accomplishments. The poem *Der
Goldkäfer* may serve as an example of Brockes's approach, the
description and teaching by analogy:

> Der Monat Junius beblümte Feld und Auen,
> Als ich, die Wunderpracht der Blumen zu beschauen,
> Im Garten wandern ging. Mein Söhnchen liefe mit
> Sein reger Fuss hüpft' immer hin und her
> Als er nun ungefähr
> Ein güldnes Käferchen auf einer Rose fand,
> [. . .]
> Ich lobte seinen Fund und nahm ihn lächelnd hin,
> Betrachtete mit fast erschrocknem Sinn
> Die Schönheit, Farben und Figur
> Mit welcher ihn die bildende Natur
> Begabt und ausgeziert.
> Durchs Auge ward mein Herz gerührt,
> Als ich mit höchster Lust erblickte,
> Wie ihm Smaragd und Gold den glatten Rücken schmückte,
> [. . .]
> Als ich mich lange nun an seinem Glanz ergetzet
> Und diese Schönheit hochgeschätzet,
> Verspüret' ich, wie die veränderliche Pracht
> Mich allgemach auf die Gedanken bracht':
> Was sind die Farben doch? Nichts als ein blosses Nichts;
> [. . .]
> Dies heisst mich weiter gehn und auch: Was ist die Welt?
> Was ist das Irdische, was ist die Kreatur?
> Was sind wir selber? fragen,
> Worauf mir Gottes Wort, Witz und Erfahrung sagen:

[...]
Ohne Gott, den Brunn des Lichts
Sind wir und ist alles nichts;
[...]

[*DNL* XXXIX, 307–8]

Here the analogy leads to an acknowledgement of man's utter dependence on God. But what if the analogy engenders a feeling of discontent?
In describing the crocus Brockes points to the short-lived nature of this
flower, an observation that would, of course, by way of analogy, lead to
lamenting the brevity of human life. This analogy is actually drawn, but
its potentially negative impact is obviated by a rhetorical appeal to the
underlying rationalist principle that it can never be right to lament the
natural course of events as ordained by God. In this instance, therefore,
the poet is forced *a priori* to conclude, even in contradiction to the
spontaneous feeling, that brevity of life *must* be preferable to longevity:

So muss die flüchtige Beschaffenheit
Der Dinge besser sein als die Beständigkeit.

This example shows how Brockes emerges as a stout defender of the
Enlightenment concept that our world is the best of all possible worlds.
He does not prove this concept, he postulates it, just as he postulates
God's existence. Where the limitations of human reason prevent us from
fully understanding the basic goodness of creation, feeling can be
depended upon to do the rest. In this way Brockes assigns to feeling a
positive value and uses and reconciles the principles of both Enlightenment and Pietism. This reconciliation may help to show that there was
not as sharp a division between cold intellect and spontaneous emotions
as is sometimes asserted of the early years of the eighteenth century.
Brockes does not find it difficult to unite a rather strict rationalism with
views the Pietists held, including the possibility of *rapport* with a
personal God. In particular, he espouses Johann Arnd's *Vier Bücher
vom wahren Christentum*, as Weichmann — Brockes's friend and editor
— asserts in his preface to the second part of the *Irdisches Vergnügen*.[4]
To Arnd, too, nature is a book that tells us about God. Nature is not the
ultimate object of human praise, but merely the means for spurring man
on to praise God. And this praising results in a feeling of enjoyment and
happiness. Arnd subordinates such feelings to higher religious insight,
but Brockes allows them to function as an end in themselves.
   It hardly need be emphasized that Brockes in his didacticism often

belabors the point and tires the reader. It is probably more appropriate to point to Brockes's true lyric ability, his deftness in the handling of verse and meter, and his awareness of sound. Perhaps his best-known poem, 'Kirsch-Blühte bey der Nacht', can serve as an illustration of the ease with which he writes, of the rich imagery he employs, and of his careful choice of vowels:

> Ich sahe mit betrachtendem Gemüte
> Jüngst einen Kirschbaum, welcher blüh'te,
> In küler Nacht beym Monden-Schein;
> Ich glaubt', es könne nichts von gröss'rer Weisse seyn.
> Es schien, ob wär' ein Schnee gefallen.
> Ein jeder, auch der klein'ste, Ast
> Trug gleichsam eine rechte Last
> Von zierlich-weissen runden Ballen.[5]

[*EDL*, V, 105–6]

It is a bit playful in its effect, yet serious in its intent, when he prefaces 'Die auf ein starkes Ungewitter erfolgte Stille' with the information that the 'r' sound is rather masculine and harsh and should therefore be totally avoided in describing the calm before and after the storm. He adheres to this theory throughout the poem, in fact achieving the desired sound effects. The two closing lines of the poem illustrate this theory. One line has no 'r' sound whatsoever and is intended to evoke an atmosphere of calm delight, the other using the 'r' sound deliberately to create a feeling of threatening power:

> Es ist die helle Sonn ein Bild von Gottes Liebe,
> So wie des Donners Grimm die Probe Seiner Kraft.

[*DNL* XXXIX, 330]

Brockes is rightly credited with relegating the Alexandrine verse, which had been the dominating meter in German Baroque poetry, to a much less important position. In his own poems he makes use of different meters, frequently employing the dactyl and trochee, often changing the meter within a poem, favoring the looser madrigal, yet occasionally using the Alexandrine to express his philosophical refections. It is this ability to control rhythm and sound that enables him to write some exceptionally beautiful poems, pure and subtle, moving and yet light, in his *Irdisches Vergnügen*, and this in spite of some extremely awkward lines and titles. That same quality moved the contemporary composer

Georg Philipp Telemann to set Brockes's verse to music. In fact,
Telemann praised the mastery of Brockes's nature poetry in a poem of
his own. The composer felt that the Hamburg poet's lines create in the
reader an imagined scene of beauty from nature:

> Die Andacht/so sich hier den Worten mitgetheilet/
>   Zieht meinen Blick noch mehr ins Reich der Creatur.
> Dann merk' ich/wie mein Kiel zum Componieren eilet;
>   Da such' ich/voller Brunst/die mir gezeigte Spur.[6]
>
> [*EdL*, V, 96]

In 1724 Brockes founded a second literary society, the *Patriotische
Gesellschaft*, which existed until 1748, publishing a weekly journal, *Der
Patriot*. Brockes also wrote an autobiography and continued with his
translation work. He published in translation parts of Milton's *Paradise
Lost* and Pope's *Essay on Man* (1740), and in 1745 James Thomson's
The Seasons. In part, Brockes himself, through his nature poetry, had
helped create the receptivity for the works of these English writers in
Germany. His poetry exhibits a deep kinship with Thomson's nature
poetry. It must have provided personal satisfaction to know that he
had ventured into nature poetry even before Thomson had published
The Seasons (1726). Brockes was not the only translator who introduced
contemporary English literature in Germany. Still, the fact of his translating English literature at all, and the specific selections he made from
that literature, show Brockes to be a leading figure in his time.

Brockes helped shape a new literary consciousness and style through
example — his poetry has not lost its appeal in spite of its prosaic
moralizing — and through active intervention in the literary affairs of
the age, rather in keeping with the image of an influential Hamburg
senator in the eighteenth century for whom writing poetry was much
more than a pastime. It was a means of educating the people, even of
involving them in the arts. Thus it is no accident that Hamburg, a
commercially active city with strong ties to England, plays such an
important role in the beginnings of the literary Enlightenment in
Germany. Nor is it surprising to discover that the poet who must be
considered in chronological order after Brockes is also from Hamburg.

2 *Hagedorn*

Friedrich von Hagedorn (1708–1754), especially well versed in English
philosophy and literature, brought to German poetry the kind of wit
and urbanity which were to become the most prominent attributes of

Enlightenment verse. Indeed, Hagedorn's memory lives because of his remarkable ability to write fluent poetry with a bent for the witty, something which was new and welcome in the 1730s, and which fascinated his contemporaries. An ever closer attention to formal aspects in his writing allowed him to achieve a polished smoothness which is not a merely gratuitous exercise in form.[7] Rather, the poet's technique reflects his positive view of a polished urban social structure whose order may help one to find purpose and fulfillment. Yet Hagedorn recognizes the irony whereby social approval may lead to the vanity or self-pride that undermines any sense of purpose or fulfillment. While he uses satiric wit to describe such vanity in human actions, he resolves the negative outcome inherent in satire by contrasting empty vanity with situations in which simple and unassuming wisdom prevails. Thus it is that Hagedorn's interest is not restricted to the urban and sophisticated, but encompasses also the less complex man who can find happiness even in want and satisfaction in song. Hagedorn accepts the idea of enjoyment as life's purpose without limiting this enjoyment to religious or aesthetic feelings.[8] We may, therefore, regard his song 'An die Freude' as exemplary of the general tone of his poetry. The first and the last stanzas speak of the importance of joy in human life:

> Freude, Göttin edler Herzen! Höre mich!
> Lass die Lieder, die hier schallen,
> Dich vergrössern, dir gefallen:
> Was hier tönet, tönt durch dich.

> Du erheiterst, holde Freude! Die Vernunft.
> Flieh auf ewig die Gesichter
> Aller finstern Splitterrichter
> Und die ganze Heuchlerzunft!

'An die Freude' was published in 1744 in the second part of his *Sammlung neuer Oden und Lieder*. Some of Hagedorn's poems written for special occasions appeared in print as early as 1720 (he was only twelve then), but his first small volume of poetry, *Versuch einiger Gedichte oder Erlesene Proben politischer Nebenstunden*, dates from 1729. The word 'Versuch' may be derived from the then widespread English term 'essay', but also may reveal an uneasiness about the reception of the poems. Moreover, the alternate title suggests a defensive attitude: Hagedorn stresses that the poems are imitations of things he had liked in his leisure reading. Implicitly he is appealing to established models, in this way arguing indirectly that he should not be viewed as an innovator but as one following a tradition, albeit a new one.

In 1729 Hagedorn was appointed secretary to Baron von Söhlenthal, the Danish ambassador in London. As his outlook became more cosmopolitan he developed greater self-confidence and stylistic independence. It was at this time that he gained his extensive knowledge of English philosophy and literature, which in turn led him to French sources. After his return to Hamburg in 1731 he accepted the position of manager of the local branch of an English trading house and remained with this company for the rest of his life.

Graceful in his manners, always intent on maintaining his personal freedom in artistic and political questions, standing aloof from the literary feud between the Leipzig professor Gottsched and the Swiss critics Bodmer and Breitinger, Hagedorn displayed the same qualities of elegance and sophisticated tolerance in his writing. His second collection, *Versuch in poetischen Fabeln und Erzählungen* (1738), was an immediate success and called forth many imitations. Hagedorn's emphasis in these fables and stories in verse is on a smooth and concise telling of the actual story. The most famous poem in this collection has remained 'Johann, der Seifensieder', which praises the sang-froid and contentedness of an industrious yet happy soap-boiler; but this idyllic picture does not preclude criticism of the society and culture in which Hagedorn himself lived. For instance, Hagedorn chastizes voluptuous living and material greed when he says of one of Johann's neighbors:

Der stets zu halben Nächten frass
Und seiner Wechsel oft vergass.

This neighbor contrasts strongly with the soap-boiler who sings even when he is eating:

Und wann er ass, so must er singen;
Und wann er sang, so wars mit Lust,
Aus vollem Hals' und freier Brust.

Annoyed by Johann's singing, the neighbor seeks to instill in the happy soap-boiler his own greed for money by giving him a sizable sum if only he promises not to sing any more. Johann, who has never cared about money, discovers how worrisome it can become to guard his new treasure:

Er lernt zuletzt, ie mehr er spart,
Wie oft sich Sorg' und Reichthum paart,
Und manches Zärtlings dunkle Freuden
Ihn ewig von der Freiheit scheiden,
Die nur in reine Seelen stralt
Und deren Glück kein Gold bezahlt.

[*EdL*, V, 147—150]

Of course, Johann returns the money and regains the freedom of singing.
Hagedorn prefers such deceptively simple fable material and presents it
in equally simple-seeming language. Close analysis shows that the fable
reads unusually well because the diction fits the action perfectly, so that
the moral appears to follow inevitably, without being forced. The theme
of this particular story was not original with Hagedorn. He did invent
many of his fables, but many others are based on traditional narratives,
usually going back to French sources. However, these are not merely
translations of well-known fables, such as had been published earlier,
among others by Brockes, who had added some of de la Motte's fables
to the first part of the *Irdisches Vergnügen* in 1721. Rather, Hagedorn
speaks of fables *and* narratives, thereby indicating that both genres
are very similar in nature: both serve to teach a moral and both must
lead up to and prepare for the intended *pointe*, offering the reader in
the Horatian sense profit as well as delight. Hagedorn achieved his aims
so well that his 1738 collection of fables marked the beginning of the
strong interest that the eighteenth century developed in that genre. To
be sure, the fable was well suited to express the sentiments of the
bourgeoisie. Its predominance in an age that also produced the bourgeois
tragedy is therefore not surprising. Hagedorn's second collection of
fables appeared in 1750 under the title *Moralische Gedichte*.

During the 1740s Hagedorn published two collections of poems,
Sammlung Neuer Oden (1742—52), and *Oden und Lieder in fünf
Büchern* (1747). His odes are not grand and solemn hymns, as the term
might suggest; rather they are modest and pensive songs. After the
fables, Hagedorn devoted the entire following decade to writing odes
and songs in the Rococo style. The concern with the new genre does
not indicate a decisive break, however, since, in some of his fables,
Hamburg's surroundings had appeared as bucolic settings, typical of
those from pastoral poetry. Such settings are far more frequent in his
odes and songs, which otherwise no longer have any affinity with the
fable. The odes and songs have no particular moral to proclaim, but
convey idyllic moods by stressing the conventional features of Rococo

poetry. The element of profitableness (the Horatian *prodesse*) that was important in the fables has been almost totally neglected in favor of pure enjoyment (the Horatian *delectare*). The poem *An die Dichtkunst*, first published in the 1747 collection, seems to define for us Hagedorn's concept of Rococo poetry. These odes and songs, he claims have lessened the burden of many a worry and increased his happiness:

> Gespielinn meiner Neben-Stunden,
> Bey der ein Theil der Zeit verschwunden,
> Die mir, nicht andern, zugehört:
> O Dichtkunst, die das Leben lindert!
> Wie manchen Gram hast du vermindert,
> Wie manche Fröhlichkeit vermehrt!

Lightheartedness has become a dominant feature of his verse, confirmed by the end of this poem where he states — an unmistakable rejection of the Baroque ideal — that his verse is not intended to be immortal:

> Den itzt an Liedern reichen Zeiten
> Empfehl ich diese Kleinigkeiten:
> Sie wollen nicht unsterblich seyn.

> [*EdL*, V, 213–14]

The term *Kleinigkeiten* was later to be used frequently to describe this non-philosophical, lighthearted poetry, especially as a synonym for Anacreontic verse, a sub-type of Rococo literature to which Hagedorn's work gave strong impetus. In a sense Hagedorn can and should be regarded as the first Rococo poet in Germany, although many other poets in other parts of Germany were publishing Rococo works at around the same time. The influences were probably, therefore, reciprocal. At any rate, interest was revived in Anacreontic and pastoral poetry, and Hagedorn was right when, almost twenty years after the publication of his first volume of poetry, he pointed out the profuseness of Rococo literature that had developed in Germany. The quantity of this poetry is not matched by any great variety, however. All these works have a tendency toward the epigrammatic, the playful and the graceful in language, and toward erotic flirtation which ranges in tone from the frivolous to the sentimental to the comical to the satirical.

Although Rococo literature is an outgrowth of the Enlightenment spirit in Germany, it can also be seen as a reaction against the overly

serious philosophizing that had characterized rationalistic literature of
the 1720s and 1730s. Yet this philosophizing provided a rationale for
its own repudiation by arguing the need for enjoyment in art. As the
influence of the third Earl of Shaftesbury grew on the continent − and
Hagedorn considered himself a student of Shaftesbury's concept that
in man there exists a natural moral sense − and the interest in
aesthetics spread, the question of what is and what is not permissible
in literature, was answered by the dictum: whatever is 'gefällig', that is,
pleasing and appealing, is permitted. 'Gefällig' becomes an almost
obligatory key word in Rococo works. Hagedorn in the above-
mentioned poem *An die Dichtkunst* further defines his role as a Rococo
poet:

> Und deinem Flaccus abzulernen,
> Wie man durch echten Witz gefällt.

What he terms 'echter Witz' was soon to be called *Scherz*. In the
strictest Enlightenment sense 'Witz' referred to a poet's power of dis-
cernment, and his intellectual acumen, his ability to state things clearly,
logically. Rococo redefines 'Witz' to denote much more the actual
witticism, the intellectual joke.

3 *Haller*

While Brockes renewed nature poetry in Germany and Hagedorn proclaimed the right of enjoyment in his Rococo poetry, a third voice
added to the diversity of early Enlightenment literature. Albrecht von
Haller (1708−1777) promoted the overtly philosophical poem. His
approach to poetry shows unusually strong parallels to that of Brockes.
Both were didactic in their work and scientifically exact, as might be
expected of Enlightenment poets: Brockes, the careful observer of
nature, and Haller, the outstanding scientist who devoted most of his
life to the study of botany and medicine. Haller was somewhat of a
universal genius, and writing poetry appears to have claimed his fancy
only as a side interest, something for which he was very gifted and
which he took very seriously, but which he practiced only as a young
man.

Haller studied in Tübingen and Leyden, receiving his doctorate at
the age of nineteen. It was important that when he went back to his
native Switzerland, in 1728, to complete his studies in Basel, he found
men who encouraged him to study language and literature. Especially
Karl Friedrich Drollinger (1688−1742), whose own poetry reflects

the stylistic changes from late Baroque to Enlightenment, influenced
Haller decisively. Drollinger had introduced Brockes's poetry to
Switzerland and thus could direct the young poet to the new impulses
of the early Enlightenment literature. When Haller, in the summer of
1728, took his famous trip through the Swiss Alps to study the botany
of the region, he was prepared to undertake scientific observation of
nature, but also to engage in philosophical and theological reflections
about what he saw and experienced. These reflections make up the long
poetic treatise 'Die Alpen', written in 1729. The work embodies a
good deal of analysis and cultural criticism, rather dominant in this
particular poem, but not necessarily characteristic of all of Haller's
work. Haller ascribes to the villager of the Alps a happy, innocent, and
natural life, in contrast to the life of the city-dweller. He praises the
shepherd, who despises material wealth; and the folk song, as an
example of unconscious art. The entire poem is arranged around the
four seasons. The poet enumerates the differing but always severe
challenges the villagers face in each season, and stresses that the
difficulty of life in the Alps has strengthened the moral soundness and,
hence, the happiness of these people:

> Der lange Winter kürzt des Frühlings späte Wochen,
> Und ein verewigt Eis umringt das kühle Tal;
> Doch eurer Sitten Werth hat alles das verbessert,
> Der Elemente Neid hat euer Glück vergrössert.[9]

[37–40]

'Die Alpen' is written in Alexandrines, in a language that above all
strives for clarity and precision, and that reflects through its very
orderly yet seemingly dynamic sentence structure Haller's concept of
harmony between man and nature. It is in the shaping of the German
language for literary expression that Haller, according to his own
contemporaries, as judged by Gellert, Bodmer and Moses Mendelssohn,
made his greatest contribution.

After the trip through the Alps Haller spent a few years in Bern as a
practicing physician, at the same time very much involved in writing
poetry. The success of the first edition of his collected poems, bearing
in part the same title that Hagedorn's first volume bore, *Versuch
Schweizerischer Gedichte* (1732), spurred the poet on to expand this
little volume gradually and to publish it in a total of eleven editions
over the next four decades.[10] He added love poems as well as
satirical verses about the moral and political corruption in Bern.

Perhaps the most important poem in the second edition (1734) is 'Vom Ursprung des Uebels'. Its title reflects the influences of Leibniz's theodicy, and it is an example of Haller's strict philosophical poetry. Haller, like Lessing later, distinguishes between the philosophical poet and a poetic philosopher, and this distinction was essential to him because he saw himself more as a poet than a philosopher. He thus felt no need to offer in the poem a complete treatise on the question of the origin of evil, as the title might lead one to believe. In fact, the poem must be classified as a fragment, if viewed from the standpoint of the philosophical argument. The poet appeals more to emotions than to reason by simply asserting rather than demonstrating that ours must be 'Der Welten würdigste' even though it appears to be dominated by evil. Haller's reference to the most worthy of all possible worlds suggests Leibniz, as does his use of the image of a clock. But whereas Leibniz had used the analogy to explain his concept of pre-established harmony, that is, the absence of direct influence between spirit and matter, Haller argues that a world seen as analogous to a clock mechanism would eliminate the possibility of doing evil because it would not allow for personal choice. By the same token, of course, virtue would be as impossible as vice:

> Gott, der im Reich der Welt sich selber zeigen wollte,
> Sah, dass, wann alles nur aus Vorschrift handeln sollte,
> Die Welt ein Uhrwerk wird, von fremdem Trieb beseelt,
> Und keine Tugend bleibt, wo Macht zum Laster fehlt.
>
> [II, 53—56]

Haller himself suggests that he never fully developed the religious aspects in this poem. From his later religious experience this statement sounds plausible, since he began to devote himself much more to religious questions, following the death of his first wife. Characteristically, his religious interests took on an increasingly Pietistic attitude with a stronger emphasis on religious feeling than on intellectual belief, as is borne out by his *Tagebuch religiöser Empfindungen*, which he began writing in 1736. In 'Die Alpen', published before his serious involvement in religious issues, the poet had viewed civilization as the main cause of evil. Now, in 'Vom Ursprung des Uebels', Haller regards evil as an outward manifestation of something inherent in human nature. Inherent virtue, on the other hand, can bring into harmony the frustration arising from the conflict between the unquenchable desire for new experiences on the one hand, and the simultaneous wish to enjoy passively what one already possesses, on the other. Goethe's Faust later complains of man's being thrown back and forth with no resolution between desire and enjoyment:

> So tauml' ich von Begierde zu Genuss
> Und im Genuss verschmacht' ich nach Begierde.
>
> [3249–50]

Haller, foreshadowing Goethe's poetic language, perceives balance in this dichotomy when he says of those who are close to God in thought:

> Ihr Stand der Gottheit naht und keinen Ekel zeugend
> *In der Begierd geniesst und im Genuss begehrt*
> Und ihren Geist mit Licht, das Herz mit Wollust nährt.
>
> [italics mine] [III, 30–32]

In 1736 Haller accepted a professorship at the university of Göttingen, which had opened its doors the previous year. This position was to bring him many honors during the next seventeen years, and it directed his energies almost exclusively to scientific studies. However, his poems now began to inspire many young poets in Germany, among them Lessing, Ewald von Kleist, and Klopstock. Contemporary critics cited Haller's work as the kind of poetic writing worthy of imitation. Important for the development of literature in Germany are also his many critical reviews, which he published in his role as editor from 1747 to 1753 of the famous journal *Göttinger Gelehrten Anzeigen*. In its columns he reviewed many new literary publications, and he was the first to hail Klopstock's far-reaching accomplishments, which will occupy us later.[11] Yet his strong ties to his native city were reason enough for him to give up the influential position in Göttingen and accept a much less prestigious appointment in Bern. He did continue, however, with his enormous scientific projects, as he continued to write reviews for the Göttingen journal. Because of his religious experiences, Haller stresses in his reviews more and more those qualities in literary works that have to do with the heart and with feeling, and less and less those that appeal merely to the mind. While it may be difficult to ascertain how much he influenced the literary taste of the period, it can at least be argued that his new emphases were soon to become representative of the increasing stress on sentiment in German literature.

His three novels (*Usong*, 1771; *Alfred, König der Angelsachsen*, 1773; and *Fabius und Cato*, 1774) are political novels written by a man who, by this time, because of many disappointments in Bern and possibly many illnesses also, had become conservative and anti-democratic. He discussed forms of government in them: absolutism, constitutional monarchy, and aristocratic-republican rule. The creative, novelistic element is suppressed in favor of open didacticism, and the content often follows slavishly the historical sources. During these years Haller also completed two apologetics on the book of Revelations. But his contemporaries did not receive these later works with the same enthusiasm with which they were still reading his poems, which had meanwhile become frequent objects of discussion in the literary feud between the Swiss critics Bodmer and Breitinger on the one side, and the Gottsched circle in Leipzig on the other.

4 *Schnabel*

Haller's turn from poetry as a young man to novels in his later years may serve as one indication that the novel as a genre was coming into literary prominence as a result of having undergone changes during the Enlightenment, changes which deserve close scrutiny. In an age that sought to establish and uphold the ideal of broadening education by removing barriers that kept the citizenry from knowledge, the novel was ultimately to reflect the new philosophical and sociological emphasis more comprehensively than any other genre. The novel as an art form and as a carrier of new ideas developed more slowly than other forms, in part because it was a slow outgrowth of an 'uneducated', popular tradition that had exploited adventurous and improbable narration for its own sake. Accordingly, the novel was viewed as a mere pastime, incompatible with the high aims of poetic arts. However, its fictional narrative content and its everyday prose became advantages, lending themselves to vivid portrayal of the feelings, experiences, and thoughts of the growing audience of bourgeois readers. The gradual increase in respectability of the novel during this age is confirmed by the publication, in 1774, of the first book-long, critical treatment in German of the novel as an art form, Christian Friedrich von Blankenburg's *Versuch über den Roman*.

As Brockes, Hagedorn, and Haller were the first to express the new sentiments and philosophical tenets through poetry in the twenties, thirties, and forties, Johann Gottfried Schnabel (b. 1692, d. after 1750) incorporated some of the new ideas in the novel *Insel Felsenburg*, which he began publishing as early as 1731. Little is known about the life of this author. He was orphaned at an early age, and seems to have studied medicine, without formally concluding his education. His

experiences and activities are varied and include the military campaigns
of Prince Eugene of Savoy, whom he admired greatly, and journalism,
which he took up while in the service of the Count of Stolberg – in the
Harz mountains – as editor of the journal *Stollbergische Sammlung
Neuer und Merckwürdiger Welt-Geschichte* (1731–1741).[12] This title
and that of the novel *Wunderliche Fata einiger See-Fahrer, absonderlich
Alberti Julii, eines gebohrnen Sachsens* (1731–1743) – as *Insel
Felsenburg* was titled – point to the form and nature of the Baroque
novel of adventure. The full title of the novel includes, in Baroque
fashion, a brief plot summary, characterizing the story as one built
around the Robinson Crusoe theme.[13] The title further informs us that
the main hero, Albert Julius, was shipwrecked on an island, where he
discovered the most beautiful land, married his companion and became
the patriarch of a family which eventually numbered over three hundred.
Schnabel is intent on making the novel contemporary, as shown by his
inclusion of the date of 1728 in the title. In that year the hero reached
his hundredth birthday on the island state, with its exemplary form of
government and utopian life.

Schnabel's preface, a polemical address to the public rather than a
traditional dedication to the ruler, shows the extent to which the social
class of the readers he anticipated had grown to include the middle
classes as well as the aristocracy. This preface, functioning as a brief
treatise in defense of the novel as an art form, discusses the problems of
believability and verisimilitude in fiction. In defiance of the Baroque
tradition of vouching for the veracity of the often unbelievable content,
Schnabel asks the reader to regard the function of fiction as separate
from that of factual truth. He thereby provides a rationale for using the
fictional plot as a vehicle to discuss ideas, in this case on the state and
on contemporary society. The novel is no longer to be read for the
mere story line:

Aber mit Gunst und *Permission* zu fragen: Warum
soll man denn dieser oder jener, eigensinniger
Köpffe wegen, die sonst nichts als lauter Wahrheiten
lesen mögen, nur eben lauter solche Geschichte
schreiben, die auf das kleineste *Jota* mit einem
cörperlichen Eyde zu bestärcken wären? Warum soll
denn eine geschickte *Fiction*, als ein *Lusus Ingenii*,
so gar verächtlich und verwerfflich seyn? Wo mir
recht ist, halten ja die Herren *Theologi* selbst
davor, dass auch in der Heil. Bibel dergleichen

Exempel, ja gantze Bücher, anzutreffen sind.[14]

Schnabel uses the combination of familiar Utopia and Robinson Crusoe motifs, known from the start by the reader to be fictional, so as to focus attention on the theme beyond the plot. Furthermore, Schnabel uses the novel's structure to encourage detached objectivity by appearing merely as an editor whose role is to introduce the main narrator. The novel abounds in didacticisms and moralizings, criticizing the terrible conditions in Europe by contrasting them with the harmonious government of the island. The result is the usual one in Utopian novels: individual character traits disappear under the need for stereotyped conformity to a pragmatically proven set of ethical values. Consequently, the functional landscape of the island is easily imbued with allegorical religious meanings understood and accepted by all. The smooth continuity of this insular state in a paradisiac setting triumphantly vindicates the former sufferings of its individual members, uniting them in a patriarchal society whose continuation depends upon excluding all those who might threaten its values, its harmony, and the moral purity of its members, who have no desire to return to the world of luxury, strife, and godless living. Those few Europeans who are invited to become members of the *Felsenburg* state have no difficulty adapting to its way of life, which is Protestant in religion with a strong Pietistic bent, and enlightened in its government, teaching high regard for the individual while preserving a hierarchical structure.[15] In this land neither want nor superabundance is known. Just as the land will yield the proper and needed amount of food, so a balanced human society will keep evil in check, and prevent moral deterioration by not allowing luxury to rule.

It is an indication of this novel's success that such a stout defender of Enlightenment ideals as the Berlin book-dealer Friedrich Nicolai took it for granted that the *Insel Felsenburg*, as well as Schnabel's other novel, *Der im Irr-Garten der Liebe herumtaumelnde Cavaljer* were among the most popular novels of the time. Nicolai mentioned these works in his 1773 novel *Die Leben und Meinungen des Herrn Magister Seb. Nothanker* as examples of good reading.

Schnabel wrote additional novels, but he did not achieve similar success. His *Der im Irr-Garten der Liebe herumtaumelnde Cavaljer* appeared in 1738, and *Der aus dem Mond gefallene und nachhero zur Sonne des Glücks gestiegene Printz* in 1750. Judging from the fact that contemporary sources do not have much to say about these later novels, it appears that Schabel did not permanently break out of the Baroque tradition. Nor did he develop further the early model he had presented in *Insel Felsenburg*. Still, Schnabel's novel was an early indication as to how the novel in general was to become a major vehicle for the dissemination of the philosophical tenets of the Enlightenment.

II New Norms: Gottsched

The didactic rationalistic tenets of this new literature impelled its authors, even if only implicitly, to strive for clear definitions of feelings, thoughts, and world views. The case is analogous to Pope's line: 'What oft was thought, but ne'er so well expressed.'[16] This same striving was bound to produce comprehensive revolutions of aesthetic rules, critical and conscious presentations of the goals and forms of Enlightenment literature. The name that deserves foremost mention here is that of Johann Christoph Gottsched (1700–1766), a dynamic defender of the philosophical ideas of the period, a successful teacher who inspired young men to write poetry and drama according to his rules, a prolific critic, translator, and writer with a strong and forceful commitment to the improvement of such a basic institution as the theater and such fundamental means of communication as language. Unfortunately for his subsequent reputation, he went about his mission with a sense of authority and pedantry that eventually alienated many of his admirers and involved him in a bitter and long-lasting feud with the contemporary Swiss critics Bodmer and Breitinger, and caused him to be seen as no more than a narrow-minded, self-serving dictator in literary matters, insensitive to the creative process and insisting on banal correctness. It is quite true that Gottsched became more and more doctrinaire and intolerant in the course of the feud. Nor can it be denied that some of Gottsched's disenchanted disciples experienced literary success after leaving Gottsched's sphere of influence. Nonetheless, it would be misleading to see Gottsched as the caricature his enemies made him out to be.[17] The difference between him and the Swiss critics was not so much in philosophy and convictions about literature, as it was in temperament and, to a degree, even in general cultural orientation.[18] Gottsched looked more to French models, while the Swiss critics were more receptive to English literature. It was precisely because Gottsched had given strong impetus to the development of literature in Germany, and because his impact was felt so keenly that his position was challenged.

Gottsched knew few classic models of German literature worthy of emulation; he, therefore, felt called upon to provide normative rules in his *Versuch einer kritischen Dichtkunst vor die Deutschen* (1730), the work for which he is best known. The work gives instructions which, if followed closely, will supposedly result in an acceptable compositional exercise. Gottsched formulated detailed rules to show how the same theme might be developed within the special strictures of the various genres. However, his training in philosophy, and particularly his admiration for Leibniz and Wolff with their systematic and all-encompassing explanations of life, soon caused him to attempt to state a unifying principle which would be applicable to all poetic art. For only if literature could be shown as enhancing the role of philosophy would literature and the study of it become academically acceptable. This widespread view helps further to account for the growing body of literary theory in this age. The chief task of literature according to Gottsched was to popularize philosophy so that a broader reading public would understand philosophical truth and moral teaching. The awkward title of an ode which Gottsched wrote in 1733 stresses this point: 'Dass die Poesie am geschicktesten sey, die Weisheit unter den rohen Menschen fortzupflanzen.' Gottsched felt that in Baroque poetry rhyme had become an end in itself, and that it had distracted from poetry's primary function, the communication of ideas. His didactic nature leads him to argue this point in the above-mentioned ode:

> Die Dichtkunst kömmt, ihr altes Lob zu retten,
> Das wir ihr fast entwendet hätten,
> Seitdem an ihrer statt die Reimsucht bloss gelärmt.

He wanted to upgrade the quality of literature, so that the study of it would become a worthwhile field of academic investigation.

Gottsched defined as the dominating principle of literature the theory of probability, or imitation of nature. Events described, characters portrayed, the level of diction employed, feelings evoked, historical narrative presented — all must be not only probable but also consistent with each other to yield artistic unity. Much of the discussion of literary criticism during that decade and the following one revolved around this principle. On the grounds of the theory of probability Gottsched rejected the opera as a form of art since opera portrays events which belong more to the realm of magic than of reality. Not that Gottsched disallows events simply because they do not occur in reality; even animals may speak in a fable if their speeches support the philosophical 'reality' that the moral of an animal fable is intended to portray. The reality of nature need not be strictly factual. Rather, Gottsched looks for 'die Ähnlichkeit des Erdichteten, mit dem, was wirklich zu geschehen pflegt.'[19] Similarity is the criterion. The poetic creation that parallels some truth found in nature is judged to be probable and, therefore, in conformity with the principle of imitation.

Among other questions that the principle of imitation raises are the following: Is verse permissible in a comedy, since ordinary citizens do not normally employ rhyme in their everyday speech? Can the miraculous in any form be incorporated into literature? How literally must the three unities be observed? While Gottsched addresses himself to many such questions, all the answers serve to reflect his overriding concern, the desire to make literature the object of a creditable academic discipline by equipping it to be an effective carrier of Enlightenment ideas and attitudes. Accordingly, the quality of any literary work is judged by the success of its 'fable', by which Gottsched means the core of content which most clearly embodies the author's abstract ideas or views.

> Ich glaube derowegen, eine Fabel am besten zu beschreiben, wenn ich sage: sie sey die Erzählung einer unter gewissen Umständen möglichen, aber nicht wirklich vorgefallenen Begebenheit, darunter eine nützliche moralische Wahrheit verborgen liegt.[20]

The term 'fable' as Gottsched uses it includes the plot outline, but goes beyond it. As the carrier of ethical principles and abstract teaching the 'fable' is for Gottsched the 'Ursprung und Seele aller Dichtkunst'. Yet Gottsched does not slight the aesthetic implications of the 'fable', since it must be constructed in the poetic form most appropriate to the presentation of moral teaching. The 'fable' determines whether a work is literature or mere historiographical narrative. The quality of the 'fable' is used to measure the literary quality of a piece.[21] In fact, the 'fable' is considered by Gottsched to be the highest form of imitation of nature, and is the standard by which both the abstract truth and the concrete form of any work may be evaluated. Mere description may be true to reality, but there is no guarantee that it will go beyond the boundaries of historiography. For this reason lyric poetry is not regarded highly by Gottsched, who argues that its form of imitation is usually limited to enumeration. His favorite genres are the epic poem and the drama. To these he devotes long chapters; to the remaining types of poetry only relatively short comments.

Gottsched's *Kritische Dichtkunst* was a milestone in the development of literary criticism in the eighteenth century in Germany. It established Gottsched's considerable and powerful influence during the

1730s and 1740s; it was the abstract foundation on which he built his practical innovations. By no means was his theoretical program in all aspects forward-looking. Nor did he always perceive accurately the nature of the creative process and so did not really allow for poetic imagination. Yet, at the height of his career, around 1740, Gottsched could look back on substantial achievements, such as having provided the theater in Leipzig with twenty-seven plays, most of them trans-lations, to be sure, but also including six original tragedies.

It is a remarkable oddity of German literary history that Gottsched's unusual height determined some of the influences on his life. A native of Juditten near Königsberg in East Prussia — like so many eighteenth century writers in Germany, he was the son of a Protestant minister — Gottsched fled from there in 1724, since he was subject to being drafted by force into the special royal guard of tall soldiers, the pride of Prussia's king. He completed his studies in Leipzig and began his teaching career there in 1725, eventually holding the chair of poetics and metaphysics. Leipzig offered Gottsched's energies a wide field of activities. This city away from the coast was a major trade center between the east and the west, and was known for its fairs, to which businessmen and visitors came from numerous countries and diverse traditions. When young Goethe arrived in Leipzig as a student he found the contrast between 'Klein-Paris', as he called it, and Frankfort overwhelming, particularly in the areas of fashion and social elegance. Unlike Berlin and Hamburg, Leipzig had a university, founded in 1409, and was jealous of its role in higher education. As the Enlightenment encouraged the writing of books and journals, and as the members of the middle class bought more books, Leipzig attracted more and more of the book-business, and in the process outdid Frankfort in this area. Music and theater were cultivated here. After all, it was the town in which Johann Sebastian Bach had been serving as the famous Thomaskantor since 1722. It is not surprising then that Leipzig was the first German town to have public concerts, beginning in 1736. Gottsched quickly became involved in the life and culture of the city of Leipzig, bringing more activity in literature and theater to the city. He was soon made a member of a literary society, the 'Deutschübende Gesellschaft', became its president in 1727, and changed its name on the model of the 'Academie française' to 'Deutsche Gesellschaft'. The society was a significant forum for his work in advocating the use of a simple, clear German prose. His style is an adaptation of the Meissen dialect, the German spoken in and around Leipzig. Gottsched's first significant publications appeared in Leipzig. He founded and wrote two moral weeklies, *Die vernünftigen Tadlerinnen* (1725–26) and *Der Biedermann* (1727–28). The first journal employed the fiction of being edited by three women who disclaim learnedness. Simple, lively style and down-to-earth, common sense rationality are Gottsched's aim. His fictional three women ridicule superstitious beliefs, condemn drunkenness, and rebuke gossip and vanity. Topics of discussion include theology, literature, and philosophy. While *Die vernünftigen Tadlerinnen* is consciously aimed at women, *Der Biedermann* addresses itself more to a male audience. In these periodicals Gottsched shows that a good literary style, marked by simplicity and clarity, need not include the colloquial in order to be popular.

Another fortuitous coincidence in Gottsched's move to Leipzig came about when he found himself able to put his theories regarding the reform of drama into practice. In the *Versuch einer kritischen Dichtkunst* he had already called for a radical improvement of the German stage. These reforms included a closer interaction between actor and playwright, a banning, from the stage, of improvisation and extraneous clown characters, and an appeal to writers to produce for the German theater plays which in content and form would meet the standards of classical drama. The presence of Germany's best theater troupe in Leipzig gave Gottsched the forum he needed for the implementation of the reforms during the 1730s. He found willing, even enthusiastic collaborators in Friederike Karoline Neuber and her husband, Johann Neuber, the directors of the troupe. They, too, were interested in raising the quality of theater production and discovered in Gottsched an energetic promoter. As early as 1728 the Neubers had excluded the harlequin from tragedies. At Gottsched's prompting, in 1737 they performed a play in which the harlequin was banned from the stage altogether. That event impressed itself strongly, although rather negatively, on the minds of Gottsched's contemporaries. The harlequin was gone from the stage, but Gottsched's authority was now questioned. A few years later Karoline Neuber herself would make fun publicly of Gottsched and his theater reform. However, her criticism could not undo Gottsched's reforms, because these had brought about genuine and badly needed improvements. Gottsched had raised the theater to a new level of social and cultural consciousness; he had replaced the Baroque 'Haupt und Staatsaktionen' with regular tragedies; he had come to the aid of the pastoral drama and had rejected the Baroque opera; and he had proved that good comedy does not rely on the harlequin. Gottsched had published his best-known tragedy, *Der sterbende Cato*, in 1732. The play, based on Deschamps' *Caton d'Utique* (1715) and on Addison's

Cato (1713), was written in Alexandrines so that the actors were
forced to memorize their parts, and to deliver their speeches in elevated
fashion. The play demonstrates Gottsched's persistent striving for
stylistic purity, metrical regularity, and completely logical plot development.[22]

Gottsched had no aptitude for writing comedies. His wife, Luise
Adelgunde Victorie Gottschedin (1713–1762), however, seen generally
as the more skillful and gifted playwright of the two, is the author of
several comedies, among them *Die Pietisterey im Fischbein-Rocke oder
die doktormässige Frau* (1736). For this play she borrowed from a
French comedy which had utilized the subtle religious differences
between the Jesuits and the Jansenists to develop a humorous plot. Her
version is successful because she was able to adapt the play skillfully to
the religious differences between Pietists and orthodox Protestants in
Germany, and because of her ability to create a fully rounded character
who is tellingly criticized for hypocritical piety. *Die ungleiche Heirat*,
Die Hausfranzösin, *Das Testament*, and *Herr Witzling* are her other
comedies. The critic and author Lessing found *Das Testament* to be the
most worthwhile of these plays. All are written in prose, and all concentrate on rewarding virtue and ridiculing vice. Gottsched could point
to his wife's comedies as examples of the kind of comedy, derived from
the classic high styles, that he had in mind.

Three other major works should at least be mentioned to round out
Gottsched's contribution. These are the periodical *Beyträge zur
Critischen Historie der deutschen Sprache, Poesie und Beredsamkeit*
(1732–1744), the anthology *Deutsche Schaubühne* (1740–1745), and
the grammatical treatise *Grundlegung einer Deutschen Sprachkunst
nach den Mustern der besten Schriftsteller des vorigen und jetzigen
Jahrhunderts* (1748). Both the *Beyträge* and the *Sprachkunst* document
his efforts to arrive at a commonly accepted standard German. Just as
the development of literature must start by adhering to exact rules, so
also good usage of the language is predicated on knowing, stating, and
applying the proper grammatical rules. Gottsched laid them down in the
Sprachkunst. This method is explained in the opening statement:

> Eine Sprachkunst ist eine gegründete Anweisung, wie man die
> Sprache eines Volkes, nach der besten Mundart desselben, und nach
> der Einstimmung der besten Schriftsteller, richtig und zierlich,
> sowohl reden als schreiben sollte.

Gottsched continued to regard the Meissen dialect as the normative standard for proper High German. He further calls upon the best writers, not only to accept but also to provide authority by deciding what is and what is not correct usage. His approach proved effective. Gottsched soon became the respected authority in matters of language. He addressed himself in the *Sprachkunst* to orthography, word usage, syntax. His pedantic rules were followed and applied, again because they met a real need. His German became the basis for almost all literary works, thus codifying and regulating standard High German, even in areas which at the time used only regional dialect.[23]

It is of course interesting to note that Gottsched's *Sprachkunst* had a more lasting impact on the development of German literary prose than his literary criticism had on the development of German literature. He was effective in both areas, but the rules he set up for writing and evaluating literary works were soon rejected. Before that happened, though, Gottsched had provided in his *Deutsche Schaubühne* a collection of dramas which he considered to be models. They included translations of French plays, some plays of his own, those of his wife, and those of young playwrights who had bowed to his authority. The *Deutsche Schaubühne* made available, in printed form, to all theater troupes in Germany, a number of plays selected according to their adherence to Gottsched's 'correct' rules.[24] Gottsched specifically rejected Shakespeare's because of their irregularity. He was a practical pedagogue and as such he was influential. His writings were significant not only in themselves. They provided the impetus for conscious and forceful efforts to create literary works that would match those of the French. His fear, confirmed by subsequent trends in German literature, was that the wave of enthusiasm for English literature would under-mine the ideals of regularity and correctness that he had so carefully formulated. And indeed, those authors who were later to question his authority, to attack his rule books and his translations, and to accuse him of insensitiveness to artistic and creative urges, would often do so in the name of English models and types.

Notes

1.   For this reason Johann Christian Günther (1695–1723) is considered a Baroque poet in this literary history. His contributions are summarized in the preceding volume. The concept of modernity to describe the eighteenth century is most cogently employed by Robert Mollenauer (ed.), *Introduction to Modernity: A Symposium on Eighteenth-Century Thought* (Austin, 1965). He sees the eighteenth century 'generally acclaimed as an age of change and of modernity' (p. 4).

2.   Harold Jantz, 'Brockes's Poetic Apprenticeship', *MLN*, LXXVII (1962), 439–42.

3.   For a detailed treatment of Brockes's philosophical and religious views see H. M. Wolff, *Die Weltanschauung der deutschen Aufklärung in geschichtlicher Entwicklung*, 2nd ed. (Bern und München, 1963), pp. 120–37.

4.   H. M. Wolff, 'Brockes's Religion', *PLMA*, LXII (1947), 1124–52, analyzes Brockes's indebtedness to Johann Arnd, and concludes that Brockes did not anticipate deism.

5.   The poem was first published in 1727, in part II of *Irdisches Vergnügen in GOtt*. The quotation here follows the original as reprinted in EdL.

6.   Telemann's poem, written in 1723, appeared under the title 'Gedanken über (S.T.) Herrn Brockes Sing-Gedicht vom Wasser im Frühling/als er selbiges in die Music gesetzt hatte.'

7.   E. A. Blackall, *The Emergence of German as a Literary Language 1700–1775* (Cambridge, 1959), pp. 255–59, has shown convincingly how Hagedorn's early insistence on leaving the first version of a poem untouched gradually gave way to serious revisions of his poems, in the process establishing Hagedorn's reputation for polished smoothness.

8.   For a fuller discussion see Wolff, *Die Weltanschauung der Deutschen Aufklärung*, 2nd edn. (Bern und München, 1963), pp. 175–79.

9.   The quotations from Haller's poetry are taken from L. Hirzel, ed., *Albrecht von Hallers Gedichte* (Frauenfeld, 1882).

10.   While Haller was influenced by Brockes, he was also impressed by the formal and linguistic achievements of Hagedorn. In 1768, in the preface to the tenth edition of his volume of poetry, Haller remarked: 'Ich kam in den Zeiten der leichten . . . Art zu reimen, unter die Dichter: bloss ein Hagedorn fieng in fast eben diesen Jahren in seinen geistvollen und mit vieler Sorgfalt ausgemahlten Gedichten ein neues Muster zu zeigen an.' *Hallers Gedichte*, ed. Hirzel.

11.   Haller's important contributions to literary criticism have now been documented by K. S. Guthke, ed., *Hallers Literaturkritik* (Tübingen, 1970). Cf. also K. S. G., 'Neues zu Hallers Literaturkritik', *LY*, V, 198–218.

12.   The family of Stolberg, active on political assignments in Denmark, developed strong interests in literary matters, especially during the next generation, when Countess Auguste von Stolberg was for a time Goethe's correspondent and confidante, and when her two brothers Christian and Friedrich Leopold, in 1775 Goethe's travel companions to Switzerland, contributed significantly to the *Sturm und Drang* poetry. None of them, however, was born in Stolberg or ever lived there.

13.   It might be well to remember that Defoe's *Robinson Crusoe*, first published in 1719, had been translated into German as early as 1720.

14.   *Insel Felsenburg*, ed. W. Vosskamp (Hamburg, 1969), p. 10.

15.   W. Vosskamp, 'Theorie und Praxis der literarischen Fiktion in J. G. Schnabels Roman *Die Insel Felsenburg*', *GRM* [N.F. 18], XLIX (1968), 131–52, cites evidence that the political convictions of Albert Julius were akin to the conventions and rules of the Moravian Church, a major group within the Pietistic movement.

16.   *Essay on Criticism*, II, 1, 298.

17.   Fortunately, it is no longer necessary to defend Gottsched. His accomplishments have been recognized in recent publications, not least by a critical edition of his works: J. Birke, ed., *Ausgewählte Werke* (Berlin, 1968 ff).

18.   E. Cassirer, *Die Philosophie der Aufklärung* (Tübingen, 1932), emphasizes that even Gottsched's contemporaries had difficulty understanding what the point of contention was between the feuding factions. He explains the difference as one of approach: 'Die eigentliche Differenz zwischen Gottsched und den Schweizern lässt sich nicht von aussen, sondern nur von innen her bezeichnen; sie

lässt sich nicht durch die Art der Einwirkungen, denen beide unterlagen, sondern nur durch den verschiedenen Ansatz ihres systematischen Problems erklären,' p. 448.

19. Gottsched, *Kritische Dichtkunst*, 4th edn. (Leipzig, 1751; facsimile rpt. Darmstadt, 1962), p. 198.

20. Ibid., p. 150.

21. Cf. K. R. Scherpe, *Gattungspoetik im 18. Jahrhundert* (Stuttgart, 1968), who defines Gottsched's 'fable' as 'dichterisches Formprinzip', p. 37.

22. For a discussion of *Cato* in the context of the development of tragedy during the Enlightenment see R. R. Heitner, *German Tragedy in the Age of Enlightenment* (Berkeley, 1963). Heitner shows how the play meets Gottsched's own criteria for rationalistic tragedy; how a virtuous Cato can incur guilt when he is obstinate, 'the tragic guilt (so to speak) as a practically unavoidable imperfection in the exercise of human reason', p. 30.

23. For a full treatment of Gottsched's contribution to the development of German prose see Blackall, *The Emergence of German*, pp. 107–148.

24. The *Deutsche Schaubühne* was a six-volume publication, with each volume containing six or seven dramas. The last three volumes were made up entirely of original German plays.

SENTIMENTALISM AND THE SPIRIT OF ROCOCO

I The Challenge From Switzerland: Bodmer and Breitinger

The most prominent adversaries of Gottsched, the Swiss critics Johann
Jakob Bodmer (1698–1783) and Johann Jakob Breitinger (1701–
1776), had begun to play their roles as critics before Gottsched, and
until 1740 a friendly exchange of ideas and common concerns marked
the correspondence between Leipzig and Zurich. Bodmer and
Breitinger were life-long friends and colleagues at Zurich's Gymnasium,
Bodmer as historian and Breitinger as philologist teaching Greek and
Hebrew. They co-authored a number of books, and attained an unusually
high degree of mutual consultation as all of their publications were
being prepared. Bodmer was the more eloquent and more daring in
presenting his thoughts, while Breitinger was more cautious. From
the beginning their critical work received strong impulses from English
models, most notably from Addison's *Spectator* and Milton's *Paradise
Lost*. Bodmer's various translations of Milton into German — the first,
in prose, appeared in 1732 — brought the English poet many
admirers in Germany, inspired German poets, and established Bodmer
as a critic so solidly that in time his authority became a threat to
Gottsched. Although the literary feud often consisted of Gottsched's
attacks on, and Bodmer's defense of, *Paradise Lost*, Milton's epic
served only as the battleground on which an important power struggle
was taking place.

  Their interest in English literature was similar to that of the Hamburg
poets Brockes and Hagedorn. Indeed, Hamburg and Zurich did have
many common interests, mainly because neither city was responsible to
a territorial prince. While it is true that Hamburg's Lutheranism exhibited very strong feelings against the Reformed Swiss — it was often
the case that Germany's Lutheran theologians spoke out more strongly
against Zwingli's Reformed Christianity than against Catholicism —
there were also official cultural contacts between the two cities.[1]
Because of the political structure of both cities, literary interests and
public service awareness usually went hand in hand. Bodmer, first a
businessman, was author and politician, a member of Zurich's
'Grosser Rat', and a proponent of the establishment of the 'Helvetische
Gesellschaft' in 1761. The ideals of the Enlightenment were embraced
easily and supported fully in Hamburg and Zurich. During the seven-

teenth century Zurich's social and cultural life was controlled strongly
by the strict standards of the Reformed churches of that town. The
town had even issued a law against theaters, whereas Hamburg had a
city opera in the seventeenth century. The eighteenth century, however,
is marked by a rise in philosophical, literary and general cultural
activity in Zurich. Its contributions to the early Enlightenment literature
were most influential and long lasting.

Bodmer and Breitinger brought to literature a new English trend of
the period with the foundation of their moral weekly, the *Discourse
der Mahlern* (1721–1723). The plan for the journal was Bodmer's,
following the example of Addison's *Spectator* which Bodmer had read
in French. The special form of current art criticism in Italy, to which
Bodmer had been exposed during a visit there, suggested the idea of
using famous painters as the ostensible authors of his journal articles.
Since 'painters' wrote about philosophical, moral and literary topics, it
seemed natural to compare painting and writing as art forms, to
employ criteria used to judge painting and apply them to writing. In
general, critical theory in this period was not concerned to separate
the arts on the basis of the media employed. Thus the Swiss critics were
more eager to stress the similarities than to distinguish the differences
between painting and literature:

> Ihr sehet aus diesem, worinne die Verwandtschaft der Schreiber,
> der Mahlern und der Bildhauer besteht, nemlich in der Gleichheit
> des Vorhabens; sie suchen sämtlich die Spuhr der Natur, sie
> belustigen durch die Aehnlichkeit welche ihre Schriften, Bilder und
> Gemählde mit derselben haben, sie machen sich lachenswidrig,
> wenn sie davon abtretten. Aber sie unterscheiden sich von einander
> in der Ausführung ihres Vornehmens . . . .
>
> [*DNL*, XLII, 8]

They also used such phrases as 'redende Malerei' and 'stumme Poesie'.
Discourse der Mahlern was a successful undertaking. Because it predates
both Brockes's *Der Patriot* and Gottsched's *Die Vernünftigen
Tadlerinnen*, its stylistic accomplishments, even though not as smooth
and convincing as those achieved by Brockes and Gottsched, must not be
underestimated.[2] Bodmer and Breitinger strove for a style that would be
pleasing to and easily understood by a larger reading public. In contrast
to Gottsched they retained dialect features in their prose. Gottsched
criticized them severely for this, but it added to the expressiveness of
their language. While the Swiss accepted grammatical advice from

Gottsched, they tirelessly defended the use of powerful and suggestive words (which they called 'Machtwörter') from local dialects.[3] Their position on this matter gradually became accepted practice, reaching culmination as one of the most noticeable hallmarks of *Sturm und Drang* literature.

Bodmer's prolific literary career stretched over fifty years. His publications were mainly critical and theoretical from the twenties to the forties, but he turned to plays, poems and prose narratives during the fifties, sixties, and seventies. In addition, he also edited several important medieval German manuscripts, including *Parzifal* and the *Nibelungenlied*. In this latter endeavor Bodmer's and Breitinger's interests overlapped with those of Gottsched, but the Swiss were much more successful in discovering old manuscrips, not only because they lived closer to the monasteries that housed these manuscracts, but also because their Swiss dialects were closer to the Middle High German in which they were written.

Bodmer's and Breitinger's first joint theoretical work, *Von dem Einfluss und dem Gebrauch der Einbildungskraft* (1727), attempted to investigate the role of imagination in literary creation. The term 'Einbildungskraft' is their rendering of the English 'imagination', and reveals their indebtedness to Addison, who had written about the topic. Bodmer and Breitinger did not use the term to refer to creative productivity or 'inspiration'; they were referring more to the analytical ability to shape works of art out of informed insights and experiences. Like Gottsched, the Swiss critics operated strictly within the limits of a rationalistic approach. Accordingly, Gottsched was in agreement with Bodmer and Breitinger, and praised Bodmer's prose translation of *Paradise Lost* (1732). Enmity did not develop until the Swiss critics brought out four voluminous and comprehensive works of literary criticism, in 1740 and 1741. Besides showing concern for the pre-eminence of his position, Gottsched asked whether Bodmer and Breitinger were not abandoning the critic's task, which he felt to be so essential, of formulating rules within whose guidelines the poet could work securely and correctly. Gottsched's objections to Bodmer's and Breitinger's work are formulated in the preface to the third edition of his own *Critische Dichtkunst*: 'Man wird daraus weder eine Ode, noch eine Cantate; weder ein Schäfergedicht, noch eine Elegie . . . weder eine Epopee, noch ein Trauerspiel, weder eine Komödie, noch eine Oper machen lernen.' This reaction by Gottsched was bound to evoke counter-attacks from all sides, for it was now obvious that his concept of and his approach to literary criticism was too narrowly pedagogical,

and too exclusively concerned with formal correctness. Bodmer and
Breitinger had taken great care in the preparation of their decisive works
so that their failure to deal with prescriptive rules indicates that rules
were not their concern. They were more interested in philosophical and
linguistic issues, in whether elements of the marvelous have any place in
literature, in the use of metaphor, and in discovering what makes a work
of literature a piece of art. Breitinger first published in 1740 the
*Critische Abhandlung Von der Natur, den Absichten und dem Gebrauch
der Gleichnisse*, and then the two volume *Critische Dichtkunst
Worinnen die Poetische Mahlerey in Absicht auf den Ausdruck und die
Farben abgehandelt wird*. In the same year, Bodmer's *Critische
Abhandlung von dem Wunderbaren in der Poesie und dessen Verbindung
mit dem Wahrscheinlichen* was printed, and in 1741 his *Critische
Betrachtungen über die poetischen Gemählde der Dichter*. The
appearance of these four works in such a short period calls attention to
the amount of critical thinking that was going on at the time in Zurich,
while their titles document the authors' interest in dealing with specific
questions. Bodmer and Breitinger confirmed and encouraged those
poets and authors who wanted more freedom of imagination. Their
theoretical work offered not so much prescribed formulas; it encouraged
the reader to reflect and formulate on his own. With this, however, it
should be stressed that Bodmer's and Breitinger's views were not as
opposed to Gottsched's as the feud between the two factions might
indicate. It was more a difference of emphasis. Gottsched's inflexibility
was pitted against Bodmer's and Breitinger's encouragement of
independent thinking. Basically, the Swiss critics, too, demanded that
every aspect of literary art conform to the rational standards, applicable
even to the marvelous, which Breitinger defended as integral to literary
writing. The marvelous is not exempted from the need to be probable
or possible. Like Gottsched, Breitinger does not restrict the principle of
imitation of nature to a slavish description of the real world, but allows
for depiction of any possible world, just as Leibniz had spoken of many
possible worlds, of which our real world is only the best possible one.
Breitinger is innovative by arguing that the effect of poetry is even
heightened if not merely the ordinary is presented, but also the
marvelous, which will imbue the work with a sense of newness, because
it is outside of our normal experience. His famous definition puts it
well:

Denn was ist Dichten anders, als sich in der Phantasie neue Begriffe
und Vorstellungen formieren, deren Originale nicht in der

gegenwärtigen Welt der würcklichen Dinge, sondern in irgend einem andern möglichen Welt-Gebäude zu suchen sind.[4]

Gottsched had recommended a sparse use of metaphor, but Breitinger valued a language rich in imagery as requisite to the accomplishments of his aims.[5] Much of the discussion of language by both Bodmer and Breitinger amounts to a defense of Milton's form of presentation, and of course their analysis of the form and language of Milton's poetry shaped their own views. Considering the radical conclusions drawn by Bodmer and Breitinger, Gottsched changed his position, and attacked not only Bodmer and his translation of *Paradise Lost*, but Milton himself as well. Yet Bodmer and Breitinger did not merely cite examples from past literature, they frequently found much to extol in contemporary poetry. They especially liked Brockes and Haller. Their praise of poets of their own age expressed their confidence in the significant development of recent German literature.

This development was increasingly to reveal Bodmer's meager accomplishments as poet and dramatist. Breitinger never tried his hand at creative literary writing. By the time Bodmer began publishing literary works German literature had produced a number of superior examples. The first three cantos of Klopstock's epic, *Der Messias*, had appeared in 1748, much lauded by Bodmer, who now wrote lengthy epic poems on Biblical themes himself: *Noah ein Heldengedicht* (1750), *Jacob and Joseph* (1751), *Die Synd-Flut* (1751), *Der Noah. In Zwölf Gesängen* (1752), *Jacob and Rachel* (1752) and many others. Later he also wrote historical plays, his own versions of plays of antiquity, and plays treating topics from national history, including the William Tell theme. Despite these literary works his main contributions remained his theoretical reflections which stimulated and encouraged those who had talent. It was to Bodmer's and Breitinger's credit that the 1740s witnessed a burst of literary activity in Germany and Switzerland, bringing diversity to the literary scene. Increased literary production also generated more discussion about literary theory, leading to greater independence on the part of poets and authors from either Gottsched or the Swiss critics, and this independence in turn led to noteworthy advances in literature.

II The Challenge from Germany

1 *Schlegel*

Among the most prominent of those who showed an interest in

Gottsched's reform program, at least initially, was Johann Elias Schlegel (1719–1749). In recent years scholars have examined his critical and dramatic works with increasing appreciation, and have convincingly shown the complexities and artistic depth of his writings. In spite of his good rapport with Gottsched and his admiration for his work, Schlegel maintained his independence. He was the more gifted of the two, and a close examination of his plays and critical essays reveals that a variety of approaches to literature was possible in a so-called rationalistic period. Schlegel was particularly successful in moving away from a rule-conscious, rigidly normative approach to one that included emotional and playful aspects. Johann Elias Schlegel, an uncle of the famous Schlegel brothers of the Romantic period, was long over-shadowed by the far more famous Lessing, primarily because his writings were not edited and published until after Lessing's position had been firmly established. This publication date obscures the fact that his important contributions in criticism pre-date Lessing's. Chronologically speaking, Schlegel was the first to voice a positive critical evaluation of Shakespeare, the first to define more accurately than any of his contemporaries what constitutes a work of art, and the first to anticipate in his own writings the features and characteristics of the *Sturm und Drang* movement.

The young Schlegel received his education at the famous boarding school in Pforta, Saxony, where he was inspired by the literature of the classics to base his own initial attempts at tragedy on the themes and plots of the plays of antiquity. The encouragement to do so came mainly from two sources, Gottsched's *Critische Dichtkunst*, which he read in Pforta, and contemporary French versions of these ancient dramas. These early tragedies reflect the stilted rationalistic approach. In his use of Alexandrine verse as well as in his strict observance of the unities he followed Gottsched. His earliest play, *Orest und Pylades* (1737), originally under the title *Die Geschwister von Taurien*, was performed by his fellow students in 1738 and in 1739 in Leipzig by the Neuber troupe. A rationalistic mood dominates the dialogue, which turns into an exchange of witticisms. The characters outdo each other in clever phrases. As a result the real action of the play lies in the language, in the attempts of the characters to interpret each others' actions. Iphigenia questions Pylades' apparently strong expressions of friendship for Orest. Her words indicate a detached rational examination of Pylades' actions:

Nun fass ich, was du sagst. So bist du auch ein Freund,

Der darum redlich ist, damit er redlich scheint?
Du hast dich ihm getreu und ohne Falsch erwiesen;
Doch du hast es gethan, nur dass es andere priesen.[6]

[IV, 1]

Schlegel's concern in these early plays was with developing the German language as a critical and sharp tool for expressing precise thoughts. That is of greater importance to him than the absolute adherence to the three unities. His next drama, *Dido* (1739), and the following one, *Die Trojanerinnen* (originally planned as *Hekuba*), were also written while he was still in Pforta, although they were not published until 1744 and 1747 respectively. Schlegel continued to revise his plays in later years. *Die Trojanerinnen* is of interest because it echoes the concern of the period with the problem of explaining the existence of evil, which seemingly is in conflict with the notion of God as creator. Schlegel uses the cool reflection of his characters as a device to tone down the cruel elements of the play, and to achieve a distance from the immediacy of the plot. When Agamemnon contemplates in the fourth act whether or not to give his consent to human sacrifice, he describes his dilemma in analytical detail:

Jetzt denk ich: Soll ein Blut, das Unschuld schützt, erkalten?
Jetzt denk ich: Soll ich Blut den Geistern vorenthalten?
Bald denk ich, dass ein Gott kein Unrecht fordern kann,
Bald denk ich, er begehrts, drum ist es recht gethan.

[IV, 4]

For nine more lines Agamemnon continues this debate in his own mind. This thinking out loud is essentially undramatic, so that neither Schlegel's depiction of the characters nor his plot line hold fascination for the reader. But the use of German as a means of precise presentation of thoughts and feelings stands out as Schlegel's major achievement in his early works.

In 1739 Schlegel enrolled at the University of Leipzig. His move to Leipzig coincided with his finding the literary *métier* in which he was to be most successful, the comedy. The promise to his father that he would forgo writing plays during his university years was soon forgotten. The year 1740 saw his first comedy, *Die entführte Dose*, in rhymed Alexandrines. Only a few scenes of this early play are extant, but they give significant proof that the comedy allowed Schlegel to make full use of his witty language. Schlegel himself viewed the dialogue

as the major accomplishment of a comedy.[7] Of course, he was familiar
with the repertoire of the Neuber troupe, and realized that there was a
scarcity of German comedies. The use of verse in his first comedy was
startling. It was against Gottsched's rules. Schlegel defended his decision
to produce a rhymed comedy in the treatise *Schreiben an den Herrn
N. N. über die Comödie in Versen* (1740).[8] However, his eloquent
argument for the use of verse in comedies did not prevent him from
employing prose in most of the comedies he wrote after 1740. This is
not altogether surprising, for Schlegel had maintained that the question
of verse or prose is not one of primary importance, as it does not
pertain to the nature of a work of art. Of the Leipzig comedies the text
of only one, *Der geschäftige Mussiggänger* (1741), is available in its
entirety. Schlegel burnt *Die Pracht zu Landheim* (1742), a play that
castigated the wastefulness of the Saxon country nobility, and he never
finished *Die drei Philosophen* (1742). In spite of their incompleteness
these comedies underline his theoretical concept that a work of art
represents a new kind of reality, not one measured and established by
the principles of either imitation or probability. Nor is it the main
function of a work of art to demonstrate moral teachings. He allows
for intellectual and aesthetic enjoyment, and sees the moral and
didactic principles as being subordinate to the broader concept of art
as an aesthetic expression.[9] In developing this literary theory Schlegel
pursued and defended his own individual approach; at a time when all
of Germany's critics were divided into two camps, he sided neither
with the Gottsched group nor with the Swiss critics, but rather
continued to define and refine his own views, independently of the
fighting factions which showed less and less objectivity in delineating
their respective positions. Again and again Schlegel formulated his
conviction that a work of art must not be judged by the same criteria
which are used to understand outward reality. A work of art has its
own set of laws and must be judged accordingly. It would be wrong,
however, to say that Schlegel rejected all of Gottsched's theories about
literary criticism. He did not claim that art has no didactic function,
merely that the moral lesson is not the essence; nor did he claim that
imitation of nature should not be a guiding principle. What he rejected
was Gottsched's inflexibility. It is therefore understandable that their
friendship lasted only as long as Schlegel remained in Leipzig.

In the fall of 1742 Schlegel completed his studies, and early in
1743 he went to Copenhagen. He was to spend the remainder of his
short life in Denmark, first as secretary to the Saxon ambassador, later
as professor of history and political science. During 1745 and 1746

he published a weekly journal, appropriately named *Der Fremde*. In Copenhagen Schlegel directed his full attention to practical aspects of the theater, writing a short play, *Die Langeweile* (1747), in which Comedy is presented as a young woman, not yet grown.

The same interest in the theater is suggested by the title of his famous essay *Gedanken zur Aufnahme des dänischen Theaters*. In it he expresses his feeling that the predominance on the German stage of French comedies in translation had hindered the development of German comedy and had introduced foreign standards and customs into Germany: 'Die Deutschen haben den Fehler begangen, dass sie ohne Unterschied allerley Komödien aus dem Französischen übersetzt haben, ohne vorher zu überlegen, ob die Charaktere derselben auch auf ihre Sitten sich schickten.' It is in this context that his earlier pioneering essay, *Vergleichung Shakespears und Andreas Gryphs* (1741), must be mentioned. The comparison of the two poets and dramatists — Gryphius was born the year in which Shakespeare died — prepared Germany for the enormous influence Shakespeare's works were to exert over the next few decades. Not that Shakespeare is seen as a genius, setting his own rules. Schlegel points out that Shakespeare's strength lay in his ability to create characters rather than in his con- centrating on the plot. Because the plot is not of primary concern Shakespeare should not be expected to pay special attention to such matters as the three unities. While defending Shakespeare's dramas Schlegel does criticize the English author for employing language not in keeping with the accepted high level of discourse so suitable for tragedies. From the point of view of the rationalistic Enlightenment critic, both Shakespeare and Gryphius display a certain pompousness in their works which Schlegel cannot accept. Schlegel compared neither of these two undervalued dramatists to the then standard-setting Racine or Corneille but to one another. This indicates that further renewal of the drama had to come from non-classicistic approaches. Long before Lessing, Schlegel questioned the ascendency of translated French plays in the German theater at that time.

He continued experimenting with new styles in his writing of plays. In Leipzig he had written the tragedy *Hermann,* which was published in Gottsched's *Deutsche Schaubühne* in 1743. That was the first time he chose a topic from national history. Much more important in this respect, however, is his *Canut* (1746), treating an event from Denmark's history and written for the opening of Copenhagen's theater. Through cunning, Ulfo had gained the hand of King Canut's sister, Estrithe. Her love for him and her absolute faithfulness to him stemmed from her

mistaken belief that it was the king's will that she marry Ulfo. Therefore, she quietly accepts and even supports Ulfo's evil actions, all of
which have only one goal, to make him king instead of Canut. It is only
when Estrithe and Ulfo return to the king's palace — the entire play
takes place there — to receive his pardon for Ulfo's actions against
Canut's army that Estrithe learns how she had been tricked into
marriage. There is little action in the play and there are no unexpected
events. Ulfo's responses are entirely consistent with his stated goal, the
overthrow of Canut. To that end he will use any means, except self-
humiliation. He will not beg for leniency or forgiveness and will not ask
that his life be spared:

> *Ulfo.* Doch ich bin ungebeugt. Es schwimmen in der Flut,
> Durch meine List ersäuft, die Völker des Canut.
> Trotzt' ich nicht ungestraft die Stärke seiner Flotten?
> Ein Boot beschützte mich, ihn sicher zu verspotten.
> Der keinem Feinde sonst vergebens nachgejagt,
> Hat in der Wüsten mich zu suchen nicht gewagt.
> Und ich, ich käme selbst und wollt' um Gnade bitten?
> Dies heisst zu viel verlangt; wofür hätt' ich gestritten?
>
> [I, 1]

Ulfo's honesty in admitting to his wrongdoings gives substance to his
character. When confronted by Estrithe he admits to his trickery, and
when asked by Canut about the plan to overthrow the king he confesses
to the crime:

> *Canut.* Und du gestehst die Tat?
> *Ulfo.* Wie sollt' ich sie verhehlen?
> Mein Anschlag war so gross!-ach! musst er denn verfehlen!
> *Canut.* Haquin, befiehl der Wacht, das sie ihn mit sich führt.
> *Ulfo.* Was hilft es, dass ein Herz der Trieb nach Ehre rührt,
> Wenn andre träge sind, und sucht man sie zu heben,
> Doch immer mit Gewalt zur Erde niederstreben?
> Wenn es der schönsten Tat stets an Gehülfen fehlt.
>
> [IV, 4]

Canut is a play in the Enlightenment tradition if judged by the amount
of time that is devoted to rational discourse about vice and virtue.
Schlegel still observed the unities, still used Alexandrine verse — even
though he was by then advocating iambic pentameter — but he portrays,

through the two main characters in the play, the tension between the ideals of his own time and the growing attack on these ideals, the patient, modest, and very deliberate Canut on the one hand, and the egocentric, unscrupulous Ulfo on the other. In Ulfo, Schlegel created a character whose ruthless striving for power, independence, and individuality represent a criticism of the Enlightenment era that would soon be heard over and over again.[10]

Unlike Gottsched, Schlegel was equally effective as critic and as playwright, a dual role which was to be played by Lessing as well. Of the comedies Schlegel wrote in Denmark, *Triumph der guten Frauen* (1748), and *Die stumme Schönheit* (1747), the latter, a one-act play in rhymed Alexandrines, is the more important from a formal point of view, being his only complete comedy in verse. There is hardly any action in the play. Jungwitz is to meet his bride. The marriage is to take place now that the bride has spent several years living with a widow and her daughter and receiving an education. But Jungwitz finds his bride to be utterly without any intellectual ability. The clever widow exchanges the two girls, and Jungwitz is delighted when he suddenly discovers 'his' bride is well educated and intellectually his equal. The point of the play is Jungwitz's enlightened insistence that his wife must also be his intellectual companion: 'Zum Umgang nehm ich sie, nicht um bedient zu seyn.' His faith in reason is vindicated when he finds such a wife in the widow's daughter. Jungwitz is a true representative of his age when he asserts that only reason has the power to convince another:

Die Schönheit kann ein Herz wohl rühren, nicht durchdringen.
Nur der Verstand allein kann den Verstand bezwingen.

The use of verse stresses the importance Schlegel attached to language as a means of achieving the aesthetic pleasure that he saw as the main function of a play. But it must be added that such pleasure is only possible in Schlegel's view if the didactic message, in this case teaching the power and virtue of reason, is delivered at the same time.

When Schlegel died in 1749, only 30 years of age, he left a rich legacy that would only slowly be understood and appreciated. His work gives evidence of the variety of approaches possible even in such a seemingly uniform period as the rationalistic age.

2 *Gellert*

In Christian Fürchtegott Gellert (1715—1769) we meet an author easily identifiable as a representative of the German literary Enlightenment. Both as professor — he was a popular teacher — and as a successful writer he embodied the concerns of the age: preoccupation with educational efforts, emphasis on wit and gracefulness, acceptance of standardized rules and codes. Being a man of unusual integrity, Gellert demonstrated in his own life the ideals of modesty and deliberateness that his contemporaries hailed as the most important human virtues.

In his own time Gellert was known primarily as a writer of fables, continuing the tradition of Hagedorn, which had found many imitators. Gellert published fables in 1746, and in 1748, each time with success. But whereas Hagedorn had developed the light Rococo verse narrative that charmed and amused, Gellert is at all times, even in his poetic writings, the professor who uses the witty fable to illustrate his teachings, often in satirical fashion. His fables are no less witty than Hagedorn's but they do not advocate Rococo carefreeness; they rather reflect his endorsement of the ideals of a bourgoisie that is proud of its education and of its role in society. They relate how people may be easily fooled, and may for instance assume intelligence in a person simply because he is well-dressed. In 'Der Zeisig' a boy picks out the bird that looks most attractive even though he has been asked to determine the bird that sings most beautifully:

> Sagt, ob man im gemeinen Leben
> Nicht oft wie dieser Knabe schliesst?
> Wemb Farb' und Kleid ein Ansehn geben,
> Der hat Verstand, so dumm er ist.
>
> [*DNL*, XLIII, 39]

The fables also tell of the free-thinker whom fear induces to turn to the religion he had so often scorned; and of the lover who naively thinks his love will be more convincing if clothed in the rhetorical language of the Baroque. Discriminating knowledge is the ideal extolled. The person who is widely read will not as easily become a victim of man's follies as the one who eschews real learning. This ideal is carried over to Gellert's comedies, in which the young are triumphant because they have critical faculties and are well aware of the cultural and social developments of their age.[11] They frequently discuss recent literary events and important new publications. Gellert correctly gauged the temperament of the new generation and took particular care to address himself to the young. This fact may have contributed decisively to the enormous popularity he enjoyed in his lifetime.

Gellert, born in Hainichen in Saxony, came to Leipzig in 1734 as a
student and stayed there all his life except for a three-year interval
following his university studies. In 1741 he took up writing in a more
formal manner, and in 1744 he assumed a teaching position at the
university, where he remained until his death. Most of his own literary
works appeared in quick succession during the forties: the fables, the
comedies, and his novel, *Das Leben der schwedischen Gräfin von G. . .*

In a century when poets often treated in their fables topics or
incidents found in older examples of the genre, Gellert devised original
fables based for the most part on incidents he had observed in real life.
The same is true of his plays. He started out with two pastoral plays,
but soon dropped this genre in favor of comedies. Judging from his own
remarks about the nature of pastoral plays Gellert wanted to treat
issues more immediate than those found in the framework of the
pastoral life. His earliest play, *Das Band* (1744), built on the motif of
unfounded jealousy, uses the traditional landscape and characters of
the pastoral scene. Yet Gellert felt correctly that the play was not
pastoral in the strict sense of the word; for he had stayed much too
close to real farm life to have done justice to the stylized poetic
demands of the pastoral. Only once more did he try his hand at a
pastoral play, with *Sylvia* in 1745. Thereafter he turned to writing
comedies. The same year he published his first prose comedy, *Die
Betschwester*, a play he later wished he had not written. The play
was attacked because it allegedly satirized religion. The attack hurt
Gellert who was a deeply religious man, one who practiced the
'vernünftige Andacht eines frommen Herzens'.[12] To be sure, Gellert
did deal with the problem of hypocritical and superstitious religiosity
and selfish piety. That in itself could hardly have occasioned the
attack; but he also provided a contrast to this false kind of religiosity
through several characters whose generosity and fundamental goodness
is just as dominant as the 'Betschwester's' false piety. Objections to the
play arose because their generosity is in no way grounded in religious
piety.

Gellert, the enlightened critic, questions the 'Betschwester's' piety in
the opening scene:

> *Ferdinand.* Allein ihr stetes Beten und Singen bringt mich fast
> auf die Gedanken, dass sie nicht fromm ist, sondern nur fromm
> scheinen will . . . . Stets beten heisst nicht beten, und den ganzen
> Tag beten ist so strafbar, als den ganzen Tag schlafen.[13]

[I, 1]

The play then continues to reveal the 'Betschwester's' hypocrisy. What she claims to be her pious manners, namely her being dressed in clothes that were common fifty years earlier, is judged correctly as her particular fashions. Gellert delights in such subtle and scrutinizing distinctions. A sequence of events rounds out the picture of the pious 'Betschwester' as superstitious, greedy and without any understanding for the plight of those who are less fortunate than she is. Gellert appears to voice his own opinions through Ferdinand, whose task it is, on behalf of his friend Simon, to settle the matter of the dowry for the 'Betschwester's' daughter. When the 'Betschwester' accuses Ferdinand of lack of religion he replies:

> Die Religion is das Heiligste unter allem, was ein Vernünftiger hochschätzen kann. Aber die Meynungen eines übelbeschaffenen Verstandes gehören nicht zur Religion, sondern unter die Irrthümer.
>
> [I, 6]

Such a comment surely reflects Gellert's own views and explains why he felt personally attacked by the numerous criticisms of the play. It is characteristic of the Enlightenment that wealthy Simon, who had come to marry the 'Betschwester's' daughter, decides rather to marry Christianchen's intelligent friend Lorchen because Christianchen does give the impression of simple-mindedness. Yet it is merely because her mother denied her access to 'worldly' reading materials that she gives this impression. Her first encounter with contemporary thought is the moral weekly *Der Zuschauer* ('Lesen Sie mir nur oft aus dem Zuschauer vor', [II, 3]). In reality, Christianchen is a talented girl, who will be Simon's equal as soon as she is exposed to the Berlin society and its wealth of culture. It is, therefore, just as much a sign of the optimism of the period that Lorchen in the final scenes of the play convinces Simon through rational arguments that he should indeed marry Christianchen.

Two important points become obvious to the literary historian. The first is that Gellert was caught in a characteristic tension of the Enlightenment period. On the one hand prevailed a deeply rooted personal piety that was not blind to the superficiality and intolerance of a false religiosity, while on the other there prevailed a conviction that man is capable of adhering to high moral standards without any reliance on religion. The second observation is that Gellert's use of the comedy for didactic purposes, not only indirectly by satirizing vices, but just as much by portraying positive examples of goodness, is quite in keeping with Gottsched's *Critische Dichtkunst*.

However, Gellert changed the emphasis of the comedy, which traditionally exposed human weakness and folly. In his comedies he goes a step further by placing the emphasis on the exemplary action. Because such emphasis produces less laughter, the playwright seeks to engage the reader's emotions through empathy. Thus Gellert became the initiator of the sentimental comedy in Germany, strongly in-fluenced by the 'comedie larmoyante'. In 1746 Gellert's second comedy, *Das Loos in der Lotterie*, was published, again portraying characters at whom we are to laugh, but more importantly portraying others who should move us by their exemplary lives. Thus the characters satirized for demonstrating a lack of empathy and an attitude of overweening, affected French manners and language, are foils to the positive and dominating figures.

His third comedy, *Die zärtlichen Schwestern* (1747), can most clearly be placed within the 'sentimental' class. Very few amusing parts are contained in this play, which is as it should be, for according to Gellert the audience is not to react with laughter but rather with compassionate tears. It is more a play in which the characters are being tested, and their virtue or lack of it is established. Two sisters, Lottchen and Julchen, are being courted but Julchen apparently prefers her freedom to marriage. Her uncle, a typical but dull representative of the age, attempts to convince her with rational arguments why she is obligated to marry:

> Wenn Sie gleich nicht den schärfsten Verstand haben: so haben
> Sie doch ein gutes Herz. Und ich wollte wetten, wenn Sie statt
> der Bremischen Beyträge und anderer solchen seichten Schriften,
> eine systematische Moralphilosophie läsen, dass sie bald anders
> sollten denken lernen. . . . Die Liebe ist eine Uebereinstimmung
> zweener Willen zu gleichen Zwecken. Mich deucht, diess ist sehr
> adäquat.
>
> [II, 14]

Julchen's constant love for her suitor, of which her uncle is unaware, is the virtue that turns the uncle's misguided rationalism into an object of laughter. The sentimental comedy was an effective means of closely engaging the reader in the emotions and feelings of the characters. These comedies testify to the growth of a more positive attitude toward emotional reactions, making the distanced observation and rejection of vice no longer a sufficient response. When Lottchen discovers her lover to be a traitor and deceiver she lets him go. The disinterested observer would interpret this as being necessary for her happiness. Her last words, however — also the final line of the play — emphasize her loss rather than her gain: 'Bedauern Sie mich!'

The sentimental comedy was a thorough success in Germany. This is evidenced in part by Gellert's treatise on the subject, *Pro comoedia commovente*, written in 1751, several years after the comedies had appeared and had been well received. The same year Gellert published a collection of his letters, *Briefe, nebst einer Abhandlung von dem guten Geschmacke in Briefen*, which became a sort of style manual for the period, and in which he treated also literary genres, including the comedy. He supports the typical satirical comedy, yet gives preference to the sentimental play.

Gellert wrote his only novel during the same years that saw the writing of the comedies. The anonymously published *Das Leben der schwedischen Grafin von G. . .* (1747–1748) holds an important place in literary history as an example of a sentimental family novel in German. Gellert was deeply impressed by Richardson's novel *Pamela*, which had appeared in a German translation only two years after the original publication in 1740. It was inevitable that Richardson's tremendous success in Germany would produce imitators. Gellert, with a keen eye for Richardson's artistic innovations, was among the first. In Gellert's judgement Richardson was the first to make the novel acceptable as a form of literature. In a letter to one E. v. Schönfeld he includes the epigram:

> Wie lange war für dich, o Jugend,
> die Liebe des Romans ein Gift!
> Und sieh, ein Richardson, der Freund der wahren Tugend
> macht den Roman für dich, o Jugend,
> zum Wercke des Geschmacks, der Weisheit und der Tugend,
> zum frömmsten Werke nach der Schrift.[14]

He summarized his insights into Richardson's works: 'Sie sind Natur, Geschmack, Religion.' Gellert paid special attention to these three aspects while working on his own novel. The first person narrator expressly states that this is not to be just another adventure novel of the kind that was still favored in Germany. The intention is to produce a work in which the realistic elements of life, 'Natur', force the characters to understand themselves as complex human beings. The moral issues, 'Religion', provide perspectives for judging the actions of the characters, and Gellert deals with the formal problems, 'Geschmack', in such a way that the novel does not turn merely into a moral guide. Still, the novel does not constitute a unified whole, mainly because the author concentrated more on the abstract issues than on portraying consistent individual characters. The theme of the novel is that of human reaction to extraordinary events. Ideally there are always rational solutions, yet human beings, especially the young, are not always capable of finding and accepting such solutions.[15] The sentimental element in Gellert's comedies and in his novel broadened the means for literary expression by providing an appropriate approach to the artistic portrayal of feelings and emotions.

Gellert produced all of his major works of literature during the forties. In the fifties he concentrated more on critical essays. But the famous collection *Geistliche Oden und Lieder* originated in the fifties also (1757). Some of these hymns which gave expression to Gellert's personal devotion to the Christian faith became extremely well known. There can be no question that this commitment to religion grew more prevalent at this time. This explains why immediately after his death people would write more about Gellert's faith and moral life than about his literary achievements.

3 The 'Bremer Beiträger'

Gellert contributed much to the prominence of Leipzig in the mid-forties in the history of literature in Germany. As professors at the university both he and Gottsched directed many students toward the study and the writing of literature. As a consequence, Leipzig attracted many an aspiring young author. The city offered cultural activities that were conducive to their literary projects. When Lessing started his writing career there, towards the end of the decade, he remarked about the representative, non-provincial nature of the town: 'Ich komme nach Leipzig, an einen Ort, wo man die ganze Welt in kleinen sehen kann.'[16] This statement is all the more understandable if one keeps in mind the cosmopolitan character of Leipzig, established by the merchants who came here in large numbers from all parts of Europe. Lessing's arrival in Leipzig coincided with the decline of Gottsched's power, a decline which had started in the mid-forties. Some minor authors, disciples of Gottsched's broke away from the tyranny of his influence, probably prompted by the example shown by such independent writers as J. E. Schlegel and Gellert. One group of poets in particular, the so-called 'Bremer Beiträger' must be mentioned here, as they established their independence from Gottsched, preferring to function as their own authorities, without joining forces with the Swiss critics. Even though as individual authors they did not set new standards or develop new models, they took the primary stress away from theoretical writing about literature and placed it on the literary works themselves. They quickly gained respect because they were contributing to the revival of the creative aspect in literature.

Several young men in Leipzig, originally followers of Gottsched and contributors to the journal *Belustigungen des Verstandes und Witzes*, joined in a small revolt against Gottsched in 1744. The exception in this group was the ever-faithful Gottsched supporter, Johann Joachim Schwabe (1714–1784). Schwabe had founded the journal in 1741, that is to say at the height of the feud between Gottsched and the Swiss critics Bodmer and Breitinger; and he had been more than willing to open his columns for Gottsched's use in attacking his enemies. Some of the other young contributors soon became disenchanted with this feuding and demanded a journal which would publish only creative works, leaving aside theoretical and polemical discussions as secondary. They subsequently founded their own journal which appeared under the title *Neue Beiträge zum Vergnügen des Verstandes und Witzes*. Since it was published in Bremen, its founders became known as the 'Bremer Beiträger'.

The titles of both the old and the new journals acknowledge the rule of the rational in literature. But the 'Bremer Beiträger' were seeking concrete literary models and not merely theoretical advice. They looked above all to Hagedorn and Haller. Such an orientation removed their viewpoint even further from that of Gottsched, in spite of their subservience to rules and their formal adherence to his *Critische Dichtkunst*. A strong confirmation of their divergence from Gottsched was furnished by the publication in their journal of the first three cantos of the *Messias* by Klopstock, whose artistic aims were totally opposed to those of Gottsched. The break with Gottsched was complete, and that in itself opened the way for a literary development beyond the boundaries of a strictly rationalistic age.

Karl Christian Gärtner (1712–1791), a school friend of Gellert – both attended the famous St. Afra school in Meissen – was the editor of the *Neue Beiträge* which appeared during the years 1745–1748. It was originally intended as a monthly paper, but in reality was published less often. The first number of the journal contained Gärtner's pastoral play, *Die geprüfte Treue*.

Johann Andreas Cramer (1723–1788), known for his rhymed translation of the book of Psalms, was a leading figure in the group. During the active days of the 'Bremer Beiträger' he held a teaching position at the University of Leipzig. His fame is based on his success as a theologian and preacher. He was chaplain at the court in Quedlinburg, and after 1754 in Copenhagen, then professor of theology in Kiel. His biography of Gellert (1774) is a vivid source of information about the times. He also edited the well-known journal *Der Nordische Aufseher* (1758– 1761), in which Klopstock was to publish a number of essays. Cramer's religious poetry is of the reflective type so characteristic of religious lyrics during the Enlightenment.

One of the most active contributors to the new journal was Johann Adolf Schlegel (1721–1793), a brother of Johann Elias Schlegel. He held high ecclesiastical offices as a preacher, was fairly productive as a religious poet, and occupied himself with questions of literary criticism. For example, he issued a German translation of Batteux, together with a commentary, *Les beaux arts réduits à une même principe* in 1751. He left Leipzig, where he had been a student since 1741, fairly soon after the 'Bremer Beitrager' had organized, but con- tinued to work with them. His more pronounced opposition to Gottsched found expression in a satire that ridiculed Gottsched's concept of naturalness in pastoral plays: *Vom Natürlichen in Schäfergedichten*, (1746).

Johann Arnold Ebert (1723–1795) represented the Anacreontic tradition in the group. He also contributed translations of English works, introducing Glover's historical epic *Leonidas*, and the works of Edward Young, which he published in a five-volume edition, and which were to have a revolutionary effect on many German writers. English literature gained ever greater importance in the eyes of the 'Bremer Beiträger', and this preference was to bring them closer to the Swiss critics.

There were other active members: Gottlieb Fuchs (1720–1799), Nikolaus Dietrich Giseke (1724–1765), and Christian Friedrich Zernitz (1717–1745), all three writing poetry. Of the original group the most talented were Gottlieb Wilhelm Rabener (1714–1771) and Just Friedrich Wilhelm Zachariae (1726–1777), both satirists. They have had a lasting effect, and their writings are of interest even today. Satire as a literary form enjoyed considerable popularity in the age of reason, one of whose aims was to correct human weaknesses by showing them as ridiculous. Both Rabener and Zachariä brought fame to the 'Bremer Beiträger', and it is not surprising that other poets joined the group: Klopstock, Christian Felix Weisse, Johann Friedrich von Cronegk, and Johann Wilhelm Ludwig Gleim. The new journal thus provided an incentive for young authors by pointing to and creating new and different models. The most diverse views were represented in this journal as opposed to the dogmatic rigidity required of the followers of Gottsched.

III Diversity in Drama: Krüger and Weisse

The increasing criticism to which Gottsched was subjected should in no way cloud the more important recognition that his example did much to prompt creative writing in many genres, particularly in the drama. Luise Gottsched had supported her husband's stated objective of providing the theater with German dramas that exhibited the high intellectual ideals of the period. In addition, J. E. Schlegel, Gellert and the 'Bremer Beiträger' had all witnessed Gottsched's success during their student days in Leipzig and had subscribed to his program of theater reform. As they became more independent they turned to a greater diversity of models, especially in comedy, so much so that the period between 1740 and 1760 has been described as 'Blüte' of comedy.[17] Because this flowering was concentrated in the Saxon city of Leipzig, the comedy of this period is usually referred to as 'sächsische Komödie' or even 'sächsische Typenkomödie'.[18] Its characters or 'types' are for the most part portrayed as living embodiments of particular personality traits, such as the dull scholar, the obnoxious idler, the proud freethinker. Hence these comedies are an instructive social commentary on the eighteenth century, for through them we learn much about the views and customs of middle-class society. Even Lessing's early comedies conform to the basic pattern of the 'sächsische Typenkomödie', as we shall see later. He, too, interestingly enough, first became acquainted with the theater in Leipzig and wrote his first plays there. His testimony to the effect that he learned social graces from the plays he saw in Leipzig confirms that they reflect accurately the style and ideals of the period. The age did not seek to present individuality or originality in its characters. This dimension was first added by Lessing in the 1760s.

It is appropriate to the nature of comedy to make a point through overstatement, and the 'sächsische Komödie' is no exception. While it makes use of typical characters that resemble those in real society, it ridicules human weaknesses with stark exaggeration. But if the 'sächsische Komödie' exaggerates so as to induce laughter, the sentimental type of comedy exaggerates for the sake of evoking tears. This is because the authors wanted to move their audiences to a greater dedication in practicing virtue by following the example of the 'good' characters. Besides the comedies of Luise Gottschedin, of J. E. Schlegel, of Gllert, and of several of the 'Bremer Beiträger', those of two other contemporary playwrights give evidence that the comedy enjoyed great popularity during the Enlightenment period. Johann Christian Krüger (1722–1750) is best known for his *Die Geistlichen auf dem Lande* (1743), a play whose satirical portrayal of evil and hypocritical preachers who trap an honest and credulous woman caused so much opposition that it was banned. Krüger, who himself had given up the study of theology, used the comedy to expose hidden evils of the times, and proved that the comedy of types was a powerful weapon in combating society's ills. In *Die Candidaten oder die Mittel zu einem Amte zu gelangen* (1748) he draws on the strengths of the sentimental comedy which Gellert had realized only a year earlier. Like Gellert's *Die zärtlichen Schwestern*, Krüger's comedy shows the power of love to keep the lovers virtuous and bring them together in spite of intrigues. Krüger skillfully blends elements of both types of comedy, especially in *Die Candidaten* where both satirical and sentimental tones unite.

If the popularity of the numerous comedies of Christian Felix Weisse's (1726–1804) are any measure of success, then the period received the 'sächsische Typenkomödie' enthusiastically. Like most of the other dramatists, Weisse studied in Leipzig, where he became a friend of Gottsched, and of Lessing during the latter's student days there. Weisse did not develop new forms, but rather always wrote the kind of comedy he had come to know in Leipzig during the mid-forties. But his familiarity with the techniques and nuances of the 'sächsische Komödie', and his ability to shape and write ever new comedies of the same basic type, made him one of the most successful playwrights of his time. His plays demonstrated that the fundamental scheme of the 'sächsische Komödie' was vital enough to allow for many variations. Even after Lessing had created a new kind of comedy with his famous *Minna von Barnhelm*, Weisse confidently continued with his satirical and sentimental plays. Among his best are *Poeten nach der Mode* (1751), which treats the literary feud between Gottsched and the Swiss, *Alter hilft für Thorheit nicht, oder die Haushälterin* (1758), and *List über List* (1767).

Weisse was dedicated to the spirit of rationalism, especially in its Rococo form. His Anacreontic verses reflect his love for stylized forms, including the 'Singspiel'. He was a prolific librettist for this form of 'German operetta', making it successful in spite of Gottsched's ban on the opera. The 'Singspiel' had its origin in 1743 with a performance of Coffey's *The Devil to Pay* in Berlin. Christian Felix Weisse prepared his own version of the play for a performance in Leipzig in 1752, for which J. C. Standfuss composed new tunes. The successful performance made the 'Singspiel' a popular stage attraction, to be interrupted by the Seven Year War. Following the war 'Weisse recast the two [Coffey] comedies [including *The Merry Cobbler*] after the French manner . . . He extended the number of acts to three, polished the coarse language of farce, and above all considerably increased the number of songs, retaining of course the spoken dialogue.'[19] The composer who provided the music for these new versions was Johann Adam Hiller, whose tunes became particularly popular and with whom Weisse was to collaborate very closely. The librettos which Weisse wrote for Hiller include *Lottchen am Hofe* (1767), *Die Liebe auf dem Lande* (1768) and *Die Jagd* (1770).

Weisse achieved equal success with his tragedies — so, in fact, he became the most recognized dramatist during the 1760s.[20] And while severe criticism by Lessing destroyed his fame for many years afterwards, recent studies have demonstrated the significance of Weisse's contributions to the development of tragedy in the eighteenth century.[21] Weisse's concern for stylistic smoothness, a formal characteristic of Rococo poetry, benefited his tragedies, which exhibit a polished linguistic regularity. Because he was interested mainly in such formal aspects of play-writing he did not take part in the considerable argument as to whether French or English drama was more worthy of imitation. Despite his independence from Gottsched in writing opera, he followed accepted practice by composing his first two tragedies, *Eduard II* (1758) and *Richard III* (1759), in Alexandrine verse. In 1764 appeared his *Die Befreiung von Theben*, written in iambic pentameters. By recalling a historical setting of war he treated the topical experiences of war and peace in contemporary Prussia and Saxony. The Seven Years' War, which had meant a seven years occupation of Saxony by Prussia, had come to an end only one year earlier. During the war the Saxon king was exiled to his Polish territories, and the Saxon soldiers had been incorporated into the Prussian army. Saxony was treated by Frederick the Great much like a province within his kingdom, for he had hoped for a permanent annexation of Saxony to Prussia. The 1763 peace treaty, the Hubertusburg Settlement, however, restored Saxony to its pre-war status. Weisse treated the topic with understanding and wisdom, so much so that Sengle praises Weisse's tragedy for its balanced humanistic idealism.[22] The playwright's greatest success was his prose adaptation of Shakespeare's *Romeo and Juliet* (*Romeo und Julia* 1767), for which he used the special genre of middle-class drama, or 'bügerliches Trauerspiel'.

IV Diversity in Poetry

The breadth of accomplishments which Brockes, Hagedorn and Haller had achieved in the first decade of Enlightenment literature was generally not matched by the poets of the forties. While these earlier poets had successfully embodied in their verses the complex and encompassing concerns and issues of Enlightenment philosophy, as well as the range of viewpoints of the period, the poets of the forties confined themselves to more limited themes, be it that they stressed the vatic qualities of the poet, or concentrated exclusively on Anacreontic motifs, or developed the idyllic tones. These thematic emphases are indeed directly related to the major philosophical and religious points of view of the period, but there is a deliberate narrowing of scope. Individual poets usually selected only one of these emphases resulting in the subdivision of a comprehensive genre into specialized types.

1 *The Lofty in Poetry: Pyra and Lange*

Far from being concerned with universal issues Pyra and Lange felt justified in using poetry to express their personal feelings of mutual friendship. Because their friendship was rooted in Pietism they cele-brated it as something holy. In their world of imagination the poet functions as a priest who receives his message in a moment of lofty ecstasy, and whose verse is a communication of that message. The poetry of Pyra and Lange makes use of Biblical and Pietistic concepts, often veiled with allusions to classical antiquity. It also draws on contemporary Rococo and even Anacreontic models.[23] Samuel Gotthold Lange (1711–1781) the son of a Pietistic professor of theology at the University of Halle, won Jakob Immanuel Pyra (1715–1744) over to his beliefs. The friendship that developed between Pyra and the younger Lange was sustained by shared religious convictions and literary interests. When Lange accepted his first pastorate in Laublingen near Halle in 1737, this friendship did not suffer. In fact, immediately after completing his education in Halle in 1738, Pyra went to live with Lange and his young wife. They spent some three years together in Laublingen, mainly writing poetry, before Pyra took up a teaching post in Berlin in 1742, only two years before his death.

Their poems were published in one volume with the title *Thirsis und Damons freundschaftliche Lieder* (1745). The fact that Bodmer edited the volume reveals the side on which Lange and Pyra stood in the well-known literary feud.[24] Pyra is far superior to Lange as a poet. As Thirsis, Pyra writes about his feelings for Damon (Lange) and Doris (Lange's wife). Their friendship is all he needs to rise above the sordid world to the lofty heights of poetic purity where inspiration 'full of heavenly thoughts' is possible:

> Bis in den stillen Grund der Seelen,
> Vom allerreinsten Licht erhabner Zärtlichkeit
> Durchaus erhellt verkläret und durchdrungen,
> Entzückst du mich, voll himmlischer Gedancken,
> Mit dir von der unwürdgen Welt
> Vom Schwarm des Staubs, in ewig heitre Sphären.
> O göttlich schöne Einsamkeit!
> Nichst ist um mich als du und Doris.[25]

[*EdL*, V, 193]

The careful avoidance of rhyme, the use of words derived from the Pietistic view of man and world — no longer Leibniz's best of all possible worlds — prepare for further developments in lyrical poetry that were to become identified primarily with Klopstock.[26] Pyra knows of the fire of inspiration and defends it against Gottsched. His early poem 'Der Tempel der Wahren Dichtkunst' (1737), in five cantos, describes the path that leads the poet to an understanding of inspired, and hence true, poetry. Only those with sufficient dedication will eventually enter the inner sanctuary of the temple of poetry. Klopstock would soon continue with this concept, according to which a poet is seen as a priest to whom truth is entrusted.

Pyra and Lange saw in Bodmer's and Breitinger's literary criticism a position which supported their own practice. Even without such an alliance a clash with Gottsched was unavoidable. Pyra's strongly worded treatise, *Erweis, dass die G*ttsch*dianische Sekte den Geschmack verderbe* (1743) — a sequel was published in 1744 — asserted that Gottsched had never even understood the fundamentals of poetry because he never comprehended either imagination or inspiration in poetry.

2 *Anacreontic Verse*

Hagedorn had interspersed Anacreontic elements in his poetry, by-
products as it were of his muse, which aimed at light-heartedness. Yet
the writing of Anacreontic poems was not his chief aim, as it was for a
group of three young poets, all of them students in Halle during the
winter of 1739–1740, and all of them about twenty years of age:
Johann Wilhelm Ludwig Gleim (1719–1803), Johann Peter Uz (1720–
1796), and Johann Nikolaus Götz (1721–1781).

What constitutes Anacreontic poetry? For an answer we may turn
to Hagedorn, who in his poem 'Anacreon' lists the chief Anacreontic
traits: singing of wine and love, of roses and spring, of friendship and
dancing. Even if their songs of wine and love contain frequent
references to the mythological figures Bacchus and Amor and Venus-
Cythere, they are still writing about and for eighteenth-century
middle-class society and its social life; and if they extol spring and roses
they are describing lush and colorful, but stylized pastoral landscapes:

> In Tejos und in Samos
> Und in der Stadt Minervens
> sang ich von Wein und Liebe,
> Von Rosen und vom Frühling,
> Von Freundschaft und von Tänzen;
> Doch höhnt ich nicht die Götter,
> Auch nicht der Götter Diener,
> Auch nicht der Götter Tempel.
> Wie hiess ich sonst der Weise?
> Ihr Dichter voller Jugend,
> Wollt ihr bey froher Musse
> Anacreontisch singen;
> So singt von milden Reben,
> Von rosenreichen Hecken,
> Vom Frühling und von Tänzen,
> Von Freundschaft und von Liebe.
> Doch höhnet nicht die Gottheit,
> Auch nicht der Gottheit Diener,
> Auch nicht der Gottheit Tempel.
> Verdienet, selbst im Scherzen,
> Den Namen echter Weisen.

[*EdL*, V, 214]

The Anacreontic poets emphasize that the love of which they sing is not experienced, that they are merely following a literary tradition. The tradition was based on an edition of sixty poems in Greek, published under Anacreon's name and edited by Henricus Stephanus (Henri Estienne) in 1554.[27] Well into the nineteenth century it was assumed that this collection contained the actual songs of the Greek poet Anacreon of Teos, who had lived in the sixth century B.C. Even though Gleim and Götz occasionally admitted to certain reservations as to the genuineness of Estienne's collection, they began, in 1739, to prepare an unrhymed translation of these poems. Gottsched had translated a few of these verses in 1733. In his translation he had also discarded rhyme in an attempt to reproduce the same number of syllables in German as there were in the Greek original. His was a conscious effort in achieving Anacreontic meter in German, not just using Anacreontic motifs in contemporary songs.[28] While Gottsched had reversed his position meanwhile on the question of rhyme, others, especially Pyra and Lange, now saw great virtue in eliminating it, preferring un-rhymed verse instead. The translation by Götz and Uz of Estienne's edition was published in 1746 under the title: *Die Oden Anakreons in reimlosen Versen.* They explained that rhyme, in their opinion, would destroy the divine fire in Anacreon's poetry. 'Hektors Schwert' may serve as an example of the success of their translation:

Es raste vormahls Ajax,
Das Schwerdt des tapfern Hektors,
Nebst seinem Schilde, schwenkend.
Versehn mit einem Becher,
Und Kränzen um die Locken,
Und nicht mit Schwerdt und Bogen
Will ich, will ich auch rasen.[29]

The contrast of the sword with the cup is a frequent image in Estienne's poems. Götz states in his notes about these translations that it had been the aim of him and Uz to render Anacreon's thoughts in a manner 'scherzhaft, satirisch und deutlich'. In time there would be a return to rhymed Anacreontic poetry. For the moment, however, these young poets wrote in unrhymed verse, including Gleim who otherwise is known for his smooth rhymes. His emphasis was on paralleling the graceful style that people admired in the pseudo-Anacreontic odes they knew from Estienne. Götz spoke of 'feine, leichte und anmuthsvolle Bilder' when he described the language of Anacreontic poetry.

Gleim, Götz, and Uz were together only for a short time as students,

and actually did not cooperate much later on, although all of them
continued to write poetry. The only justification for grouping them is
that their relatively brief association in Halle left a marked influence
on all three, and on the further development of poetry in the
Anacreontic fashion. Gleim's most important collection of poetry was
his first, the *Versuch in scherzhaften Liedern* in two parts (1744–1745).
Since Gleim in the first poem in the collection refers to Anacreon as
his teacher it is clear that 'scherzhaft' is to be taken as synonymous with
Anacreontic. Far from referring to a jesting tone, the term encompasses
the witty, the pungent, the humorous and the epigrammatic. It is likely
that the use of this particular word was suggested by G. F. Meier, whose
book *Gedanken von Scherzen* had appeared in 1744, and who had been
one of Gleim's teachers in Halle. 'Scherz' in poetry, Meier taught, can
and does cheer the reader. Gleim engages our imagination by presenting
deliberately unrealistic and unusual scenes of love and happiness which
elicit the reader's smile:

> Anakreon, mein Lehrer,
> Singt nur von Wein und Liebe;
> Er salbt den Bart mit Salben,
> Und singt von Wein und Liebe;
> [...]
> Soll denn sein treuer Schüler
> Von Hass und Wasser singen? [30]

In Gleim's poem 'Zefir' the poet waits in vain for the spring breeze —
the appearance of Zephyr is one of the most frequently employed
motifs in Rococo literature in general — to rustle the flowers so as to
create the impression that the roses are kissing each other. Instead,
Zephyr, laughing at the poet, chooses to blow into the light silk
clothing of a girl, revealing part of her figure. But there are only rare
touches of such erotic hints, and they are always dropped abruptly.
Gleim maintains interest by the tempo and diversity of his language.
His striving for the simplicity of folk-song-like verse deserves mention.
One of his numerous collections of poems is entitled *Lieder für das
Volk* (1772). Even his poetic romances have a ballad-like tone that
occasionally reminds us of folk songs. His *Preussische Kriegslieder von
einem Grenadier* (1758) are also of documentary historical interest
to us. These are songs written during the Seven Years' War in praise
of Frederick the Great and the cause of Prussia. Those first two years
of the war, 1756 — the war started on 1 October when Frederick the

Great invaded Saxony — and 1757 had been successful for the Prussian army, which was always outnumbered. The songs brought Gleim considerable fame, especially because he successfully and consistently held to his artistic fiction of having a grenadier tell of his experiences with the famous king in the major battles. Gleim had mainly used the meter of the 'Chevy Chase' ballad-form for the *Preussische Lieder*, the stringency of which forced him to be precise in his diction. It is well to remember in this connection that Addison had recommended the Chevy Chase stanza for folk-song-like poetry. Gleim lived a long life, enjoyed financial independence, and is remembered as a friend of poets, for he offered protective patronage to many an aspiring poet.

Upon leaving Halle, Uz withdrew from the project translating Anacreon's odes, and Götz completed the collection by himself. Uz wrote his own Anacreontic poems and turned to philosophical and religious poetry as well. In 1749 he published his well-known volume *Lyrische Gedichte*, containing only twenty-nine odes and songs, a mere sampling of his writing, but remaining to this day one of the most often cited collections of Anacreontic verse. He employed rhyme, deepened the seriousness of Anacreontic poetry, and proved to be exceptionally critical in stylistic matters. Besides the pseudo-Anacreon he claimed Horace as a model, whose odes, satires and epistles he translated in prose and published in 1773–1775. In imitation of Horace, Uz included in his 1755 edition of *Lyrische Gedichte* letters in prose and verse. They soon became popular standard form for letters in the eighteenth century. Blackall has correctly observed that Anacreontic motifs had become for Uz a sort of backdrop to his poetry, and not an autonomous *raizon-d'etre*.[31] The poem 'Der Weise auf dem Lande', for example, does not make use of the usual epigrammatic ending. The last few lines are rather straightforward:

> Mir genügt ein zufriedenes Herze
> Und was ich hab und haben muss
> Und, kann es sein, bei freiem Scherze,
> Ein kluger Freund und reiner Kuss,
> Dies kleine Feld und diese Schafe,
> Wo, frei von Unruh und Verdruss,
> Ich singe, scherze, küsse, schlafe.[32]

Poetry, and especially Anacreontic poetry, Uz claimed, has the ability to teach us the true nature of things. The extension of such a view from Anacreontic poetry to overtly philosophical poems is not difficult to image. Uz wrote his own 'Theodicee', a presentation of Leibniz's ideas, and credited Leibniz with 'enlightening' him about the mystery of life:

Es öffnet Leibniz mir des Schicksals Heiligtum,
Und Licht bezeichnet mir des Schicksals Pfade.[33]

Thus the Anacreontic was merely one of several forms of Uz's poetic endeavor; later he also wrote religious poems based mainly on the book of Psalms. In Uz's best of all possible worlds were no tensions among these various approaches.

Uz remained aloof from the literary feuds of his day. In his satirical epic *Sieg des Liebesgottes* (1753), in Alexandrine verse, he criticized the Germans not only for imitating the French indiscriminately in their *mores* and in their taste, but also for believing that conformity to the English literary models would automatically raise the cultural standards in Germany. This view points up his sceptical distance from both schools of critical thought. In his *Poetische Briefe* — the one addressed to J. F. Christ (1755) — he points out the highlights of recent German literary development and credits Opitz, Canitz, Brockes, Haller, Hagedorn, J. E. Schlegel, Gleim and Lessing with improving the quality of German literature. At the same time he is fearful that the strong English influence advocated by the Swiss critics and their friends could once again deflect this development toward an indigenous literature: 'Aber in diesen Tagen. . . fängt jener so schöne und sichere Pfad von neuem zu verwildern.' Of course, such a view evoked criticism from Bodmer, which hardly affected Uz, who by now had climbed to high positions in the judicial administration of Ansbach, his birthplace.

Throughout the 1750s Anacreontic verse flourished; Götz was able to publish a second edition of his translation in 1760. Götz himself had advanced in the meantime to high ecclesiastical office as minister in the Lutheran Church, but continued to write and publish Anacreontic verse. By trying their hand at Anacreontic poetry these poets learned to use the German language with greater precision, sophisticated wit, and a more graceful flow. Both Lessing and Goethe were to begin their careers by writing in this accepted form of poetic expression.

3 *The Idyllic in Poetry: E. v. Kleist and Gessner*

The writings of Ewald von Kleist (1715–1759) and Salomon Gessner (1730–1788) successfully combine the ideals of nature poetry and

sentimentalism with the light-heartedness and playfulness of Rococo
art. The respect these two poets had for each other is typified in a
letter from Gessner to Kleist: 'Wie wird die Sprache unter Ihren Händen
so sanft.'[34] Critics have usually used the word 'weich' to characterize
Kleist's poetry, a word which may be suggestive of sentimentality,
whereas Gessner's use of 'sanft' refers to that cultivated refinement of
feeling that the era of sentimentalism desired to find in human beings
as a sign of their moral acumen and intellectual maturity.[35] Gessner's
term recognizes Kleist's ability to describe emotions with understated
subtlety, rather than in outbursts of passion. Kleist's poems praise the
even temper, particularly a state of quiet, happy feeling, a contentment
described more as an ideal than as something actually experienced. Kleist
was inspired to find his individual poetic voice through acquaintance
with the comparatively light Anacreontics of Gleim. Kleist met Gleim
in 1743 in Potsdam. Gleim took a personal interest in the young
Prussian officer, who at the time was recovering from a wound he had
received in a duel. As a member of the Pomeranian nobility Kleist was
destined for a military career, which he began with the Danish army
after several years of study at the University of Königsberg. When
Frederick the Great ascended the throne in 1740 all Prussian military
serving foreign governments were recalled, and Kleist was forced to
take up service with the Prussian army. He was an unhappy soldier,
mainly because he never had an opportunity to fight and therefore felt
he was unable to prove his bravery. A certain melancholy is
characteristic of his poetry, as personal experiences are reflected in his
writings. Thus the poem 'An Wilhelminen', written in May 1744, does
not recount a typical Rococo love experience, including initial
rejection and final acceptance of the lover. It does not create a playful
situation under a bucolic mask which allows the unhappy lover to
take his rebuff lightheartedly and find another girl. For the title Kleist
uses the real name of his lover, Wilhelmine — whom he could never
marry because he never became financially independent — but in the
poem itself he calls her Doris in bucolic fashion. The final lines,
although not altogether avoiding the epigrammatic ending, suggest
tragedy rather than relief:

> Denk Doris, dann: Ich macht' ihn so betrübt;
> Er lebte noch hätt' er mich nicht geliebt.
>
> [*DNL*, XLV, (pt. II), 133]

These lines demonstrate Kleist's ability to fuse an Anacreontic, Rococo-

like poetic form and a somber emotional posture toward a situation
from his own life. He also draws on his war experience in his poetry.
The well-known poem 'Sehnsucht nach Rune', which first appeared in
1745, tells how war changed the field, which used to look like a
bucolic landscape, into a vista of horror. Kleist generally prefers the
longer elegiac poem to the short, playful type. In 1746 he began
writing his best known work, *Der Frühling*. Thomson's *Seasons*,
published in German in 1745 in the translation by Brockes, had given
him the idea. The publication of *Der Frühling* in 1749 — the title was
taken from Thomson via Gleim — was received by the reading public
with enthusiasm. In this poem Kleist successfully found words and
metaphors in German which could adequately describe impressions
one might gain on a walk through a spring landscape. Brockes's and
Haller's influence is clearly discernible in this respect. Like Brockes he
describes in detail what he sees in nature, although not with the same
scientific accuracy, and like Haller he praises the peasants for being
happier and living a more enviable life than the city and castle
dwellers. Kleist's tendency toward the idyllic drew him to Haller.
But Kleist is different in that he seeks out the picturesque adjective
to set the right mood. Most of the motifs he found in Thomson's
The Seasons, and many of the expressions were those Brockes had
employed when he rendered Thomson's poem into German. Kleist
chose the hexameter for *Der Frühling*, thereby introducing this meter
into German almost simultaneously with Klopstock but independent
of him. *Der Frühling* remained a fragment, but an important one in
the development of German nature poetry. The idea of the poem, the
fascination with the idyllic found in a spring landscape, is expressed
well towards the end of the fragment:

Grünt nun, ihr holden Gefilde! Ihr Wiesen und schattichte Wälder
Grünt, seid die Freude des Volks! Dient meiner Unschuld hinfüro
Zum Schirm, wenn Bosheit und Stolz aus Schlössern und Städten
   mich treiben!

[389–91]

During the Seven Years' War Kleist joined Gleim and others in
writing patriotic poems, mainly to praise Frederick the Great, who was
becoming the national hero. His 'Ode an die preussische Armee' (1757)
is the first of such patriotic poems, and it served as a direct inspiration
for Gleim. In 1757 he also attempted a tragedy, *Seneca*, and a heroic
epic, *Cissides und Paches*, an idyllic work praising true friendship.

Several years earlier, in 1749, he had rejected Thomson's blank verse
for his *Der Frühling*. But with *Cissides und Paches* he adopted this
metrical pattern borrowed from England. The work was not published
until 1759, and was hailed at the time because it nourished patriotic
feelings as it described friendship and virtue in a war setting.

In 1752 Kleist spent some time in Zurich, where his military duties
as a recruiting officer had taken him. Although he met Bodmer there,
the close understanding that developed between Kleist and the young
Salomon Gessner was more important for his poetic development.
Kleist became Gessner's favorite author, and Gessner in turn would
prompt Kleist to write idyls. Gessner had just returned from a stay in
Berlin (1749–1750) where he was to have learned the bookdealer's
trade, only to have his desire to become an artist reinforced. When he
returned to Zurich in 1750, Klopstock was there at Bodmer's
invitation.

During his lifetime Gessner was famous throughout Europe, and
admired in France by Rousseau and Diderot. He too combined Rococo
and sentimental motifs — so successfully that his contemporaries saw
him as setting a new beginning in literature, as recapturing the form of
the idyl. This high esteem was soon superseded by harsh criticism,
first enunciated by Herder, Goethe and Schiller, later strongly reiterated
by Hegel. Yet in his time his poetry, and his paintings and etchings as
well, were felt to express fully the sentiments of the age. Gessner's first
significant encounter with literature was his reading of Brockes's
Irdisches Vergnügen. The adolescent Gessner, banned from attending
school in Zurich because he had been unwilling to do acceptable work,
happened to be in the countryside under the supervision of a minister
when he discovered Brockes. In this setting he saw an almost line by line
correlation to the descriptions in Brockes' work. Brockes's poems
inspired Gessner to write poetry, and also to try his hand seriously at
sculpture. Gessner began publishing in 1753, much later than Klopstock.
Of course, Gessner was influenced by Klopstock, but he did not seek
to imitate *Der Messias*. Rather he worked on pastoral romances,
leaning more and more toward idyls. Gessner's first successful
publication was the pastoral romance *Daphnis*, along with a group of
idyls in 1754. These twenty poems mark a turning point in the history
of the idyl in German literature. The strictly bucolic literature had not
met the desire of the period for idealism harmonized with naturalness.
There was a growing awareness of the artificiality that characterized
most bucolic plays, and of the contradiction between what was
envisioned as a peaceful country scene and the reality of country life. A

contrast existed also between didactic nature poetry (Brockes, Haller,
E. v. Kleist) and the seemingly frivolous, playful nature of Rococo
literature in general. Gessner in his idyls seems to present a unified
image. His characters strike the reader as realistic figures whose
language, feelings, and actions are compatible with the actual life they
lead. Yet the idyls move beyond the bucolic description to evoke an
idealism based on the timeless forms of human existence. The bucolic
certainly remains an important element in these idyls, but it is not
their essence. That is found in man's harmonious response to nature;
and while Gessner does not find such harmony in his own age, he
believes that it corresponds to something man longs for and must
have experienced some time in the past. The shepherd in the idyl
'Amyntas' exhibits harmony as a result of his understanding of
nature:

> Bei frühem Morgen kam der arme Amyntas aus dem dichten Hain,
> das Beil in seiner Rechten. Er hatte sich Stäbe geschnitten zu
> einem Zaun und trug ihre Last gekrümmt auf der Schulter. Da
> sah er einen jungen Eichbaum neben einem hinrauschenden Bach,
> und der Bach hatte wild seine Wurzeln von der Erd' entblösset,
> und der Baum stund da, traurig und drohte zu sinken. . . . ich
> kann mir andre Stäbe holen, sprach er, und hub an, einen
> starken Damm vor den Baum hinzubauen, und grub frische Erde;
> . . . aber die Dryas rief ihm mit lieblicher Stimme aus der Eiche
> zu: Sollt' ich unbelohnet dich weglassen? gütiger Hirt! sage mir's,
> was wünschest du zur Belohnung, ich weiss, dass du arm bist und
> nur fünf Schafe zur Weide führest. O wenn du mir zu bitten
> vergönnest, Nymphe, so sprach der arme Hirt; mein Nachbar
> Palemon ist seit der Ernte schon krank, lass ihn gesund werden!
>
> [*DNL*. XLI (pt. I), 74–75]

The conceptions of insular purity, Robinson Crusoe beauty, and
philosophical optimism reveal a longing for an idyllic closeness to
nature on the part of rationalistic eighteenth century Germany.
    Gessner did not know Rousseau's writings at the time of his
preface to the idyls, in which he says of the characters: 'Sie sind frei
von allen den Bedürfnissen, die nur die unglückliche Entfernung von
der Natur notwendig machet.' This statement explains Rousseau's
admiration for Gessner's idyls. Gessner contrasts Theocritus' method
with the epigrammatic method of his own day, thus hinting at the
fact that the idyls are an indirect criticism of eighteenth-century

society that desires happiness without the willingness to limit its moral freedom and make the necessary sacrifices. The idyl is typically possible only in the closed-off landscape, but it does not simply offer pure happiness. In Gessner's world, only suffering and expressed concern for others makes the idyllic experience possible. Such a view was in keeping with the personality of Gessner, who spent much of his life in idyllic surroundings, living a life that was admired by others for its outward harmony. Gessner along with Theocritus soon became the accepted model for the writing of idyls, for he had been able to use the various elements of the bucolic literature and adapt them to the needs of his own time. To him the definition does not include a paradisiac setting, rather a realistic view of nature, for example, Amyntas' hard work. However, it does require the portrayal of the highest moral sense in man, for example, Amyntas' concern for the needs of nature and man. The fact that Amyntas is a shepherd is accidental; it is no longer a characteristic of the genre.[36]

When Gessner published *Der Tod Abels* (1758), a work often alleged to be inspired by Klopstock, whose *Der Tod Adams* had appeared in 1757, he made it clear that with this work he had aimed at the so-called higher form of literature, the portrayal of the tragic in nature. Indeed, *Der Tod Abels* was widely read and much admired, yet it was hardly the kind of work appropriate for Gessner. It is important only because in it he demonstrated that he could effectively use his rhythmical prose in a longer work. The idyllic prose narrative *Der erste Schiffer* (1762), as well as his second group of idyls (1772), showed him again working in his favorite genre. But by 1772 the idyllic as a subject matter no longer responded much to the needs of the times, nor was Gessner able to recapture the melodious rhythm of his earlier prose.

V The Use of Satire: Liscow, Rabner, and Zachariae

We have already said that the fable proved to be an ideal literary genre to effect the moralizing that was considered an important challenge of eighteenth century rationalistic philosophy. The Enlightenment felt constrained by its pedagogical orientation also to employ satiric prose as a means of bringing about moral improvement and intellectual tolerance. In that respect satiric essays fulfilled a function similar to the 'sächsische Komödie', which relied to a large degree on the satirical portrayal of stereotype characters. Christian Ludwig Liscow (1701–1760) was the first to publish satires during the early Enlightenment period. In the preface to his *Sammlung Satyrischer und Ernsthafter*

Schriften (1739) he defends his predilection for the genre: 'Was habe
ich denn gethan? Ich habe einigen elenden Skribenten, die sich dünken
liessen, sie wären etwas, da sie doch nichts waren, im Lachen die
Wahrheit gesaget. Sollte dieses eine so grosse Sünde sein? ' Liscow, a
native of Mecklenburg, had done a thorough study of French literature,
particularly of Boileau, Montaigne and Bayle. Familiarity with their
prose may well have influenced his style and his emphasis on satirical
treatment of common situations and viewpoints, although he always
did so by attacking individuals. His contemporaries held that against
him, especially because he persisted in destroying the reputation of
his victims. He made Gottsched and his followers the particular
object of his derision and is responsible, in part, for creating the image
of Gottsched as a prosaic and superficial critic. We find such treatment
in the satire *Die Vortrefflichkeit und Notwendigkeit der elenden
Skribenten gründlich erwiesen* (1734). With it he made a name for
himself. From his repeated insistence that satirical writing is not
incongruent with Christian principles we infer that he was attacked
for his persiflage.

The satirical writings of Gottlieb Wilhelm Rabener (1714—1771)
were much more sophisticated, and in keeping with the period's high
ideals. His sharp wit denounced the same foolish and bigoted actions
that were commonly exposed in the satirical comedy.[37] However,
whereas Liscow's attacks on known individuals forced him frequently
to single out notorious characters who were outcasts anyway, in order
to avoid the charge of slander, Rabener castigated the common vices
of the period without becoming personal. His *Sammlung satyrischer
Schriften* appeared in four volumes (1751—1755), and must be
judged as an immense success. He made use of the satire as a pedagogical
device, and avoided the destructive *pasquil* into which the genre often
degenerated. The satire 'Kleider machen Leute' contrasts an unassuming,
yet educated and honest representative of the middle class who is denied
an audience by his prince with the man who because of his fashionable
appearance finds open doors at the court. The satire ends, characteristically for Rabener, with the narrator watching a tailor cutting out
coats and gowns for such personages as a high church official and a
squire. In his vivid imagination he sees the tailor actually creating a
church official and a squire, understandably so in a satire which claims
that clothes determine the value of a human being. The narrator
assumes a pose of respect in the tailor's simple shop, for, so he reasons,
as long as we are wont to admire the clothing of those who are powerful
and, therefore, have little regard for them as human beings, we are

obliged to show respect even when we happen to see these clothings
without the persons in them.

There is a clarity and compelling logic in Rabener's prose. He was
Gellert's close friend and a member of the 'Bremer Beiträger', by
training a lawer who held government positions as an internal revenue
agent in Saxony. His definition of satire in *Sendschreiben von der
Zuverlässigkeit der Satire* (1742) clearly characterizes the genre as a
vehicle of moral admonition: 'Ich getraue mir so gar, zu behaupten,
dass sie bey unterschiedenen Fällen, und bey einer gewissen Art von
Lastern beynahe nützlicher sey, als die ernsthafteste Strafpredigt.' The
ideal of human improvability by rational arguments, which we have
come to see as a basic tenet of the age, lends saliency to satire as a
prevalent literary form, but at the same time dulls its sharp cutting
edge. That in turn undermines the didactic intentions of satire if its
scurrility leaves no room for emotional sympathy. The majority of
his satires expose vices of the middle class, pedantry in scholars, greed
in lawyers, hypocrisy in clergymen, and generally the desire to imitate
foreign customs. Rabener's *Versuch eines deutschen Wörterbuchs*
(1746) is a good sample of his cautious satire, and is significant as a
commentary on the times. The entry 'ewig' in this dictionary offers
the author opportunity to lash out against writers who want to
immortalize themselves in their works, and the article 'Kompliment'
leads him to speak out against subservience.

No German writer reached the artistic heights of Jonathan Swift in
satire. However, the satirical epic reflects somewhat the stylistic
achievements of the genre in England. The satirical epic *Der Renommist*
(1744) of Just Friedrich Wilhelm Zachariae (1726–1777) owes its
irony to the empty conflict between pretense and lack of substance. By
using Alexandrine verse Zachariae creates thoughts of grandeur, similar
to those that the epic's hero entertains. The rough and unpolished
student from the university of Jena, which was known for its noisy
and coarse student life, arrives in fashionable Leipzig. A former friend
from Jena who was completely adapted to Leipzig's elegance
persuaded the newcomer to have his hair done in Leipzig fashion.
However, his clothing still identifies him as coming from Jena, and the
girl whose favor he was out to win only mocks him. His anger leads him
into a duel with the former friend. Zachariae saw bragging and boasting
as motives for action in both characters. Moralizing is kept to a
minimum. Important is the fact that Zachariae introduced the satirical
epic into German literature and used a plot which was particular to the
German cultural scene of the period. He was a productive writer,

publishing also a comedy, *Der Adel des Herzens oder die ausgeschlagene Erbschaft* (1770), but his fame is based solely on *Der Renommist.*

Notes

1.   See W. H. Bruford, *Germany in the Eighteenth Century*, p. 312.
2.   For a thorough analysis of the stylistic achievements of the *Discourse der Mahlern* see Blackall, *The Emergence of German*, pp. 69–82.
3.   Breitinger actually included a chapter on 'Machtwörter' in his *Critische Dichtkunst.*
4.   In the same context – the statement is taken from the chapter on 'Nachahmung' in the *Critische Dichtkunst* – Breitinger calls the poet a creator. That merely shows to what degree he applied Leibniz's thinking to the field of literature. The poet who can present glimpses of another possible world is the creator of that world.
5.   For a fuller treatment of Breitinger's and Bodmer's views on the use of metaphor see Blackall, pp. 278–80.
6.   Quotations from Schlegel's plays follow the 1771 edition, which was published by his brother Johann Heinrich Schlegel.
7.   F. Martini, 'J. E. Schlegel: *Die stumme Schönheit*', *DU*, XV (1963), pp. 7–32, stresses this point when he argues: 'Die Einsicht Schlegels, dass das bestimmende "dramatische" Element sich weniger in der Handlung als in dem Dialog darbietet, liess die Fabel schmächtig werden', p. 15.
8.   Both the attack on Schlegel's use of verse and Schlegel's reply appeared in Gottsched's *Beiträge.* In this treatise Schlegel advances the view that the dialogue is the most significant and characteristic feature in a comedy.
9.   This willingness on Schlegel's part to scrutinize the then current concept in literary criticism appears to have caused E.M. Wilkinson to call her monograph *J. E. Schlegel: A German Pioneer in Aesthetics* (Oxford, 1945).
10.   K. May, 'J. E. Schlegels *Canut*', *Trivium* VII (1949), 257–285, interprets the play wholly from its forward-looking *Sturm und Drang* features.
11.   W. Martens, 'Lektüre bei Gellert', in: *Festschrift für R. Alewyn* (Köln, 1967), pp. 123–150, points out also that the negative characters in Gellert's plays do not read or spend money on books. According to Martens, Gellert taught young people to read critically; he even provided them with suitable reading lists.
12.   From Gellert's preface to his comedies in *Sämtliche Schriften*, 2nd edn. (Berlin und Leipzig, 1867), III.
13.   The quotations from *Die Betschwester* follow the 1747 edition. C. F. Gellert, *Lustspiele*, Faksimiledruck nach der Ausgabe von 1747, mit einem Nachwort von H. Steinmetz, in *Deutsche Neudrucke* (Stuttgart, 1966).
14.   As quoted by W. Martens in 'Lektüre bei Gellert'.
15.   Cf. R. H. Spaethling, 'Die Schranken der Vernunft in Gellerts *Leben der schwedischen Gräfin*', *PMLA*, LXXXI (1966), 224–235.
16.   Letter to his mother, dated 20 January 1749.
17.   H. Steinmetz, *Die Komödie der Aufklärung* (Stuttgart, 1966), p. 1.
18.   It would appear that the use of the term 'Typenkomödie' is justified historically. See H. Steinmetz, p. 2. Besides, the term 'Typenkomödie' is a clearer indication of the nature of Enlightenment comedy and points to its many traditions that relate it to the 'Commedia dell' arte', the 'Theatre italien', and the seventeenth-century 'Wanderbühnen'. For a full treatment of its development see D. Brüggemann, *Die sächsische Komödie: Studien zum Sprachstil* (Köln,

Wien, 1970).
19. Anna Amalie Abert, 'berman Singspiel', in *The New Oxford History of Music*, vol. VII: *The Age of Enlightenment 1745–1790*, ed. E. Wellesz and F. Sternfeld (New York and Toronto, 1973), p. 81.
20. F. Sengle, *Das historische Drama in Deutschland*, 2nd end. (Stuttgart, 1969), p. 28.
21. Brüggemann, in *DLE, Reihe: Aufklärung*, XII, 22; and Sengle, *Das historiche Drama*, pp. 28–29.
22. Sengle, *Das historische Drama*, p. 29.
23. W. P. Hanson, 'Lange, Pyra and "Anakreontische Tändeleien" ', *GLL*, XVIII (1965), 81–90.
24. Lange, being the true friend he was, prepared a second expanded edition in 1749, in which he included additional poems by Pyra, among others the significant 'Der Tempel der wahren Dichtkunst'.
25. L1. 10–17 from the poem 'Des Thirsis Empfindungen, da er ihnen entgegen gehet'.
26. The lines:

Vom allerreinsten *Licht* erhabner Zärtlichkeit
Durchaus *erhellt verkläret* und *durchdrungen*
[italics mine]

appear to reflect Pietistic vocabulary. August Langen, *Der Wortschatz des deutschen Pietismus* (Tübingen, 1954) describes the verb 'durchdringen' as a very common composite verb in Pietistic literature. One of the quotations from Pietistic writings which he cites to document the use of 'durchdringen' interestingly enough includes the words 'Licht', 'hell' and 'klar', all words or parts of words which Pyra employs in the above two lines. Langen's example reads: ' . . . als ich in aller Einfalt zu lesen anfing/ wurde mein Hertz von dem *Lichte Gottes* dermass en *durchdrungen*/ dass mir alles . . . *hell* und *klar* war.' [italics mine]
27. Estienne brought out a second expanded edition of the poems in 1556 in which he provided also Latin translations of the poems. The Greek songs represent different periods.
28. Addison's translation of Estienne's collection appeared under the title *The Works of Anacreon* (London, 1735).
29. The text follows Johann Nikolaus Götz, *Die Gedichte Anakreons und der Sappho Oden*, ed. Herbert Zeman, *Deutsche Neudrucke*.
30. The text follows the original as reprinted in: *Neudrucke deutscher Literaturwerke*, NF 13, ed. A. Anger (Tübingen, 1964).
31. Blackall, *The Emergence of German*, pp. 400–401.
32. *Deutsche Dichtung im 18. Jahrhundert*, ed. A. Elschenbroich (Darmstadt, 1968), p. 72.
33. L1. 10–11 from the poem 'Theodizee', *DNL*, XLV.
34. Letter of 28 March 1758, as quoted by Blackall, p. 402.
35. Blackall, pp. 403–405.
36. For a full discussion of the genre 'idyl' see Renate Böschenstein-Schäfer, *Idylle* (Stuttgart, 1967). She treats Gessner in detail, pp. 20–68.
37. Cf. J. Jacobs, 'Zur Satire der frühen Aufklärung: Rabener und Liscow', *GRM*, XLIX (1968), 2.

4 NEW STANDARDS

Gottsched's hope of seeing literature accepted as a respected field of academic endeavor was fulfilled. His critical work had encouraged literary production, and the ensuing literary feud had been creative in stimulating diversity in literature. Rationalistic philosophy as well as Pietistic experience had made their influence felt in the choice of content and form. This development had its culmination during the height of the Enlightenment, beginning in the late 1740s and continuing until the 1760s, when the three most important authors of the entire period wrote and worked more or less simultaneously, although with far different concerns: the lyric poet Klopstock, representing the Pietistic tradition; Wieland, the novelist and author of verse epics, under whose hands the early Rococo devices evolved into their highest sophistication; and the dramatist and critic Lessing, whose work set new standards and inspired the generation of *Sturm und Drang* poets.

I Klopstock and the Development of Lyric Poetry

Friedrich Gottlieb Klopstock (1724—1803) represents a peculiar phenomenon in literary history. Often praised and just as often reproached for his metric innovations, for the affected solemnity of his religious epic *Der Messias*, for his extreme and not infrequently repulsive patriotism, for his undramatic plays, and for his expressive and highly individualistic language, he nevertheless, has consistently received extensive treatment in literary histories. Klopstock's historical significance is an accepted fact, even though from our perspective today it may be difficult to ascertain how far Klopstock's works actually altered the direction and form of literature in the middle of the eighteenth century. Beyond a doubt his contemporaries did recognise his works as being new and different. This newness was the basis for either rejection or, as was more frequent, acceptance of Klopstock. It is also beyond dispute that the admiration accorded him was enthusiastic, that the mere mention of the name Klopstock could be used, as in Goethe's *Die Leiden des jungen Werthers*, to express a feeling of awe, or to intimate an affinity of thought. Goethe's words capture fully the enthusiasm the young shared for Klopstock's poetry:

Es donnerte abseitswärts, und der herrliche Regen säuselte auf
das Land, und der erquickendste Wohlgeruch stieg in aller Fülle
einer warmen Luft zu uns auf. Sie stand auf ihren Ellenbogen
gestützt, ihr Blick durchdrang die Gegend, sie sah gen Himmel
und auf mich, ich sah ihr Auge tränenvoll, sie legte ihre Hand auf
die meinige, und sagte — Klopstock! — Ich erinnerte mich sogleich
der herrlichen Ode, die ihr in den Gedanken lag, und versank in
dem Strome von Empfindungen, den sie in dieser Losung über
mich ausgoss.

[Book I, letter of June 16]

Johann Martin Miller included in his novel *Siegwart*, which appeared in
the mid-seventies, a high number of references to Klopstock. This
reflected the positive reaction of even Catholic readers in Germany to
the northern Protestant poet, and also indicated how well young lovers
felt their own thoughts and feelings were expressed in Klopstock's
poetry. He was a dominant figure during the fifties and sixties, writing
not only poetry but also essays on his prosody. Yet it can hardly be
said that Klopstock started a literary movement. The young poets of
the *Göttinger Hain* revered him and spoke of him even in the early
seventies as 'Vater Klopstock', but their movement did not owe its
existence to him. Klopstock, in fact, soon after his initial successes, cut
himself off more and more from the continuing evolution of poetry in
Germany, partly because he had enveloped himself in the aura of a
vatic poet. But because of Klopstock, it was easy for the *Sturm und
Drang* poets of the seventies to experiment with meter and with
coining new words, to stress feeling and nature, to idealize friendship,
and to herald originality in poetic invention. Even today every
anthology of German poetry includes a few of Klopstock's odes, which
have been enjoyed by readers ever since because they invite
participation in a lofty flight of thoughts and feelings.

Born in the idyllic town of Quedlinburg in the Harz mountains,
Klopstock attended the famous secondary school in Pforta, and from
an early age could boast a thorough familiarity with Greek and Latin
and with the literatures in these languages. This knowledge was to
translate itself quickly into the writings of German hexameters, and
into imitations of the complicated metrics of Greek odes. He was
somewhat older and presumably somewhat more mature than his
classmates. Even before he left Pforta in 1745 at the age of twenty-
two, he had sketched out what was to become his major life's work,
the epic *Der Messias*, which was not completed until 1773. Klopstock's

graduation speech, which he delivered in Latin and in which he calls for
a German poet to rise up and write a German national epic, is evidence
of the patriotic pride and ambition which together with his religious
enthusiasm constituted the actual motivation for his writing. Klopstock's
graduation speech occurred in the same year in which Frederick the
Great won his second war against Maria Theresa, in the famous battle
of Hohenfriedberg. Popular support for the Prussian king was strong at
this time throughout Germany, for the victory meant recognition of
Prussia as an important political power in Europe. It was also the year
when, upon the king's return to Berlin, the people afforded him the
attribute 'the Great'. There is little doubt that Klopstock was inspired
by the political and geographical growth of Prussia. Prussia's rise
politically may well have prompted him to attempt a similar
accomplishment in the intellectual realm. At the same time, Frederick
the Great's love for the French language and for French culture, and
his concomitant contempt for German, influenced Klopstock deeply
to stress the need for a *German* national epic. It is not without irony
that the same Klopstock, who more than anyone else elevated the
social standing of poets in Germany, who stressed sublimity as a hallmark of literature, and who put so much emphasis on the concept of
the poet's calling, should himself have been spurred on by such
unartistic goals as national prestige. We might consider it even more
ironic that Klopstock, whose poetic talents were in the area of lyrical
poetry, devoted most of his time and energies to writing a religious
epic which had no real epic content, and to writing patriotic dramas
which lacked any dramatic structure in plot and form. One of
Klopstock's most knowledgeable and most admiring critics, Richard
Hamel, admits that Klopstock misjudged his poetic gift when he
concentrated on epic and drama.[1] Yet his contemporaries were pleased
with the patriotic theme in Klopstock's work. Even Hamel, writing in
the early 1880s only a decade after Germany's unification in 1871,
praises the poet precisely for his strong patriotism, as though patriotic
ambition were somehow enough to justify Klopstock's worth as a poet.

The spring of 1748 saw the publication of the first three cantos of
Der Messias. It was mainly Bodmer's strong and unreserved praise for
the German hexameter verses that persuaded the editor of the 'Bremer
Beiträger', to publish them, one year before Ewald von Kleist's
hexameters of *Der Frühling* were made known. It should be
remembered that Gottsched had recommended the use of this meter a
few years earlier. By and large, *Der Messias* was well received, both as
a religious poem — there were not many who would criticize the choice

of the subject nor the manner of treatment – and as an epic poem in hexameters. It is understandable that Klopstock's epic was seen as supporting the Swiss critics, and judgements were influenced by this fact. Gottsched, upon seeing these hexameters, regretted having published some of his own because he abhorred the many 'un-German' expressions that Klopstock had introduced. However, Gottsched's opinion was no longer valued, and Klopstock's achievement appeared to transcend the literary feud, especially when young forceful critics, such as Lessing, spoke in favor of the hexameter. Young Lessing was deeply moved by the first three songs of *Der Messias*. In his early fragment 'Die Religion' he speaks of the powerful and emotional effect of Klopstock's lines:

> Nimmt mich, ans Pult geheft, der ewige Gesang,
> Durch den der deutsche Ton zuerst in Himmel drang. .
> In Himmel . . frommer Wahn! . . Gott . . Geister . . ewig
>   Leben . .
> Vielleicht ein leerer Ton, den Dichter kühn zu heben! . .
> Nimmt mich dies neue Lied . . zu schön um wahr zu sein,
> Erschüttert nicht belehrt, mit heil'gem Schauer ein:
> Was wünscht der innre Schalk, erhitzt nach fremder Ehre,
> Und lächerlich erhitzt? . . Wann ich der Dichter wäre!
>
> [295–302]

First Lessing, and then Herder, welcomed Klopstock's reliance on British examples: Milton, Young, Addison, Pope, Rowe, Glover, and Shakespeare; and both welcomed Klopstock's approach, although by no means uncritically. Lessing, well aware that Klopstock was not the first to use hexameters in German, praised particularly the poet's sophisticated understanding of the metric details of this Greek verse, defended the difficult but logical sentence structure, and called on Klopstock's critics and readers to study with care the many excellent revisions the poet made in each edition of the poem.[2] But Lessing did not remain altogether fond of *Der Messias*. In one extensive review he sharply criticized the opening lines of the poem.[3] His close reading of these opening lines discovered in Klopstock a lyrical genius whose emotional makeup was fundamentally different from Lessing's own. Whereas Lessing insisted on an intellectual examination of all feelings, Klopstock often equated feelings with thoughts.

Herder's admiration of Klopstock was even more qualified with critical reservations. He had called for a poetic language different from prose, and found in Klopstock's poetry, at least in part, the kind of vivid language he desired. However, he could not subscribe to Klopstock's hexameters, arguing their incompatibility with the structure of German, or declaring the inappropriateness of Greek meter in German poems. Besides, he disagreed with the syntax which resulted from such meter because it made comprehension unnecessarily difficult, so much so that Lessing felt he had to defend Klopstock by saying that Homer had been just as little understood by his contemporaries, a sentiment which Herder, the champion of folk-poetry, could not possibly echo. Herder, who wanted nothing more than to see lyric poetry develop new forms, was thus forced into the uncomfortable position of having to warn against Klopstock whose genius as a lyric poet he did recognize, and who with his emphasis on inverted sentence order in German forged a language that was distinct from prose. Herder lists his critical complaints about the plan and execution of *Der Messias* in his *Fragmente über die neuere deutsche Literatur*.[4] The hero of the epic, according to Herder, is not really as human as he appears in the New Testament and, therefore, does not really move the reader. Herder concludes that Klopstock was wrong when he declared beauty to be of higher value in a work of literature than the ability to arouse the reader's feelings and sentiments. He approved the poetry in as far as Klopstock did and could arouse the reader's feelings.

It is important to state Lessing's and Herder's views briefly because they help us understand how it was possible that, despite his enormous popularity during the fifties, Klopstock's poetry could be quicly pushed into the background by the new poetic impact of the *Sturm und Drang*. The diversity of opinion over Klopstock's worth can thus be seen to reach back to his own contemporaries.

Why did Klopstock choose Christ as the hero of his 'national epic'?[5] Klopstock had been reared in a Pietistic atmosphere where he learned to reflect intensely on the subject of salvation in general, and on the suffering and victorious Savior in particular. Such experience had certainly prepared him for treating this topic. That is not to say that he approached the subject solely from a Pietistic point of view. The first few lines of Klopstock's epic demonstrate the intended sublime tone of the entire work as well as the scope of its content:

Sing, unsterbliche Seele, der sündigen Menschen Erlösung,
Die der Messias auf Erden in seiner Menschheit vollendet.
[. . .]
Aber, o Tat, die allein der Allbarmherzige kennet,

Darf aus dunkler Ferne sich auch dir nahen die Dichtkunst?
Weihe sie, Geist Schöpfer, vor dem ich hier still anbete,
Führe sie mir, als deine Nachahmerin, voller Entzückung,
Voll unsterblicher Kraft, in verklärter Schönheit, entgegen.

[1–12]

Even though Klopstock made many changes in the text the first two
verses were never changed.[6] The usual prepositional construction 'von
der Erlösung singen' has given way to the characteristic Klopstockian
transitive use of a normally intransitive verb, 'Erlösung singen', thereby
imbuing these words with a sense of the majestic. That the poet calls on
his own immortal soul to tell how the salvation of sinful man was
accomplished underscores Klopstock's vatic image of the poet. It also
demonstrates strikingly how Klopstock's sentimentalism really results
from a conscious mental or rational decision to talk about the thoughts
and feelings that must have been God's and the Messiah's as the plan of
salvation unfolded. The poem in its entirety could be viewed as another
eighteenth-century theodicy. The notion expressed at the beginning of
his ode 'Der Zürchersee', that a human engaged in re-thinking the great
idea of divine creation is more beautiful than nature itself, may well
serve as a motto to Klopstock and his kind of sentimentalism. This
means also that imitating nature is no longer the highest principle.
Accordingly, there is a great deal of emphasis in *Der Messias* on the
emotions attributed to Jesus, and much less concern with any action.[7]
The epic poem is divided into twenty cantos with a total of nearly
twenty thousand lines, beginning with Christ's struggle on the Mount of
Olives and ending with his taking his seat on the right hand of God.
Klopstock uses the New Testament account as his major source,
drawing a great deal on the Book of Revelation for details. At no point,
however, does he allow his imagination free reign; the characters,
therefore, do not develop a literary existence of their own. The work
as a whole is thus not easily readable. The poem exerted its great
influence less because of its ideas than because of its meter and its
language. The number of unusual words and neologisms is impressive.
The hexameter is used with relative ease, with some exceptions to
the strict rules of antiquity. But each foot regularly begins with an
accented syllable, and each line usually has the two obligatory
unaccented syllables after the fifth accent in the line.

Still, the publication of the first three cantos of *Der Messias* was
reason enough for Bodmer to support Klopstock, and for the Danish
king to assure for many years the poet's financial independence.

Klopstock requested Bodmer's patronage, and Bodmer in turn graciously invited the seraphic young poet to Zurich, only to be bitterly disappointed by the unexpected worldliness the guest displayed. Klopstock, who in his letter of petition to Bodmer had spoken of his fragile health and of his strong love for his cousin Marie Sophie Schmidt — whom he addressed in his poems as Fanny and who never returned his love — turned out to be exceptionally fit physically and uncommonly interested in meeting girls. Only ten days after his arrival he was invited to join a boating expedition on Lake Zurich. It was a day of unbounded joy and produced the famous and very beautiful ode 'Der Zürchersee' (1750). He addresses joy as follows in the third strophe:

> Komm, und lehre mein Lied jugendlich heiter sein,
> Süsse Freude, wie du! gleich dem beseelteren
>   Schnellen Jauchzen des Jünglings,
>   Sanft, der fühlenden Fanny gleich.

The theme of joy as the dominating motif of the ode gives the poem its power to engage the reader even today:

> Jetzo nahm uns die Au in die beschattenden
> Kühlen Arme des Waldes, welcher die Insel krönt;
>   Da, da kamest du, Freude
>   Volles Masses auf uns herab!
>
> Göttin Freude, du selbst! dich, wir empfanden dich!
> Ja, du warest es selbst, Schwester der Menschlichkeit,
>   Deiner Unschuld Gespielin,
>   Die sich über uns ganz ergoss!

                                                            [25–32]

It is, however, characteristic of Klopstock that the theme and word 'Freude' toward the end of the ode gradually changes to 'Freund' and 'Freundschaft', a topic which is treated frequently by him. The beginning 'Freundschaftskult', which was in evidence also between Pyra and Lange, is a sign that the strict rationalistic literature is giving way to more and more emphasis on feeling.

The young poet stayed only a few days in Bodmer's house, and only a few months in Zurich. He arrived in July 1750, and by May 1751 he was located in Copenhagen, drawing an annual grant from the Danish king, Frederick V. Klopstock's welcome in Denmark was due in no

small measure to the positive impression that Johann Elias Schlegel had
made on Danish academic circles. Copenhagen was to be Klopstock's
place of residence until 1770 when his special protector at the Danish
court, the powerful Count Bernstorff, lost his influential position.
Klopstock returned to Germany and lived in Hamburg, the birthplace
of his wife, Meta Moller. She inspired several odes and poems, in which
he addresses her as Cidli.

In Denmark Klopstock had been exposed to the so-called bardic
literature which flourished in the sixties. He was immediately fascinated
by the concept and defended it with ardent patriotism. The joining of
art with patriotism to reproduce the glorification of the tribe and the
war caught Klopstock's imagination. This interest led to his writing
dramas about Teutonic history. He had already published several lyric
dramas, *Der Tod Adams* (1757) and *Salomo* (1764) — the tragedy
David was written in 1763–1764 although not published until 1772 —
when he began work on a trilogy, treating the life of Herman the
Cheruscan. The choice of this particular subject matter was not new;
Johann Elias Schlegel had written his drama on the Cheruscan in 1743.
His enthusiasm for bardic poetry led Klopstock to develop a whole
Germanic mythology. In this endeavor he often fell victim to historical
and linguistic misunderstandings of the mythological tradition. He
coined the term 'Bardiet' to designate dramatic poems dealing with
events from the time of the bards, deriving the expression from
Tacitus, among other sources, who used the term 'barditus' to describe
the battle cry of the Germanic tribes. The trilogy consisting of
Hermanns Schlacht (1769), *Hermann und die Fürsten* (1784), and
Hermanns Tod (1787) was planned and partly executed in the sixties
as an example of the 'Bardiet' type of drama. In the trilogy Hermann
emerges as the preserver of cultural and political freedom. For
Klopstock saw the Germanic tribes in a glorified light, even going so
far as to revise earlier poems by substituting allusions from Teutonic
mythology for allusions to Greek mythology. Instead of the Greek
temple he spoke now of the 'Hain'. The representativeness of
Klopstock's poetic practice and concerns is best evidenced in the name
several young poets in Göttingen chose for their circle: *Göttinger
Hainbund*. However, the idea of writing 'Bardiete' found no followers.
And Klopstock himself appears to have returned to a more traditional
dramatic form by the time he wrote *Hermanns Tod*, the last play in
the trilogy. It deserves mention that Klopstock combined his interest
in Teutonic mythology with his call for political freedom in the present.
Klopstock portrayed the events of the American battle for independence,

and also of the French Revolution, enthusiastically and vividly.

In all his works Klopstock consciously avoided an Anacreontic smoothness and Rococo playfulness. Strength rather than elegance was his aim. He developed his views on language in several essays, most notably in *Die deutsche Gelehrtenrepublik* (1774), a work planned for several volumes of which only the first ever appeared. As against the seventeenth-century utopian idea of an international republic of scholars, Klopstock preferred a company of German scholars, again a nationalistic-patriotic goal. German is declared to be more capable of the highest literary expressiveness than other European languages. He proposes changes in the grammatical and orthographical structure of the language, declaring usage to be the factor that decides correctness.[8] Of such a nature was his individualism that he wanted to have a theoretical base which would assure the continuation of his elevated poetic language. His experiments in language provided a foundation for the exploration of deeper poetic expression, most notably in Hölderlin and Rilke, as Blackall points out.[9]

II Wieland and the Development of The Novel

Christoph Martin Wieland (1733–1813) represents in his many creative and critical-essayistic writings the full range of the thoughts and forms that dominate the literature of the Enlightenment. The cosmopolitan Wieland admired both French and English literature in an age that seemed to demand a preference for one or the other. This breadth of vision elevated him above partisanship; his refusal to join any literary movement befitted his subtle and ironic temperament. He produced a formidable array of novels and verse epics as well as translations and reviews, developing the German language into an instrument capable of the finest irony and of an heretofore unknown elegance.

When his novel *Agathon* appeared in an English translation in 1773, the anonymous translator, in reviewing contemporary literary achievements in Germany, comments, no doubt with particular reference to Wieland's prose: 'But the greatest improvement made by the Germans of the present century, is in the cultivation of their own language.'[10] This same translator acknowledges the wit, urbanity, and satire in Wieland's style, even though he does fault Wieland for his excessively long sentences, possibly not realizing that Wieland employed the long sentence patterns in the German legalistic tradition precisely for the purpose of irony. Because Wieland achieved his elegance of style and melodious flow of words in his verse epics, he has often been described as having perfected the literary Rococo. Of all the authors of the

Enlightenment period Wieland was the most prolific.

In an age that was preoccupied with literary theory he preferred artistry to criticism. As we have seen, it was not at all uncommon in the eighteenth century to create literature mainly to prove a certain theory. The struggle to define and describe the various genres was in harmony with the belief of the age that a rational explanation is possible for all phenomena, including that of artistic creativity. Writing toward the end of the period, as it were, Wieland exhibited those characteristics the philosophers of the age had been extolling: tolerance, kindness, and understanding. Yet a literary history must note that Wieland's influence in the development of German literature was in some ways indirect. Even a cursory look at Wieland scholarship will demonstrate that very little Wieland research was carried on through most of the nineteenth century; most of it has been done only recently, especially since the 1940s;[11] Just prior to the full impact of *Sturm und Drang* literature Wieland was the most widely read author in Germany. But then his reputation was attacked by the young Goethe[12] and Schiller, and later by the Romantics August Wilhelm Schlegel and Ludwig Tieck, who in 1799 accused him of plagiarism. Their accusation in effect destroyed Wieland's reputation, discouraging even scholars from studying his works seriously. The attention that as of late has been given to Wieland has significantly altered our understanding of the eighteenth century in general, particularly of the development and nature of Rococo literature, but also of the later classicism. Wieland's concept of the whole person was very much like Herder's, Goethe's, and Schiller's. He accepted Shaftesbury's view of man as much as Herder did.

Almost as soon as Wieland, the son of a Pietistic minister in the Swabian town of Biberach, escaped the influence of his parents' home and the confines of Pietistic schools, he surveyed current philosophical thought and turned agnostic. While he had given early evidence of his literary talent, the student Wieland now expressed even his philosophical thoughts in poetry, as in the poem 'Die Natur der Dinge' (1751), in which he shows himself to be an idealist by rejecting a materialistic explanation of the world. He was formally a student in Tübingen (1750–52) but really studied mainly on his own, concentrating on his writing. This surge of literary productivity was no doubt due to his engagement to his cousin Sophie Gutermann just prior to his going to Tübingen. His love for her spurred him to write, and also aroused his keen interest in Hagedorn and his Anacreontic poetry. Soon the pursuit of a literary career became his only aim. He could not hope for marriage, and although Sophie broke off the engagement under pressure from her family, Wieland's love and admiration for her never died. Instead, the aspiring poet looked for recognition and decided that Bodmer's approval was the most desirable.

His attempt at a national epic *Hermann* (he wrote the fragment in 1751) was meant to please Bodmer, and his early *Erzählungen* (1752), verse narratives along the lines of his later verse epics, were written in the sentimental style, capturing the mood of the idyl and of the fairy tale. Bodmer was pleased and Wieland received an invitation to come to Zurich and live with the famous author. In return Wieland was quite willing to do away with his agnosticism and Rococo-like poetry. For some two years Wieland lived and worked as Bodmer's disciple, producing the sublime poem *Der gepryfte Abraham* (1753) in hexameters; in this he described Abraham's feelings as he prepares to sacrifice his son Isaac. The most important document of this period is a group of psalms he wrote and published under the title *Empfindungen eines Christen* (1757). In the preface to this collection, he addresses the Prussian court minister Sack in Berlin. This letter has probably been more often read and discussed than the collection of poems itself, because in it Wieland sought official sanctioning from the Church by condemning the Anacreontic poetry he had admired only a few years earlier, singling out Uz as the object of his attack. It can hardly be argued that these psalms, published in 1757, do not represent his own ideas about the value of religious poetry, since Wieland had in the meantime gained his independence from Bodmer and did not have to tailor his stance to the dictates of a patron. Reviews critical of Wieland soon appeared, most clearly phrased by Lessing in the *Literaturbriefe*, accusing the young poet of having changed his style and tone at someone else's bidding, and of dabbling in a subject-matter foreign to his nature. Basically, Wieland accepted this criticism and soon began to concentrate on the novel and the verse epic, which were more to his liking, even though they were not very popular at the time. But during this period of transition Wieland also wrote the first German drama in blank verse, the bourgeois tragedy *Lady Johanna Gray* (1758), an adaptation and occasionally even a direct translation of Rowe's *Lady Jane Grey*.[13] This play about a martyr is written in the style of the sentimentalists, all but eliminating the figure of the villain.

In 1760 Wieland returned to his native Biberach after a year (1759–1760) in Bern, where he had made his living by tutoring, as he had done in Zurich after 1754. The city of Biberach had elected him to be senator and later appointed him as director of its chancellory. These positions assured Wieland of an adequate income and of free time for his writing. He stayed there during the decade of the sixties and produced or conceived in Biberach most of his well known works. It was there that he translated and published twenty-two of Shakespeare's plays (1762–1766), thus introducing the German reading public to the British author who was to become the idol and model of the *Sturm und Drang*. Wieland's Shakespeare translation has been sharply criticized, partly because it is in prose, and partly because he left untranslated much that was offensive to his enlightened sense of decency in literature.[14] But Wieland did see in Shakespeare the greatest of all poets and recognized in his dramatic 'irregularities' a way of depicting true life, a goal that Wieland hardly aimed for in his own works. In fact Wieland experienced in the castle of Warthausen – near Biberach – the style of a small Rococo court. Its openness to the arts, specifically its appreciation of Italian and French literature, its delicate taste in furnishings and fashions, and its wit in all intellectual matters, were too representative of the Enlightenment to have induced Wieland to abandon them and to imitate Shakespeare. He admired Shakespeare but the 'reality' he knew and liked was Warthausen, where Count Stadion, who had been influential in the service of the elector of Mainz, was enjoying his retirement. Wieland was brought into this circle by his cousin Sophie, who by now was married and whose husband La Roche was in Stadion's service.[15] There can be no question that the atmosphere at Warthausen inspired some of Wieland's works and that it was a crucial factor in Wieland's adopting a Rococo attitude in his writing. Eventually, Count Stadion helped him get the position as a professor of philosophy at the University of Erfurt. That was in 1769 at the end of a decade of fruitful literary production in Biberach.

In 1765 Wieland published the novel *Der Sieg der Natur über die Schwärmerey, oder die Abentheuer des Don Sylvio von Rosalva*, usually known as *Don Sylvio*. The intentional similarity of the title to Cervantes's *Don Quixote* has often been noted and is underscored by the burlesque Spanish setting of the novel. The word 'Schwärmerey' in the eighteenth century was used mainly to describe the dominance of feeling among the religious enthusiasts. And, clearly, Wieland includes under this slightly deprecating term not only many enthusiasts of his age but also such of his own works as he had produced during the years in Zurich. Don Sylvio seeks after the 'reality' of the fairy tales he has read and actually finds in Donna Felicia the 'princess' he is looking for. Her expectations are not much different, since she believes in the reality of the literary genre of pastoral plays and takes Don Sylvio to be the shepherd she had hoped to meet. Both characters leave behind their 'Schwärmerei' and sentimental seclusion and accept the physical and psychological realities of this world. Wieland may have written this novel with his friends at Warthausen as the audience in mind. He certainly wrote it for an audience with a refined taste in literary matters, because he included so many allusions to other works of literature. The novel was well received for its Rococo wit and playfulness. But much more significant is the fact that Wieland now had discovered not only the novel as his particular talent, but also irony as his way of being didactic. His next novel would be a masterpiece.

However, before beginning work on *Agathon*, Wieland published his lighthearted *Comische Erzählungen* in 1765. These four verse narratives, *Das Urteil des Paris, Endymion, Juno und Ganymed*, and *Aurora und Cephalus*, are reminiscent of the Anacreontic tradition: the setting in antiquity, the unexpected twist at the end, the natural and even roguish playfulness, the lightness of tone, the sensuous attitude, and the hedonistic outlook on life. Wieland had admired Anacreontic poetry before his stay in Zurich, had then rejected it on moral grounds, and now seemed to embrace it all the more, as though he wanted to reject all sentimental literature. In the *Comische Erzählungen* he perfected his Rococo style. This in itself allowed him to gain the necessary ironic distance from his earlier sentimental works, but also from the literary and philosophical movements of the century in general, and he was now ready to attempt to bring both world views together. His strongest interest still was in the Greeks and in their philosophies. It was partly for this reason that Shaftesbury's philosophy appealed to him more and more. Shaftesbury's concept of 'moral grace', based on a harmony of man's mental and physical powers, became Wieland's ideal, and it constitutes the philosophical basis of his work, dominating content and form. In this way Wieland was able to perceive the seeming opposites of sentimentalism and rationalism, or Pietism and Rococo, as aspects of the larger unity of the age of Enlightenment.

The novel *Geschichte des Agathon*, first published in 1766–1767, reflects convincingly not only Wieland's fascination with Greek life and philosophy, but also his desire to include and even stress in his depiction of Greek civilization human frailties and vices. Thus it was possible to imbue the story of Agathon, a young man living in the age of late antiquity, with allusions to Wieland's own time. The plot is Wieland's invention and is in part autobiographical. Wieland published a second edition of the novel in 1773, and still another edition in 1794, each time adding new material. That the novel was so well received in

Germany may have been due to its philosophical content, which made
for difficult reading but which also properly echoed the expressed
concern of the age with rational philosophical systems. The statement
expressed early in the novel, 'ob ich einen Ort finden möchte, wo die
Tugend, von auswärtigen Beleidigungen sicher, ihrer eigentümlichen
Glückseligkeit geniessen könnte, ohne sich aus der Gesellschaft der
Menschen zu verbannen', [Book I, chapter 10] echoes the concern of
the Enlightenment period. Will i⁺ be possible, Agathon seems to ask,
for any society to practice the ideals of an enlightened philosophy?
The novel does not describe such a society, nor does it offer a philosophical base for one. Wieland rejects idealistic enthusiasm as much
as mere sensualism, but is a fusion of the two possible? The question
of the novel: ' . . . und warum sollt es unmöglich sein, Liebe und
Tugend miteinander zu verbinden? Sie beide zu geniessen, das würde
erst eine vollkommene Seligkeit sein', sounds more like a rhetorical
question and scarcely an answer to the problem.[16] Ambiguity is
essential to Wieland's work, for it is central to the ironic view. To
Lessing, *Geschichte des Agathon* was the first great German novel, as
important for German literature, he argued, as Fielding's *The History
of Tom Jones, A Foundling* (1749) had been for English literature.[17]
The resemblance of the two titles is of course intended. The title does
not imply, however, that we are dealing with a historical novel as such,
but rather with a psychologically realistic account of man and his
ideas. Agathon, a young idealist who believes in Platonic love, is
exposed to the wickedness of the priests, is challenged by a cynical
but elegant spokesman of hedonism, and is introduced to erotic
pleasures. He is defeated in his efforts to change the life of a corrupt
ruler, and he gives up trying to be a political reformer, yet as an
individual he passes all his trials. Putting aside the idea of Platonic
love, he instead withdraws from society and leads a contented family
life.

The criticism of the age was still not sure about the criteria for a
novel. Hence the critics often hesitated to voice their reaction to
Agathon. Yet in 1774 Friedrich von Blanckenburg, a Prussian officer
and not a trained literary critic, inspired by Wieland's *Agathon*,
attempted a theory of the novel in his *Versuch über den Roman*
(1774). Blanckenburg successfully insisted that the modern novel
describing the actions and feelings of the individual had replaced the
classical epic that depicted public deeds and events. Lessing and
Blanckenburg thus recognized and acknowledged Wieland's accomplishment in allowing the reader to perceive the complicated nature of

human personality.

While *Agathon* was Wieland's most important achievement during
the sixties in the genre of the novel, *Musarion oder die Philosophie der
Grazien* (1768) must be considered his most important verse narrative
of this period. In its stylistic innovations and in its treatment of themes
it ranks among the finest Rococo literature, with its humerous yet
touching account of how the beautiful and clever Musarion succeeds in
persuading Phanias to forget his hasty renunciation of all pleasures of
this world, a renunciation induced by Musarion's passing attention to
another. As a result Musarion and her converted lover achieve a full
measure of earthly happiness. Her dispassionate love reveals as mere
contempt for this world Phanias' alleged renunciation which he had
learned from his teachers, the stoic philosopher Kleanth and the
Pythagorean Theophron. Not their seemingly lofty idealism but
Musarion's ideal love teaches him to recognize the beauty of a normal
earthly existence.[18] The ironic narrator summarizes his point when he
identifies love as Phanias' successful mentor:

> Die Liebe war's. — Wer lehrt so gut wie sie?
> Auch lernt' er gern und schnell und sonder Müh
> Die reizende Philosophie,
> Die, was Natur und Schicksal uns gewährt,
> Vergnügt geniesst und gern den Rest entbehrt;
> Die Dinge dieser Welt gern von der schönen Seite
> Betrachtet, dem Geschick sich unterwürfig macht
> [. . .]
> Den Irrenden bedaurt und nur den Gleisner flieht;
> Nicht stets von Tugend spricht, noch, von ihr sprechend, glüht
> Doch ohne Sold und aus Geschmack sie übet.

[Book III, 334–349]

Musarion's love is based on more than a frivolous Rococo quest for
pleasures. She combines wit with grace, seriousness and lightheartedness, is witty and pert in her language, yet full of love. The narrative is
divided into three relatively short books — the narrator ironically
speaks of the three acts of a comedy — and is marked by a lively style
that keeps alive the reader's tension. Wieland's *Idris. Ein Heroisch-
comisches Gedicht* (later retitled as *Idris und Zenide. Ein romantisches
Gedicht*) (1768), a verse epic using the Italian *ottava rima*, was also
written, although never completed, in Biberach, and another verse epic,
Der neue Amadis, Ein comisches Gedicht in Achtzehn Gesängen, was

begun there. Wieland enjoyed the *ottava rima* which he used in free adaptation because it offered him an ironic cover for his ideas and his portrayals of man.

Wieland, by now married, moved to Erfurt in 1769 and only three years later went on to Weimar to tutor the two young princes there. As professor of philosophy in Erfurt he was a popular teacher, but since he was not really a philosopher he could not be expected to be happy in such a position for long. The works he wrote in Erfurt throw some light on the frame of mind of Wieland as professor. His *ΣΩΚΡΑΤΗΣ MAINOMENOΣ* [Socrates mainomenos] *oder die Dialogen des Diogenes von Sinope* (1770) portrays Diogenes, considered a fool by his contemporaries, as having reached the state of absolute intellectual independence, and hence of complete equilibrium. Wieland must have felt that the dual role of philosopher and poet was detrimental to his poetic writings, that he needed total·intellectual independence. The offer he received from the Weimar court did not give him this independence immediately. But there was the prospect of a life pension after three years of tutoring. To be sure, the offer was made to Wieland the educator, not to Wieland the poet, especially since he had shown himself to be knowledgeable about the task of educating young princes to become ideal rulers when he wrote his voluminous novel *Der goldene Spiegel, oder die Könige von Scheschian. Aus dem Scheschianischen übersetzt* (1772). The duchess Anna Amalia wanted Wieland to supervise the education of her two sons, the heir-apparent, Prince Karl August who was to become the ruling duke in 1775 when he reached his eighteenth birthday, and the younger, Prince Konstantin. As it turned out, Karl August soon married, and Konstantin's education was assigned to Knebel. Wieland did not meet the duchess's expectations. Goethe would become the close friend of the duke, upon his move to Weimar in the fall of 1775.

Wieland arrived in Weimar in September 1772, and in January 1773 the first issue of the very successful literary journal *Der Teutsche Merkur*, appeared. The publication was of utmost importance to him, partly as a means of preserving the great strides that German literature had made in the eighteenth century, but also as a way of protecting these accomplishments against the emotionally harsh criticism of the beginning *Sturm und Drang*. The title was chosen from the French journal *Mercure de France*; the choice underscored the idea that it was no longer necessary to bemoan the state of things literary in Germany. From then on Wieland published all of his new works first in the *Merkur*. Besides, Wieland, an extremely versatile and gifted journalist,

now had a forum in which he could voice his critical opinion on a wide
range of intellectual matters through essays, reviews, letters, and
translations.

In Weimar Wieland also tried his hand at the so-called 'Singspiel'. It
lent itself to far less costly performances than the Baroque opera and
needed only a few singers. Wieland liked this combination of drama
and opera and wrote several successful plays for the stage at Weimar.
Alceste, Ein Singspiel (1773) is the most famous of these, partly because
Wieland discussed the play in a number of letters in the *Merkur*, partly
because the play's idealistic view of the Greeks was to become commonplace in the German Classicism of a few years later. Only a few years
earlier Christoph Willibald Gluck had written his opera *Alceste* (1767).
As was customary, the libretto was in Italian. Gluck at the time lived
in Vienna and Wieland met the composer only after he had written his
own *Alceste*, an unusually successful play on the Weimar stage. Anton
Schweitzer was the composer who collaborated with Wieland. That was
significant, for it was the first time that a German opera was performed
at a German court, where traditionally Italian actors sang in Italian
operas. Schweitzer was thoroughly familiar with the 'Singspiel', having
been a conductor in one of the travelling companies. The music he
provided for Wieland's *Alceste* did much to create interest in the German
opera. In treating the Alcestis legend, her willingness to die so that her
husband might live, and her return to earth from Elysium, Wieland
extolled the pleasures of this earth over those of Elysium, and
reiterated the Enlightenment theme of virtue rewarded. When young
Goethe attacked Wieland's treatment of this legend in his farce
Götter, Helden und Wieland (1773), ridiculing the play's dispassionate
characters, the praise awarded virtue, and the censure of all vices, and
likewise attacked the characterization of Hercules in Wieland's
'Singspiel', *Die Wahl des Herkules* (1773), Wieland countered by
proclaiming Goethe's farce in his *Merkur* as a masterpiece of persiflage.
Wieland continued writing 'Singspiele', of which his *Rosamund* (1778),
the story of Queen Elinor's murder of the secret lover of her husband,
Henry II, represents yet another example of the serious 'Singspiel'
which borders on the tragic. Only a few years later, especially after his
arrival in Weimar, Goethe, too, wrote several plays in this genre.

The criticism of Wieland voiced by the *Sturm und Drang* writers
was harsh and severe. The group of writers known as the *Göttinger
Hain* burnt his *Idris* in 1773. Yet Wieland was not really averse to the
ideals of the *Sturm und Drang*. Of course, he could not and did not
adopt their concept of genius and their striving for originality in a

literary work of art. A reaction to the criticism, if not to the critics, may be seen in his humerous novel *Die Abderiten. Eine sehr wahrscheinliche Geschichte*, which appeared in the *Merkur* between 1774 and 1780 and was published in its entirety in 1781 under the title *Geschichte der Abderiten*. This work marked a high point in the development of the German novel in the eighteenth century. In it Wieland reached the zenith of his ironic style of narration. The setting of the novel in antiquity allowed him to speak pointedly and skeptically about typical aspects of Enlightenment culture, philosophy, politics, and religion, and afforded him at the same time an opportunity to question the ideal image of the Greeks that Winckelmann had painted and that the *Sturm und Drang* writers had so enthusiastically accepted. Democritus unmasks the follies of the citizens of Abdera until they stop laughing about him and instead join his laughter about themselves; they discover that their enthusiasm for things cultural had led them to misunderstand culture itself. It is symptomatic of Wieland's bent for realism that he thus dampens the educational and cultural optimism of the Enlightenment era.

Wieland had once again become a productive writer, as he had been in Biberach. The number of his verse epics grew steadily, culminating in his famous *Oberon. Ein romantisches Heldengedicht* (1780). Goethe's praise for this epic poem was immediate. *Oberon* is a Rococo humanistic treatment of the plot of the old chivalrous novel of *Huon de Bordeaux*. The term 'humorous classicism' has been used to describe most aptly the tenor of Wieland's works of these years.[19] The witty and ironic narrator who seeks to amuse and seems to expect an occasional smile from the reader, the allusions to chivalric customs and attitudes, the oriental setting, the idyllic grottos and groves, the pastoral scenes, the world and the power of the dwarf Oberon — all of these devices fit the Rococo style. But Wieland was able to use this poetized world of Rococo lightheartedness and frivolity and fill it with the humanistic ideals of truthful love and absolute faithfulness. Wieland's modernity emerges here because the Rococo setting destroys the emotional pathos with which such classic ideals are often expressed. The degree of artistry achieved in the versification of *Oberon* is, indeed, remarkable.

Oberon is actually the high point of Wieland's verse epics,[20] appropriately continuing a group that had begun appearing in the midseventies, among them *Der Mönch und die Nonne, auf dem Mittelstein* (1775; later under the title *Sixt und Clärchen*), which is based on a folk legend and shows the poet somewhat under the influence of the *Sturm und Drang*, as does his *Ein Wintermärchen* (1776). The series continues with such titles as *Liebe um Liebe* (1776; later under the title *Gandalin oder Liebe um Liebe*), *Geron, der Adelich. Eine Erzählung aus König Artus Zeit* (1777), *Das Sommer-Märchen, oder des Maulthiers Zaum. Eine Erzählung aus der Tafelrunde-Zeit* (1777), *Schach Lolo* (1778), which has its setting in the Orient, and *Pervonte oder die Wünsche. Ein Neapolitanisches Märchen* (1778). This list is an indication of Wieland's preference for fairytale plots and for medieval and oriental settings. At the same time Wieland moved ever closer to the ideals of classical humanism. These ideals are at the heart of his verse epics, realized usually only by the help of irrational fairytale magic told by a rational ironic narrator. After *Oberon* Wieland devoted most of his time to translating his favorite Latin and Greek authors, especially Horace. Only during the last decade of the century did he once again publish works of a larger scope. The novels *Geheime Geschichte des Philosophen Peregrinus Proteus* (1791), *Agathodämon in sieben Büchern* (1799), and *Aristipp und einige seiner Zeitgenossen* (1800–1802) contain most clearly Wieland's enlightened, cosmopolitan humanism, discussing, particularly the first two, the relationship of faith and reason. There is the admission that the philosophy of Enlightenment will never fully realize the aims of its humanistic didacticism. Agathodämon in the end concludes that he has not achieved what he had set out to become and do. In comparing himself to Christ he states that only Christ by his mere existence had been able to transcend human limitations.

Wieland remained active as a writer and translator until his death in 1813. The many literary attacks forced him to withdraw for a time from Weimar society – from 1797 to 1803 he lived on the estate Ossmannstedt near Weimar – but during his last few years he was again an active member of the intellectual community of Weimar to whose prestige he had contributed so much.

III Lessing and the Development of Drama

'Ich lernte einsehen, die Bücher würden mich wohl gelehrt, aber nimmermehr zu einen [sic] Menschen machen,' wrote Gotthold Ephraim Lessing (1729–1781) to his mother two days before his twentieth birthday. The quotation has become famous, as Lessing defended with it his involvement in the theater, his association with actors, and his own early authorship of comedies. (The earliest comedy, written in 1747, incidentally drew its characters entirely from books.) Lessing's self-evaluation is important for it shows why he did not pursue the career of a scholar for which he appeared destined and for which he was

most extraordinarily gifted. Instead he chose the stage to present his
sentiments and reflections, his observations and ideas, both by his
dramatic works and by his extensive critical writings about literature in
general and drama in particular. He wanted to set new standards for
German stage productions, and he accomplished his mission so well that
Goethe, looking back at the 1760s, remarked of Lessing's comedy
Minna von Barnhelm: 'Sie mögen denken, wie das Stück auf uns
Anfänger wirkte als es in jener dunklen Zeit hervortrat. Es war wirklich
ein glänzendes Meteor. Es machte uns aufmerksam, dass noch etwas
Höheres existiere, als wovon die damalige schwache Epoche einen
Begriff hatte.'[21]

It has become commonplace to emphasize that in spite of Lessing's
dominant position in the eighteenth century none of his plays is
significant enough to have received recognition within the context of
European literature. But Goethe's high praise, along with recent revival
of interest in Lessing's dramas, acknowledges Lessing's role in the
development not only of German but, indeed, of European literature.
Nor, in fact, have Lessing's plays lost any of their stage appeal over the
last two hundred years in Germany. The effectiveness of Lessing's
plays on today's stages in Germany, it has been argued, is due to their
modernity in dealing with issues of society.[22] One might add that
Lessing's views of society are only an extension of his more basic views
of modern man. Lessing definitely used the stage as his pulpit.[23] The
choice of the term 'pulpit' is not fortuitous, for theology remained an
important aspect of Lessing's world. His theological writings provide
the basis for his views of man and society, of divine revelation, of
education, of truth and tolerance. There is then an underlying unity in
Lessing the poet, playwright, translator, literary and philological critic,
and Lessing the philosopher of religion. Lessing forever questioned
traditional concepts in all these areas. He rescued from historical
condemnation declared heretics, if he felt that they had been forthright
in stating their views, even if those views had been wrong. Similarly, he
fought those among his contemporaries whom he thought to be somewhat less than totally committed to objective and disciplined research.
Lessing, to be sure, was not always fair in his attacks, or objective in
formulating his views. Most of his expository writing was not so much a
systematic presentation of his own ideas as it was a questioning of what
others had thought and written. Just as often his own views resulted
from the need to defend himself against attacks from others. This was
the method in which he excelled and which allowed him to give impetus
to the intellectual life of his time and beyond. His impact on the last

two centuries is noticeable today if measured by the constantly high level of intensive Lessing research that has been going on since his death.

Lessing grew up in the Lutheran parsonage of the small town of Kamenz in Saxony, in an atmosphere of orthodoxy and scholarly theology. The admiration he held throughout his life for the reformer Martin Luther may well have been kindled in Kamenz. In 1741 Lessing left his home to attend the boarding school of St Afra in Meissen, where the foundations for his broad knowledge in the liberal arts, especially in language and literature, were laid. The time he actually spent as a university student was very short: two years (1746–1748) at the University of Leipzig, officially enrolled in theology to please his parents, but in reality taking courses in philosophy, the classics, and theory of the arts. Early in 1748 he changed to medicine, but left Leipzig late that spring with the intention of moving to Berlin. On the way, due to illness, he stopped in Wittenberg where Martin Luther had lived and taught, and took courses there for a few months. In December 1751, he returned to Wittenberg to complete his master's degree within a semester's time. Clearly, Lessing's interest was no longer a formal education leading towards a professional career. Rather, when he left Leipzig for Berlin in 1748, he was irrevocably determined to live by his pen as a writer-journalist, a daring step in his time but one quite in keeping with the talents he had discovered in Leipzig.

His first comedy, *Der junge Gelehrte*, was successfully performed in Leipzig, in 1748, by the Neuber troupe. He had prepared the original draft while he was still in Meissen, where he had also started writing Anacreontic verse, which he published in 1751 under the common title *Kleinigkeiten*. If these Anacreontic poems were intended as an escape from the strict classroom routine by imagining a free life, *Der junge Gelehrte* could be seen as showing what happens if such escape is not provided for in the life of a stereotype young scholar. There can be no question that he had pedagogical aims in mind when writing comedies, for he followed the model of the satirical comedy of types as Gottsched had described it. Certainly, we laugh at the comedy's main character, the young scholar, who personifies so many of the proverbial characteristics of his profession. He is an absent-minded bookworm, so eager to dazzle with his knowledge that he lacks all life-like reality. There is another aspect to Lessing's play. The constant references to the ideal of virtue attempt not merely to distinguish goodness from sham virtue, but to question virtue itself. Lessing thus demonstrates even in his first play what he later called the 'Halsstarrigkeit der Tugend', or the difficulty of defining virtue, as well as of being virtuous.[24] Juliane is willing to forget her love for Valer and marry Damis, the young scholar for whom she feels only contempt, merely out of gratitude to his father, who had provided for her when she had been without parents and without means. She is disposed to look at such a marriage as a virtuous act on her part, proving her thankfulness and self-denial. Lisette, her quick and clever maid, a typical figure in these satirical comedies, can only wonder about this kind of moral concept: 'Eine wunderbare Moral! wahrhaftig!' [II, 1]. If virtue does not lead to happiness then basic tenets of Enlightenment philosophy are being questioned. Analyzing commonly held opinions, and seeing whether the principle behind these opinions is true or not, is one of Lessing's most valuable services.

Lessing's strong interest in comedy was to continue for some time. In 1748 he completed *Der Misogyn*, originally only a one-act play, later expanded into a three-act comedy, making use of the disguise motif, and in 1749 he finished the more important *Die Juden*, a one-act play dealing with race prejudice. This satirical comedy criticizes and exposes eighteenth-century German anti-semitism. But we cannot laugh at either the baron, or his overseer, when both express openly and freely their strong prejudice against the Jews. The baron is portrayed as a good person, not deserving of scorn, but the overseer is revealed as a criminal, and hence contemptible. The play does not even totally condemn race prejudice. Both the baron and the travelling Jew, who reveals his identity only toward the end of the play, express respect for each other's humanity, but neither thinks that the barrier erected when the traveler's identity is exposed can be removed again. Minutes earlier the baron's fondest hopes had been for the unknown traveler, who had aided him against a robbery attack, to marry his daughter. Now the baron withdraws the offer, and the Jew praises the baron's generosity:

> *Der Baron:* So gibt es denn Fälle, wo uns der Himmel selbst verhindert, dankbar zu sein?
> *Der Reisende:* Sie sind es überflüssig dadurch, dass Sie es sein wollen.
>
> [Scene 22]

Lessing's play, courageous for the age, brought him considerable criticism from contemporaries who argued that the travelling Jew was too perfect to be credible, a criticism rightly rejected by the author. The play comes close to the sentimental comedy of Gellert, who was writing comedies at the very time when Lessing arrived in Leipzig. *Die Juden*, by the way, contains an interesting remark on the subject of contemporary drama in general. The Jew's servant describes his master's library as containing comedies which cause you to weep, and tragedies which cause you to laugh, a remark obviously about the contemporary literary situation in general.[25]

The other important comedy written in 1749, *Der Freygeist*, allows us an important insight into Lessing's world of thought. The play defends the thologian Theophan against the freethinker Adrast, in whom Lessing attacks intolerance and arrogance. None of these comedies appeared in print until later. The two published comedies in those early years, *Damon, oder die wahre Freundschaft* (1747) and *Die alte Jungfer* (1749) were not included in his collected works as he had come to realize that they were no better than many of the comedies he had criticized.

Lessing's decision to make his living as a writer, and thus maintain his intellectual independence, was strongly influenced by the intimate friendship he enjoyed with his cousin Christlob Mylius, his elder by seven years and a brilliant journalist, who had introduced young Lessing to the theater, and to a circle of friends devoted to discussing literary works. Mylius also introduced him to a life which was worldly, urbane, and self-confident. Mylius had published, in 1747 and 1748, some of Lessing's reviews in his weekly paper, *Der Naturforscher*. When Mylius moved to Berlin, Lessing followed. Together with Mylius, Lessing ventured his first and short-lived journal, *Beyträge zur Historie und Aufnahme des Theaters*. All four issues appeared in 1750. Lessing had in mind a sort of encyclopedic journal which would publish not only German and French dramas, but also English, Italian, Spanish, Roman, and Greek: a compilation of everything ever written on the theater, acting, and stage-setting. Here Lessing could publish his essays on the Roman Plautus, as well as a translation of Plautus' comedy *Captivi*. As editor of the prestigious *Berlinische privilegierte Staats- und gelehrte Zeitung* Mylius could and did allow Lessing to gain some income from contributions to that paper as well.

Mylius soon gave up the editorship, lost sight of his goals, began to roam through Germany, Holland, and England, and died in 1754. Eventually, Lessing became very closely associated with the *Berlinische . . . Zeitung*. Early in 1751 he assumed responsibility for the paper's book review section and from April through December of the same year he produced also the monthly insert *Das Neueste aus dem Reiche des Witzes*, under which rubric he discussed the current literary scene. After his brief stay in Wittenberg he returned, in the fall of 1752, to work again for the paper which later became widely known as the *Vossische Zeitung*. From reading Lessing's many reviews in this paper, as well as in Sulzer's *Kritische Nachrichten aus dem Reiche der Gelehrsamkeit* — it is not always possible to establish with certainty Lessing's authorship of a given review — one can tell how broad Lessing's literary interests were, and how many of his later themes occupied him even then: the defense of English literature, the attacks on Gottsched, the question of rules in dramatic literature. It is quite clear which authors he preferred, and how he viewed the development of literature, when he claimed Germany's present literary epoch had begun with the philosophical poem, a clear reference to Brockes and Haller, the two authors with whom we, too, began this account of Enlightenment literature.

Lessing's early Berlin years (1748—1755) mark the beginning of a lasting friendship with two men famed for their contributions to the cultural life of the period: the book-dealer Friedrich Nicolai, and the Jewish philosophical writer Moses Mendelssohn (1729—1786). Together the three discussed, and later corresponded about, many literary and aesthetic issues. The friendship influenced Lessing's own writing markedly. A third close friend of Lessing's was the poet Karl Wilhelm Ramler (1725—1798), who corrected much of Lessing's poetry and whom Lessing trusted completely. Lessing's literary productions continued at a rather rapid pace, so much so that he soon made plans for a six volume edition of his collected works, which was published in the years 1753—1755. Many of his poetic works appeared here for the first time, especially his plays. The first volume contained his Anacreontic songs; his German and Latin epigrammatic verse; his odes and versified fables; and his philosophical poems. Most of this was new to the public, and Lessing continued polishing his verses, and adding new songs to later editions of his works.

Young Lessing tried his hand at all the major genres that were popular in the age of Enlightenment. The philosophical poems for which Lessing chose the collective title 'Fragmente' reveal the poet's religious point of view during those early years quite sharply although not all of these poems bear out the heading 'fragments'. One of these, *Die Religion*, which did remain a fragment, suggests an ambitious plan, when Lessing first describes man's moral dilemma,

Ich brachte einen Feind in mir, mit mir herfür,
Doch Waffen gegen ihn, die bracht ich nicht mit mir.

[L1. 139—140]

and then seeks to defend man's need for religion by anticipating and refuting all possible objections. Lessing's argument is not conducted on purely rational grounds, in keeping with his feelings about the nature of poetry which he thought should convince by emotional arguments as well as by rational ones. Of Klopstock's *Messias* he claimed that the poet's greatness lay in his touching our emotions, rather than in his presenting us with knowledge. The same difference between poet and philosopher is also stressed in the essay *Pope, ein Metaphysiker!* (1755).

Lessing reserved one volume of his collected works for a type of critical writing he had grown fond of, that of rehabilitating great figures in history. Lessing started writing these 'Rettungen' in Wittenberg, as a result of his studies there. The most important of his 'Rettungen' is the one dealing with Horace. A well substantiated and carefully argued interpretation of Horace's poetry, defending the poet against the accusations of immorality and lack of religion, leads to a basic theoretical understanding of the autonomous role of poetry. Lessing's defense of Horace was occasioned by the feud he carried on with the poet and pastor Samuel Gotthold Lange. Lange's translation of Horace's odes had aroused extreme indignation in the young critic Lessing, who exposed grammatical mistakes in this translation and eventually published in 1754 *Ein Vademecum für den Hrn. Sam. .Gotth. Lange*, after Lange had attempted to refute Lessing's initial criticism, in the process attacking Lessing's personal character. The *Vademecum* destroyed Lange's reputation, but it also left its readers wondering about Lessing's tactics as a critic. Indeed, Lessing used all the sharpness of his mind and his full skill in suiting language to his aim, but his aim in this case appeared to be more the destruction of his opponent than the defense of his own honor. It has been shown, however, that Lessing merely employed familiar and traditional forms of polemical writing, when he assumed the role of a teacher writing to his wayward pupil Lange and pointing out to him the many mistakes in the latter's exercise.[26]

The last three volumes of his collected works contain the plays; only one is not a comedy: *Miss Sara Sampson*, written in 1755, and announced as a domestic tragedy, 'ein bürgerliches Trauerspiel'. The adjective 'bürgerlich', which Lessing did not use in a later edition, signaled a new genre in Germany.[27] The English title is Lessing's acknowledgement of the English tradition in this genre. Only a year before he wrote *Miss Sara Sampson*, two English domestic tragedies, George Lillo's *The London Merchant or The History of George*

Barnwell (1731, translated in 1752) and, inspired by Lillo's play, Henry Moore's *The Gamester* (1753), had been performed in Germany and had attracted wide attention. Lillo had spoken of the 'novelty' of this kind of tragedy, and Lessing intimated that Gottsched had never even mentioned the genre 'bürgerliches Trauerspiel' in his *Critische Dichtkunst*, a charge which is true only of the first edition of the work, which had appeared before Lillo's play. Lillo's often-cited influence on Lessing must have been of a very general nature, mainly providing the idea of the domestic tragedy. The most important source for *Miss Sara Sampson* has been identified as Thomas Shadwell's comedy *The Squire of Alsatia* (1688), probably much more to Lessing's liking because of its satirical approach, although the play is not without sentimental tones. Lessing, after all, did not use the term 'bürgerliches Trauerspiel' as synonymous with 'sentimental comedy'. The virtuous Lucia of Shadwell's comedy corresponds completely to Miss Sara in Lessing's play, the evil and plotting Termagant to Marwood, the seducer Belfond Junior to Mellefond, and Termagant's child plays the same role as Marwood's. But Lessing has made the virtuous Sara the main character for the play, and has raised the level of the dialogue to a serious discussion of human and, specifically, family relationships. In a period when middle-class citizens used the moral weeklies to philosophize and when Pietistic circles throughout Germany granted intellectual opportunities equal to those the nobility enjoyed, the excellent reception of domestic tragedy on German stages is hardly surprising. Neither is the rise of a German tradition of middle-class tragedy with an emphasis on the private sphere of moral responsibility; in the process traditional moral-religious concepts were interpreted for a new middle-class consciousness. Lessing had attempted his first tragedy, *Samuel Henzi*, in 1749 — the fragment was published in 1753 — based on contemporary political developments in Switzerland and written in the typical classicistic Alexandrine meter, extolling Henzi as a political hero. The tone and thematic thrust of *Miss Sara Sampson*, a prose play that sets aside the traditional unities, are totally different from this and are directed much more at the inner life, seeking to affect the audience emotionally. Lessing adopted the emotional aspects of sentimental drama for the middle-class tragedy because he felt that it is the human element that touches us and causes us to be compassionate. 'Der mitleidigste Mensch ist der beste Mensch,' he wrote in 1756 to Nicolai, because compassion will purify passion, an effect that admiration, produced by the heroic tragedy, cannot achieve.[28] *Miss Sara Sampson* was a success, not because of its plot, which lacks motivation and convincing intrigue, but surely because of its moving dialogue, and because of the sympathy the reader feels for Sara, whose virtue cannot be matched, in spite of her sinful relationship with Mellefond. This drama might be seen as an illustration of forgiveness and the Christian concept of redemption. Sara learns to accept her father's forgiveness and to overcome her own pride. Through its characters the play unites the rational mainly in the servant Waitwell, and the cult of sentimentality, mainly in Sara, and reflects the importance of these concepts in eighteenth-century Germany.

After writing *Miss Sara Sampson* Lessing left Berlin for some three years, once again going to Leipzig. Through the intermediacy of friends he had received an offer to accompany a young man from that city on a European tour in 1756, a tour they were forced to cut short when the Seven Years' War broke out. The war revealed that the Saxon Lessing had become a Prussian politically, which fact led to hostile feelings between the tutor Lessing and the family of his young charge. Lessing's pro-Prussian tendencies may, however, have been important in fostering his friendship with the poet Ewald von Kleist, famous for his poem 'Der Frühling', who came to Leipzig as an officer of the Prussian occupation. When military duty called Kleist to the battlefield in 1758, Lessing once again returned to Berlin, and, together with Nicolai as publisher, undertook a new literary venture, a critical weekly paper, *Briefe, die neueste Literatur betreffend* (1759–1765). Lessing, who wrote more than half of the letters during the first two years of this venture, defended the epistolary form as the most suitable because he was responding to the request of a wounded officer who wanted to be informed about recent developments in literature. Kleist's military rank provided the occasion for this fiction. Lessing exercised his critical faculties on a grand scale in the *Literaturbriefe*, becoming in the process a highly respected and even feared critic in Germany. Lessing attacks Gottsched, and he succinctly praises Shakespeare at the expense of Corneille and Racine by arguing that English drama is more melancholy and hence more moving and closer to the German mentality than the French. The critic's task according to Lessing is to be unrelenting, even towards authors he admires, and he follows his dictum in these letters.

In 1759 Lessing questioned the ideals of heroism in war in his one-act tragedy *Philotas*; that play, it is interesting to note was published in wartime. At this time he also worked on a dramatization of the Faust legend, only a brief fragment of which was published in 1760. He

lacked the concentration for completing any of his current projects and
he decided a change was necessary. Thus he accepted the post of
secretary to the Prussian commandant in Breslau, in this capacity
announcing the end of the war to the city in 1763. The Breslau years
provided him with considerable knowledge of the life and frame of
mind of a Prussian army officer, and this experience essentially supplied
him with the material for *Minna von Barnhelm* (1767), which has come
to be perhaps the best-known comedy in German literature. The play
was actually written in 1763, immediately after the end of the war, and
the plot, allegedly based on a real happening in a Breslau inn, highlights
magnaminity in the two major characters, Minna and Tellheim, as well
as in their servants. The Prussian major Tellheim had come to the
financial aid of the Saxon nobility during the war and was, therefore,
relieved of his command after the war and accused of treason. However,
his noble deed had earned him the love of the wealthy and charming
young Minna von Barnhelm, who is determined to marry the Prussian
and who goes to Berlin to seek him out and convince him that a union
between them is what they both desire and need. This bold yet contemporary setting engenders an action that borders on the tragic at
times, exposes pride in both of them, and through laughter causes the
two to acknowledge the realm of love, where neither honor nor disgrace,
poverty nor wealth matter, but where the heart rules. Tellheim's
insistence on his lost honor, his poverty, and his physical handicap
does not hold up against Minna's rational arguments, but neither do her
arguments nor her planned intrigue change Tellheim's point of view.

> *Das Fräulein:* . . . Eine Vernunft, eine Notwendigkeit, die Ihnen
> mich zu vergessen befiehlt? — Ich bin eine grosse Liebhaberin von
> Vernunft, ich habe sehr viel Ehrerbietung für die Notwendigkeit. —
> Aber lassen Sie doch hören, wie vernünftig diese Vernunft, wie
> notwendig diese Notwendigkeit ist.
> *V. Tellheim:* Wohl denn; so hören Sie, mein Fräulein. — Sie
> nennen mich Tellheim, den Sie in Ihrem Vaterlande gekannt haben;
> . . . Dieser Tellheim bin ich ebensowenig, — als ich mein Vater bin.
> Beide sind gewesen. — Ich bin Tellheim, der verabschiedete, der an
> seiner Ehre gekränkte, der Krüppel, der Bettler. — Jenem, mein
> Fräulein versprachen Sie sich: wollen Sie diesem Wort halten? —
> *Das Fräulein:* Das klingt sehr tragisch! — Doch, mein Herr, bis
> ich jenen wiederfinde, — in die Tellheims bin ich nun einmal
> vernarret, — dieser wird mir schon aus der Not helfen müssen. —
> Deine Hand, lieber Bettler!

[II, 9]

Minna von Barnhelm owes a great deal in its basic structure to the satirical comedy of types, but it is vastly different in that it does not aim merely to reveal flaws in the various character types and expose them to ridicule. Instead it creates strong characters, who exhibit individuality.

The other work that had its beginnings in Breslau is the treatise *Laokoon oder über die Grenzen der Malerey und Poesie*. Only the first part was completed in 1776, and Part II was never written. The study is characteristic of Lessing's approach in showing his intense desire for clarity in its seeking to eliminate the confusion which had resulted from numerous treatises in which painting and literature were discussed as if they were governed by the same aesthetic laws. Lessing wants to separate the principles that guide the creation of both arts, to be able to determine their interplay. He indicts those critics who are apt to describe a certain piece of poetry as being done in the manner of a painting or who might characterize a piece of graphic art as descriptive poetry. Against such a mixing of essentially different arts he states the often-quoted principle that poets should avoid descriptive passages and painters allegorical scenes. Painting, Lessing argues, works with figures and colors in space, concentrating on co-existing bodies, whereas poetry is built on articulated sounds in time, having as its object action. This distinction had a great effect on the development of literature in the eighteenth century and has not lost its momentum yet. That is in a sense surprising, because the distinction is by no means as logical as the clarity of Lessing's style might lead us to believe. Critics have pointed out that poetry understood as action may be an accurate description of drama, Lessing's forte, but certainly not of lyric poetry. Lessing's contemporary Herder, whose real interest was in lyric poetry, in the musical, rightly wondered in the second of his *Kritische Wälder* whether the articulated sounds in time did not define music rather than literature. Yet the effectiveness of *Laokoon* cannot be overstated. The break with traditional views that was implied in Lessing's challenge to the entrenched aesthetic principle of *ut pictura poesis* signaled freedom to a new generation of writers, the *Sturm und Drang*: foremost among them was young Goethe, who did avoid descriptive poetry and wrote true lyric lines, in stark contrast to the poetry of a Brockes or a Gessner. Although Lessing was not in agreement with the new generation and its literary aims, the influence *Laokoon* exerted on them is undeniable. Lessing had not shown them how to write poetry, rather he had shown what kind of poetry not to write.

One of the sources used by Lessing was Joseph Spence's *Polymetis* (1747). For polemical reasons he had portrayed Spence in *Laokoon* as his opponent, whereas in reality he had accepted and developed many of Spence's assumptions.[29] Lessing's method often forced him to side-step those points on which he agreed with others and to emphasize instead the points to which he took exception, thus highlighting the theoretical principle he wanted to advance. That was also the case with Lessing's treatment of Winckelmann, whose, famous characterization of Greek art as 'eine edle Einfalt und eine stille Grösse' was occasioned by reflections on the suffering Laocoön, the statue which depicts the priest and his two sons being attacked by two large snakes. Laocoön's magnanimity in spite of pain accords in Winckelmann's view with the idea that beauty is the guiding principle of art. At this point Lessing's disagreement with Winckelmann begins as he points out that in a literary work a weeping Laocoön may still possess greatness, even though in a painting or in a sculpture weeping would destroy the impression of magnanimity. Hence the thesis that we must distinguish between the arts.

Lessing had left Breslau early in 1765 and moved back to Berlin, where he hoped to be offered the court librarianship by Frederick the Great. This hope was not fulfilled. He was accordingly pleased when the city of Hamburg called him in 1767 to be critic and dramatist for its new theater, which had opened in April of 1765.[30] Within a few years' time it had to close down again for lack of support.[31] Lessing neither could nor would supply new plays on a regular basis, but for two years (1767–1769) he did publish the *Hamburgische Dramaturgie*, at first discussing each play that was performed and also criticizing the performances, but soon elaborating generally, although in frag-menatry fashion, on matters theatrical and on the theory of the drama, even though these considerations took him far beyond the scope of a mere reviewer. Many comments pertain to art or literature in general, although Lessing does return again and again to the specific genre of the drama. Nor are all of the ideas expressed original with Lessing, although they are always stated in an impressive manner, a fact which is probably particularly responsible for the influence of his *Dramaturgie*. Lessing's sharp criticism of French dramas, that is his opposition to the dominant role of French drama on the German stage, and his frequent positive evaluation of Shakespeare — he does not really present a detailed view of Shakespeare — are the major themes, as is Lessing's much discussed interpretation of Aristotle's comments on tragedy. To Lessing the Enlightenment tenet that drama, and especially tragedy, is written to make a better person out of the viewer is axiomatic.[32] The effect of tragedy on the audience according to Aristotle.was ʒοβοδ ('terror'), commonly translated into German as 'Schrecken', and ελεοs ('pity'). Lessing insisted that what Aristotle had in mind was not terror but merely fear, and that pity was to be understood as that positive ability to feel for another person in anguish. Lessing wanted neither uncontrolled terror to seize the audience nor a sort of pitying disgust for the hero, for the goal of purification — Aristotle's κάνϑροίσ — is possible only if the audience's fear is based on identification with the suffering hero.[33] Lessing has not provided an accurate translation of Aristotle's terms, but his rendering of the Greek words helped him to see tragedy within the context of the Enlightenment ideals.

In 1770 the redoubtable critic took up duties as librarian of the Duke Ernst August of Brunswick's *Bibliotheka Augusta* in Wolfenbüttel, a quiet town since the court had moved to nearby Brunswick. Lessing would remain in the Duke's services for the remainder of his life. In many ways it was an almost symbolic appointment for Lessing. His task was not so much that of cataloging books as that of buying significant manuscripts and old books. The author, whose own critical writings so often grew out of reactions to positions taken by others, and who was intent on coming as close as possible to the truth, was bound to make decisive use of the great treasure that the Wolfenbüttel library, one of Europe's largest at the time, was.[34] The library contained then and contains now innumerable manuscripts and valuable books, and Lessing soon published on a periodic basis important finds or the results of unknown manuscripts, mainly in the area of theology. Wolfenbüttel brought intellectual satisfaction, but also personal happiness, especially in his brief marriage to Eva König. For five years Lessing had to wait patiently for this marriage. He needed from the Duke a higher salary if he was to support a household of his own. The raise in salary came when the Duke sold soldiers to the British to fight in the American war of independence, one of the largest sources of income for German rulers during those years. Lessing's marriage took place in October of 1776.

Lessing's first Wolfenbüttel success was the completion of his second middle-class tragedy, *Emilia Galotti* (1772), built on the famous Virginia episode as reported by Livius, although Lessing pointedly excluded the political overthrow from the episode. Odoardo's killing of his daughter Emilia to protect her from the prince's desires because he regards her virtue to be of higher value than her life, does not, as in the Roman model, lead to an uprising of the populace and result in the abolition of tyranny.[35]

If the value of a play can be measured by the number of different and opposing interpretations which have been written about it, *Emilia Galotti* must rank among the best German tragedies. Indeed, this drama continues to hold the interest of scholars and actors alike. Is it a political drama in the sense that Lessing formulates in it his deeply felt accusation against a representative absolute prince whose actions are aimed only at satisfying his own desires? Or is it an Enlightenment contribution to the beauty of undefiled virtue as exhibited in Emilia Galotti and her father Odoardo? It is neither. Lessing's portrayal of the absolute ruler in the person of the Italian Renaissance prince — his apparent lack of concern for the feelings of his subjects, his giving in to momentary moods and whims, his maintaining a regular castle and a summer 'Lustschloss' — have invited all too easily the interpretation of *Emilia Galotti* as a political play, influenced by the model from Roman history. The effective opening scenes, including the dramatically highly successful dialogue between the Prince and the painter Conti over aspects of his two latest portraits, show a prince whose love and admiration for Emilia Galotti make him oblivious to everything else. These first scenes even betray the Prince's feelings toward Odoardo, Emilia's jealous father:

> Auch kenn' ich ihren Vater. Er ist mein Freund nicht. Er war es,
> der sich meinen Ansprüchen auf Sabionetta am meisten widersetzte.
> — Ein alter Degen; stolz und rauh; sonst bieder und gut! —
>
> [I, 4]

The prince is not simply unjust and unresponsive to human virtue. He rebukes his devilish councilor Martinelli who scorns the ideals of innocence and feeling:

> Wer sich den Eindrücken, die Unschuld und Schönheit auf ihn
> machen, ohne weitere Rücksicht, so ganz überlassen darf; — ich
> dächte, der wäre eher zu beneiden, als zu belachen.
>
> [I, 6]

Yet it is this cynic Martinelli, who has only contempt for human beings and who will use any means to accomplish his goals, to whom the prince yields in all things. His plans are to hire known criminals who will stage an attack on the carriage in which Emilia and Count Appiani, the bridegroom, are travelling to the estate where the marriage is to take place. In the ensuing chaos Emilia is to be brought to the Prince's 'Lustschloss'.

Because the Prince's admiration for Emilia is love indeed, we understand why she is touched by it, at the church where he confesses his love to her, and later at the 'Lustschloss' when she confesses to her father the reason of her real fear:

> Was Gewalt heisst, ist nichts: Verführung ist die wahre Gewalt. — Ich habe Blut, mein Vater, so jugendliches, warmes Blut, als eine. Auch meine Sinne sind Sinne. Ich stehe für nichts. Ich bin für nichts gut.
>
> [V, 7]

This fear and her accusing claim that there no longer exists a father who will protect his daughter's virtue by killing her, thereby giving her life for a second time, move Odoardo to stab Emilia in a moment of unreflecting emotion. Both the Prince and Odoardo appear to be influenced by their particular roles in society, the Prince by the power of absolute despotism, and Odoardo by an inflexible zealousness in moral matters. Now both must learn that they are human beings under God. Odoardo tells the Prince that he will go to jail voluntarily — a forerunner to Karl in Schiller's *Die Räuber* — and there await the Prince as his judge, reminding him, however, that together they will face the eternal judge. The Prince laments his human weaknesses, but regrets even more that he was controlled by his devilish adviser: 'Ist es, zum Unglücke so mancher, nicht genug, dass Fürsten Menschen sind: müssen sich auch noch Teufel in ihren Freund verstellen? ' [V, 8] .

Social and religious areas of conflict are thus aspects of the play. Seen against Lessing's own theories as set forth in his *Dramaturgie*, the strictly political interpretations would be outside the author's intentions. All the more important becomes the question of how Lessing saw in this tragic sequence of events a justification of our world order, for that is what he required of a play. It is to be found in Odoardo's and the Prince's realization that neither the Prince's political despotism nor Odoardo's stubbornly rigid and dogmatic moral stance allow virtue to develop and justice to prevail.[36]

Wolfenbüttel has become associated in German literary history mainly with Lessing's theological dispute with the Lutheran minister Johann Melchior Goeze (1717–1786) of Hamburg. In 1774 Lessing had begun publishing the so-called *Fragmente eines Ungenannten*, actually parts of an apologia which Hermann Samuel Reimarus (1694–1768) had written but never published because of its attacks on orthodox religion. Lessing's avowed reason for publishing the apologia – he claimed that he had happened upon this manuscript in the Wolfenbüttel library, whereas in fact Reimarus had given it to him – was that in the name of tolerance and truth, freethinkers' ideas should be made known. When he published in 1777, among others, Reimarus' attacks on revelation and his compilation of contradictions in the gospel accounts of the Resurrection, the orthodox theologians protested loudly. Lessing defended not so much these views in themselves as Reimarus's efforts to grasp the truth; to Lessing the effort to arrive at truth was more noble than its actual possession:

Nicht die Wahrheit, in deren Besitz irgendein Mensch ist oder zu sein vermeinet, sondern die aufrichtige Mühe, die er angewandt hat, hinter die Wahrheit zu kommen, macht den Wert des Menschen. Denn nicht durch Besitz, sondern durch die Nachforschung der Wahrheit erweitern sich seine Kräfte, worin allein seine immer wachsende Vollkommenheit bestehet. Der Besitz macht matt, träge, stolz.[37]

Lessing had at least maintained a certain disagreement with the 'unnamed' scholar, arguing that contradictions in the Biblical account of the Resurrection do not conclusively prove that the Resurrection was an invention. The quarrel became particularly bitter after Goeze attacked Lessing by name early in 1778. Lessing's answers did not aim at reaching any understanding but merely at refuting Goeze, and he continued his replies until the Duke ordered him in July 1778 to cease work on his *Anti-Goeze*. Even that order did not keep Lessing entirely from writing against Goeze. However, he now concentrated most of his efforts on writing *Nathan der Weise*.

The play, one of the first German dramas written in blank verse, was called 'ein dramatisches Gedicht'. Its setting is Jerusalem during the Crusades after the Moslem ruler Saladin had captured the city from the Crusaders. Thus three religions, Jewish, Moslem, and Christian, live side by side but fight each other. *Nathan der Weise* expresses Lessing's theological tenet, through the famous parable of the three rings, that religious truth is not supported by historical facts but by an individual's life. Therefore, tolerance is required. In the play the practice of tolerance leads to the discovery that the three religions represent one family. In this family the wealthy Jewish merchant Nathan turns out to be the true spiritual father, a moving figure who fascinates readers through his wisdom as well as his compassionate nature. The parable of the rings, which Lessing had found in Boccaccio, is used by Nathan to answer Saladin's question about the one true religion. The three rings, representing the three religions, look so much alike that they cannot be distinguished from each other. The power of the original ring to make its bearer loved by others has vanished as the sons turn to quarreling. It is now up to each bearer to prove through his life the original power of the ring he possesses:

> So glaube jeder sicher seinen Ring
> Den echten. — Möglich; dass der Vater nun
> Die Tyrannei des einen Rings nicht länger
> In seinem Hause dulden wollen! — Und gewiss;
> Dass er euch alle drei geliebt, und gleich
> Geliebt: indem er zwei nicht drücken mögen,
> Um einen zu begünstigen. — Wohlan!
> Es eifre jeder seiner unbestochnen
> Von Vorurteilen freien Liebe nach!
> Es strebe von euch jeder um die Wette,
> Die Kraft des Steins in seinem Ring' an Tag
> Zu legen!

[III, 7]

The forcefulness of the parable lies not in its logical consistency, or rather lack of it, but in the plot constructed around it, and in the crisp and lucid language of the dialogue.

The problems of tolerance and of overcoming every kind of prejudice as a way towards humanitarianism occupied Lessing also when he wrote *Ernst und Falk: Gespräche für Freimaurer* (1778). He had become a member of the Masonic order in 1771. A late work, *Die Erziehung des Menschengeschlechts* (1780), turns once again and in great detail to the relationship of revelation and rational insight. Lessing projects a development from revealed religion to a form of natural religion in which the necessity for divine revelation would be superseded by unaided operation of mankind's highly developed knowledge. The critic who had always distinguished between the religion of Christ and the Christian religion imagines revelation as a form of education. Just as education allows us to learn and understand more quickly things which otherwise would require much time, so does revelation provide man with insights into his nature and destiny more quickly than those he would be able to gain on his own. In this way, Biblical revelation aids mankind in the proper use of reason, so much so that reason now assumes the role of revelation. Lessing perceives a definite moral and ethical progress from the Old to the New Testament, a progress which he believes will continue. The process of the education of mankind is ongoing and will never be completed, just as the search for truth will never end.

The year 1780 was also the year in which the so-called 'Spinozastreit' developed. Friedrich Heinrich Jacobi met with Lessing during that summer and later made known their conversations. Because the subject of Spinoza's philosophy had come up Jacobi apparently pressed Lessing for a clear statement of his views on Spinoza. To the great disappointment of Lessing's old friend Moses Mendelssohn, Jacobi's account declared Lessing to have accepted Spinoza's faith in a pantheistic God. Christians and Jews of the period had rejected Spinoza's philosophy, a form of mysticism, and Mendelssohn could not believe that Lessing had indeed seriously expressed agreement with Spinoza's concept of God, nor that he would have kept such an important matter from him, especially since they had corresponded about Spinoza during Lessing's stay in Breslau. It is probably not possible to settle the argument whether or not Lessing was a strong supporter of Spinoza's ideas, but it is understandable that Lessing at the time of his *Die Erziehung des Menschengeschlechts* had distanced himself from any orthodox views of God.

The totality of Lessing's work makes understandable his being treated in all standard works as the single most influential figure in the literature of German Enlightenment. The complexity of his work was at least in part responsible for this view. The high praise he received for his pioneering thoughts from the *Sturm und Drang* movement as a whole furnishes another reason. The *Sturm und Drang* authors liked his sharp attacks on Gottsched and others who pedantically adhered to picayune rules, as they liked his positive evaluation of Shakespeare. But even more important was that Lessing's urbanity and modernity, his broad literary and cultural interests, as well as his philosophical insights, profoundly and permanently altered the image of the man of letters in Germany.

Notes

1. R. Hamel, *DNL*, 46, CLXXI. This is probably the major reason why the poem had lost its appeal by the time Klopstock's epic was complete in 1773. Since then the interest in this particular work by Klopstock has been mainly historical.

Cf. however the conclusion of R. Grimm, 'Marginalien zu Klopstock's *Messias*', *GRM*, 42 (1961), 294: 'Die Doppelheit von Erbauungsbuch und ins Erhabene stilisierter Passionsgeschichte liefert, so scheint es mir, eine präzisere Erklärung dafür, dass Klopstocks Werk seit mehr als hundertfünfzig Jahren so ganzlich tot und abgetan ist.'

2. See nos. 18 and 19 of Lessing's *Briefe, die neueste Literatur betreffend.*

3. See op. cit., nos. 15—19.

4. See 'Gespräch zwischen einem Rabbi und einem Christen über Klopstocks *Messias*' in Herder's *Fragmente.*

5. Blackall, *The Emergence of German*, p. 314, shows that Pyra's *Tempel der wahren Dichtkunst* prompted Klopstock to treat the theme of Christ's redemption.

6. The best available edition listing textual changes is still that prepared by R. Hamel, *DNL*. It compares the three cantos of the original edition of 1748 with the version the poet published in 1799. A historical-critical edition of Klopstock's writings, including his letters and related materials, is now being published: *Werke und Briefe. Historisch-kritische Ausgabe*, ed. H. Gronemeyer *et al*. (Berlin, 1974 ff).

7. Cf. K. L. Schneider, *Klopstock und die Erneuerung der deutschen Muttersprache im 18. Jahrhundert* (Heidelberg, 1960), p. 89. He argues that Klopstock made possible the smooth transition from rationalistic literature to the portrayal of unreflected sensation in the *Sturm und Drang.*

8. Klopstock put his own orthographical system into practice in the 1780 edition of the *Messias.*

9. Blackall, *The Emergence of German*, pp. 347—350.

10. *Agathon* (London, 1773), I, ii.

11. The marvelous monograph by F. Sengle, *Wieland* (Stuttgart, 1949), not only corrected many misconceptions about the author but inspired critics to turn their attention to Wieland.

12. Ibid., p. 133. It must be noted, however, that the old Goethe had great praise for Wieland: 'Wielanden verdankt das ganze obere Deutschland seinen Stil. Es hat viel von ihm gelernt, und die Fähigkeit sich gehörig auszudrücken, ist nicht das geringste.' Cf. *Gespräche mit Eckermann*, as recorded under 18 January 1825.

13. It should be noted that Wieland shares the honor of introducing the iambic pentameter into German with Joachim Wilhelm von Brawe (1738—1758), who wrote his *Brutus* (1758) in blank verse.

14. Actually, the first Shakespeare play he translated he rendered into verse.

15. As Sophie Marie von La Roche (1731—1807) she authored the novel *Geschichte des Fräuleins von Sternheim*, which Wieland edited for publication in 1771.

16. Book VIII, chapter 7.

17. Lessing's remarks appeared in his *Hamburgische Dramaturgie*, no. 69 (December 1767): 'Es ist der erste und einzige Roman für den denkenden Kopf, von klassischem Geschmacke.'

18. See E. Staiger, *'Musarion'*, in E. S., *Die Kunst der Interpretation* (Zürich, 1955), pp. 97—114.

19. Sengle developed the concept 'humoristische Klassik' in his monograph, using it as a sub-title for a chapter heading.

20. It is of historical interest to note that John Quincy Adams, when he was minister to the Prussian court in 1797, learned German because he wanted to translate Wieland's *Oberon* into English. The translation never appeared in his lifetime, but was published in 1940, in New York.

21. From Goethe's *Gespräche mit Eckermann*, as recorded under 27 March 1831.

22. M. Durzak, 'Das Gesellschaftsbild in Lessings *Emilia Galotti*,' *LY*, I, 60–87.
23. Letter to Elise Reimarus of 6 September 1773.
24. G. Hillen, 'Die Halsstarrigkeit der Tugend. Bemerkungen zu Lessings Trauerspielen,' *LY*, II, 115–134.
25. Scene 10.
26. N. W. Feinäugle, 'Lessings Streitschriften: Überlegungen zu Wesen und Methode der literarischen Polemik', *LY*, I, 126–149.
27. Lessing's was not the first domestic tragedy in German. That fame goes to Christian Lebrecht Martini (1728–1801), whose *Rhynsolt und Sapphira* was written in 1753, although not published until two years later. It was followed by a good number of middle-class tragedies, including *Lucie Woodvil* (1756) by Johann Gottlieb Benjamin Pfeil (1732–1800), and *Der Freygeist* (1757) by Joachim Wilhelm von Brawe (1738–1758). Cf. K. S. Guthke, *Das bürgerliche Trauerspiel* (Stuttgart, 1972), pp. 55–56; and R. R. Heitner, *German Tragedy in the Age of Enlightenment* (Berkeley, 1963), pp. 170–202. Even though Martini's play may have been more influential in setting the pattern for the domestic tragedy in the period from 1755 to 1775, Lessing's *Miss Sara Sampson* has in the long run become the classical model for this genre.
28. Letter of 2 April.
29. Cf. D. T. Siebert, Jr., *Laokoon* and *Polymetis*: Lessing's Treatment of Joseph Spence', *LY*, III, 71–83.
30. The theater reform had raised the standards of performance. Better educated actors were concerned about the quality of their art. Following the tenets of the period they looked upon their work as educational for the middle-class society. Actors, poets and audience expressed their support of these artistic and pedagogical ideals. The phrase 'deutsches Nationaltheater' was used to reflect these new ideals. The theater in Hamburg was the first to be named in this manner. Hamburg's example served to convince several princes to establish 'German National Theaters' in their realms as well. Cf. E. Ermatinger, *Deutsche Kultur im Zeitalter der Aufklärung*, pp. 290–291; W. H. Bruford, *Germany in the Eighteenth Century*, p. 85; J. Prudhoe, *The Theatre of Goethe and Schiller* (Totowa, New Jersey, 1973), the introductory chapter.
31. W. H. Bruford, p. 85, stresses the fact that ultimately the continued growth of quality theater in Germany depended on the support of the courts; for not even such a wealthy city as Hamburg was able to keep the doors of the theater open.
32. R. Heitner, *German Tragedy in the Age of Enlightenment*, pp. XIII–XVII.
33. Cf. nos. 74–78 of *Hamburgische Dramaturgie*.
34. See H. Schneider in Guthke, Schneider, *G. E. Lessing* (Stuttgart, 1967), p. 44. See also E. Ermatinger, *Deutsche Kultur im Zeitalter der Aufklärung*, p. 271.
35. Cf. Lessing's letter of January 1758 to Nicolai.
36. For a full discussion see G. Hillen, 'Die Halsstarrigkeit der Tugend', pp. 119–130; Guthke, *Das bürgerliche Trauerspiel*, pp. 60–65.
37. From *Eine Duplik*, 1778.

5 STURM UND DRANG

I A Change in Direction

Because the literary movement known as *Sturm und Drang* rejected certain tenets of rationalistic criticism and literature, it has often been viewed as diametrically opposed to the Enlightenment. The writers of *Sturm und Drang* protested against what they saw as the dogmatic rigidity of rationalistic literature and criticism, and they therefore vehemently demanded freedom from rules. The young critics of the movement invoked other standards by praising the 'old-German' traditions and the spirit of medieval times, while attacking what in their view was a monotonous, shallow and coldly rationalistic literature. This generation cherished the colorfulness of folklore, enjoyed the wilder aspects of nature, and loved being exposed to the elements. These young men defiantly exhibited their freedom by appealing to their self-styled genius in the way they lived as well as in the way they wrote. They questioned social customs and even unalterable political realities not because they wanted to repudiate the philosophical convictions of the Enlightenment but because they wanted to free them from their narrow rigidity and see them put into actual practice. It therefore seems out of place to characterize the *Sturm und Drang* movement as entirely irrationalistic, because many of its tenets were anticipated by the Enlightenment. If it assigned a high value to emotional feeling, Pyra, Schlegel and Lessing, all champions of the Enlightenment, had done the same; and if it appealed specifically to the young, so had the writings of Gellert.

Rationalism had not altogether drowned out the voice of feeling and the *Sturm und Drang* writers did not simply scout all the accomplishments of the Enlightenment period. Rather, they protested against the kind of limitations represented by Gottsched's rules, even bringing back to the stage the harlequin figure which Gottsched had banished from it. The new movement also displayed a historical consciousness — a dimension missing in the strangely a-historical Enlightenment. The critical abilities of this new movement are attested by the stature of Justus Möser, whose defense of the harlequin figure as a reflection of the grotesque-comical in human nature is considered a milestone in *Sturm und Drang* criticism. The search for universal norms led the Enlightenment to stress the similarities among epochs, whereas the positive value assigned to individuality led the *Sturm und Drang* writers to focus on the differences. This same Möser complained about the Enlightenment's lack of a sense of history in his *Patriotische Phantasien* (1774–1778), in which he characterized the difference between the seventeenth century Baroque and the eighteenth century Enlightenment:

> Die Zeit, welche ich gelebt habe, hat mir diese Veränderung mit ihren Ursachen leicht entdeckt, und ich kann sie dir mit wenigen sagen. Vordem arbeitete ein jeder für seinen Nachruhm, jetzt für den Tag, den ihm der Himmel giebt . . . . In beiden Fällen kommt es auf die Befriedigung einer Ehrbegierde an. Aber die erstere Art der Befriedigung ist dem Staate unstreitig weit nachteiliger als die letztere.[1]

From a historical perspective the Baroque period suddenly appears to be gaining in importance. The restoration of emphasis on the historical perspective is to the credit of the *Sturm und Drang*, and it suggests an awareness on the part of the *Sturm und Drang* writers that they were continuing the development of literature rather than radically breaking with tradition.

Just as it could be argued that the Enlightenment as a period encompassed diverse movements, for example, rationalism, sentimentalism and Pietism, it can be said that the *Sturm und Drang*, if the term is used to designate an epoch rather than merely an attitude or a period in a given author's life, circumscribes several literary groups which, although not strikingly different, have their own particular emphases with little mutual association. There is the famous Strasbourg-Frankfort circle with Herder and Goethe as the most notable authors. This group aimed for powerful expression and fullness of feeling in their works. Out of this circle came the name *Sturm und Drang* toward the end of the period, when the Swiss Christian Kaufmann appropriately retitled Klinger's drama *Der Wirrwarr* as *Sturm und Drang*. Simultaneously the *Göttinger Hain*, a group of close friends — students at Göttingen — who were more drawn to Gleim and Klopstock than to foreign models, added a dimension of quiet geniality in which friendship was idolized and cultivated, and where anti-feudalistic feelings were expressed. While the 'revolutionary' spirit of the 1770s in Germany did not lead to political action, as it did in France, it is noteworthy that in the southwest, in Swabia, the *Sturm und Drang* made a strong plea for political freedom. This is especially true of Schubart, whose ringing poetic indictments against tyranny led to his imprisonment. Schiller's early works also showed strong revolutionary overtones.

The dramas of the *Sturm und Drang* vividly portray the intense yearning for freedom in the spiritual, cultural, social and political realms — and all to be experienced individually. The hero-genius is usually shown as living in opposition to and in conflict with the expectations of society, so much so that he may appear as a criminal or revolutionary if measured by conventional standards, while in truth his actions are in accord with his feelings and his personality. The dramas reflect most readily the whole range of concerns of the *Sturm und Drang*, exhibit the movement's preference for strongly idiomatic language, and demonstrate well the period's disdain for rules. As a result drama has often been hailed as the *Sturm und Drang*'s most significant literary accomplishment. However, it is just as plausible to argue that lyric poetry is the characteristic accomplishment of the *Sturm und Drang*. As a group, the *Sturm und Drang* poets developed the genre of lyric poetry so that it became capable of capturing their feelings and love experiences with a direct expressiveness reminiscent of the folk song. The critic Herder, whose writings shaped and defined so many of the movement's tenets, was almost exclusively concerned with the lyric genre, having little if any sensitivity for the dramatic. Pietism with its considerable body of poetic works — Zinzendorf alone wrote more than two thousand poems and songs — gave a strong impetus to the writings of lyrical poetry, especially since so many *Sturm und Drang* poets had first-hand knowledge of the religious movement. And, of course, Klopstock's lyrical genius had found ardent admirers among the members of the *Sturm und Drang* movement. The time was ripe, it would seem, for the growth of lyrical poetry. Goethe's and Lenz's 'Strassburger Lieder' and the rich production of the members of the *Göttinger Hain*, if seen against the background of the Enlightenment period, document the great accomplishment in lyrical poetry during the *Sturm und Drang*. The term 'Erlebnislyrik', that has been used to describe this poetry, is certainly not a full characterization, but it correctly reveals an aspect of this poetry that explains its being different from the 'Gedankenlyrik' of the Enlightenment period.

1 *Hamann*

The *Sturm und Drang*, which lasted less than two decades, continues to command in literary histories a place of unusual prominence, because of the value of its own literary production, and because of the importance of its role in preparing for Germany's classic period of literature. How was it possible for the *Sturm und Drang* to exercise such enormous influence? One answer lies in the fact that the members of the movement interpreted human nature as being far more complex than either the rationalistic philosophy or the idyllic literature of the preceding decades had. Johann Georg Hamann (1730–1788) expounded such a view of the whole man through his style as well as his ideas. Hamann's puzzling style is deeply ironic and full of allusions to Biblical and classical literature. This style, even if not easily understood and even if seeming to defy any interpretive attempt, fascinated his contemporaries because it conveyed the impression of thorough knowledge and depth of thought. It was Hamann's notion that language must resort to conjuring up images so that the reader will understand an idea more fully by grasping it intuitively: 'Sinne und Leidenschaften reden und verstehen nichts als Bilder,' he wrote in his *Kreuzzüge eines Philologen* (1762).[2] In the same essay, and based on the same thought process, he made the often quoted statement: 'Poesie ist die Muttersprache des menschlichen Geschlechts.' This assumption that a nation's language was poetic and rich in imagery and idioms before it developed into rigid, logical, and abstract prose, profoundly influenced the literary style of the period.

Hamann's intellectual life as the 'Magus of the North' began with a spiritual awakening in London. He had gone there in 1756, sent by a merchant friend to take care of some business. Early in 1758, shortly before his return, he withdrew from the social life of London and read the Bible in English, and Pietistic hymns, as he reports in *Gedanken über meinen Lebenslauf* (1758–1759). He discovered the Bible to be written in a poetic language whose images appeal to our senses. When the New Testament speaks of freedom from the law, Hamann was quick to apply that thesis to the problem of literary rules and used it as proof that a genius is not bound by rules. Rather, the genius, he claimed, creates the examples from which rules can be derived:

O ihr Herolde allgemeiner Regeln! wie wenig versteht ihr die Kunst, und wie wenig besitzt ihr von dem Genie, das die Muster hervorgebracht hat, auf welche ihr sie baut, und das sie übertreten kann, so oft es ihm beliebt![3]

Hamann published these works in which he advanced views which would be widely held by the *Sturm und Drang* authors: *Sokratische Denkwürdigkeiten* (1759); *Kreuzzüge des Philologen* (1762); *Fünf*

Hirtenbriefe das Schuldrama betreffend (1763). However, when the
Sturm und Drang movement reached full flower Hamann maintained
his ironic distance. This defender of the creative faculties of the genius
found himself unable to agree with the cult of the genius of the
seventies.

2 *Möser*

As Hamann stressed the poetic qualities in the early stages of a language,
the childhood period as it was so often called in the eighteenth century,
so Justus Möser (1720–1794) praised the medieval age for its alleged
moral strength. He felt that the rule of the law of might made it
stronger and more civilized than his own. Möser studied jurisprudence
in Jena and Göttingen, and returned to his native Osnabrück to
practice law, later pursuing a distinguished civil service career, without
losing sight of his wide ranging humanistic studies about which he wrote
extensively. As a student he had joined the 'Deutsche Gesellschaft',
the society in which Gottsched had played such an important role.
Accordingly, he was influenced considerably by Gottsched. It took a
turnabout for Möser to repudiate Gottsched's views and to reject the
French cultural domination. This turnabout found its most vivid
expression in his defense of the harlequin figure on the stage (1761);
but it caused him also to see himself as a patriotic advocate of the
simple people, whose habits and cultural patterns he defended against
foreign models. His approach was historiographic. He traced the
history of the arts, of classes within society, of the separate territories
in Germany. According to Möser, a comprehensive view is possible only
if the historian first pays attention to these detailed aspects. Hence the
title of Möser's history, *Osnabrückische Geschichte* (1765, 1768). He
intentionally limited the scope of the work to the study of one small
territory. Möser's view of history inspired the young *Sturm und Drang*
authors to appreciate the Middle Ages, hitherto thought of as barbarian,
and to prefer the individual to the universal. Herder included a sample
of Möser's writing along with Goethe's and his own in the programmatic
Sturm und Drang publication *Von deutscher Art und Kunst* (1773). Yet
on the whole Möser remained more conservative and provincial than
the *Sturm und Drang* writers, possibly because he was considerably older
than the rest. His famous *Patriotische Phantasien*, which appeared in
his *Wöchentliche Osnabrückische Anzeigen* from 1766 on, and later in
book form, document Möser as a pleader for re-establishing simplicity
and hard work as common sense values.

3 *Lavater*

The literature of Germany's Enlightenment had not been anti-religious.
Rather, it had attempted to present the religious realm as part of a
rationally explainable world, and the church had responded by seeking
to make the contents of theology rationally defensible. As a result, the
Sturm und Drang writers felt no incentive to relate their work to such
a theology. The Pietistic religious movement, with its professed lack of
interest in specific theological issues and its commitment to understand
man's complex nature, offered itself to the young authors as a way of
taking into account the spiritual dimension without their having to
align themselves with the church as an institution, for Pietism existed
largely outside the official church. There were other reasons why
Pietism held a certain appeal for the *Sturm und Drang* poets. Sociologic-
ally important was the fact that Pietism minimized distinctions between
the nobility and normal citizens. Here was an ideal that could be held
up in literature. Psychologically attractive were the many Pietistic
autobiographical works, in which one theme was dealt with again and
again: the Pietist let himself be guided by feelings and sentiments after
having entrusted his life to the Savior. Such a concept could easily be
transferred to secular literature to show how a person in harmony with
nature may allow himself similarly to be guided by his feelings and
sentiments. Pietistic concepts were transferable to secular writings. In
that lay the appeal of Pietism and its language for the *Sturm und Drang*.

There were also authors who, although not strictly Pietists,
sympathized greatly with Pietistic views and whose work was strongly
religious in tone and content. Hamann is in this category, and so is
Johann Kaspar Lavater (1741−1801), whose definition of the poetic
genius, as found in his *Physiognomische Fragmente*, is analogous to
that of a religous enthusiast: 'Nenn's und beschreib's, wie du willst
und kannst; allemal bleibt das gewiss: das Ungelernte, Unentlehnte,
Unlernbare, Unentlehnbare, innig Eigentümliche, Unnachahmliche,
Göttliche ist Genie, das Inspirationsmässige ist Genie. . . . ' In his
hymnic language he comes very close to equating genius with the
divine. His enthusiasm was appreciated by the youthful *Sturm und
Drang* writers. Goethe's *Werther* contains several references to Lavater,
effectively praising his religious enthusiasm as preferable by far to the
rationalistic theology.[4] In his own time Lavater, the minister of
religion, was a much celebrated figure, in his native Switzerland as well
as throughout Germany, because of his powerful preaching, his
erudition in matters philosophical, and also his lifelong occupation

with physiognomic studies, a dabbling that caught the fancy of many a contemporary.

Bodmer and Breitinger had been Lavater's teachers in Zurich, and literature had been his main concern before he turned to theology. After that his major commitment was to his pastoral work, but his interest in the literary scene did not grow less intense. The biographical data support this impression. His several journeys through Germany include numerous meetings with groups of Pietists, but also visits with such well-known poets as Gellert, Weisse, Ramler, Gleim, and Klopstock. He met Goethe in Frankfort in 1774 — together they took a trip on the Rhine — and again in 1775 in Zurich. The friendship with Goethe lasted only a few years — it was renewed in the 1780s, again not for long — but it produced a sizable correspondence which is a significant document of the *Sturm und Drang* and its hopes and frustrations. Lavater's religious intolerance was the real stumbling block in his relationship with Goethe. The correspondence between the two was occasioned in part by Lavater's *Physiognomische Fragmente, zur Beförderung der Menschenkenntnis und Menschenliebe* (1775–1778), because Goethe cooperated with Lavater in this venture. These *Fragmente* are a collection of drawings of various historical and living people. Each drawing is followed by a description of the person's character as it supposedly reveals itself in his facial features: 'Die Schönheit und Hässlichkeit des Angesichtes hat ein richtiges und genaues Verhältnis zur Schönheit und Hässlichkeit der moralischen Beschaffenheit des Menschen.'[5] Lavater's physiognomic studies seemed to offer one highly desirable avenue toward understanding man's nature. That explains why he was such a popular figure with many *Sturm und Drang* writers.

4 Herder

The uniqueness of *Sturm und Drang* literature rests to a large degree on the lively exchanges of thought between the members of the movement. The young generation received the ideas of such men as Hamann, Möser and Lavater enthusiastically, and were inspired by them to shape a literature which contemporaries felt to be distinctively new and different. The relationships of Johann Gottfried Herder (1744–1803) to the *Sturm und Drang* authors was of this kind, but particularly close and long lasting, so much so that he might be counted an actual member of the movement. His essential contribution was that of enunciating the views that would provide the philosophical basis on which the *Sturm und Drang* writers built.

When Goethe in *Dichtung und Wahrheit* recalls meeting Herder in Strasbourg in the fall of 1770, he characterizes him most succinctly with the statement: 'Er war mehr geneigt, zu prüfen und anzuregen als zu führen und zu leiten' [Book 10]. Indeed, Herder was a fruitful critic more than a creative writer, an analyzing genius of poetry more than a poet. His first significant work was entitled *Fragmente über die neuere deutsche Literatur*, a work in which he developed his far-reaching ideas through a detailed and perceptive criticism of the literature of that day. We are here concerned essentially with young Herder, the theologian, the educator, the literary critic, and the emerging philosopher of history who was interested in the diversity and multiformity of human life, rather than in the normative existence of mankind; more in a history 'der Menschen' than in a history 'des Menschen', as he himself puts it.

Herder along with Kant and Hamann is the third major figure among German men of letters in the eighteenth century to come out of East Prussia. He grew up in the small town of Mohrungen. His father, a church organist and an elementary school teacher, was a Pietist, as was the church deacon and author of devotional literature, Tresche, in whose house Herder lived as a boy and whose library he could use, a library which contained a number of *belletristic* works. Trescho was well read in literature and introduced Herder to this vast field. In 1762 Herder arrived at the University of Königsberg well prepared to pursue studies in theology. His academic background was such that he was able to find almost immediately a position in a secondary school, where he taught languages, literature, history, and philosophy. These subjects remained throughout his life the four predominant areas of his critical inquiry. He became a theologian and was active as a Protestant minister, but was not concerned about dogmatic issues of theology. His Pietistic background made him see man rather than dogma. Herder was deeply committed to the cause of humanism, and humanity gradually came to be the key concept in his work. He spent his two years in Königsberg studying under Kant, who inspired him to read Rousseau and Hume, but he also studied in private with Hamann who taught him English, so that together they could read *Hamlet* and *Paradise Lost*. Herder felt more akin to Hamann, with his interest in English literature and his perception of genius. The beginning of his career as an author coincided with his move to Riga in 1764, where he was appointed secondary school teacher, and, after some time, also preacher. His preaching in particular was successful. There was a strong, affluent German community in this wealthy commercial Latvian town. His stay in Riga (1764—1769) saw the publication of three main works, in which he discussed the general literary situation during the 1750s and 1760s. They were Herder's attempt to come to terms with the literary criticism of his own day, and they quickly established his reputation as a critic.

Herder certainly had the personality of a critical teacher. Goethe tells us in *Dichtung und Wahrheit* that Herder introduced the group of young writers in Strasbourg to Goldsmith's *The Vicar of Wakefield*, simply by reading the novel to them without resorting at all to the technique of dramatized reading. Instead he criticized his listeners whenever they showed emotion. Goethe stresses that Herder looked only for formal aspects and for the substantive idea in the novel. This way of looking at literature was new to Goethe, but it explains Goethe's boundless admiration for Herder during those years, and it describes best Herder's fundamental goals and concerns. Three volumes of Herder's *Fragmente über die neuere deutsche Literatur* appeared between 1766 and 1777. His stated major objective was a critical discussion of language, the medium of all literature. He had intended to move to discussing aesthetics, history and philosophy, and had therefore planned a four volume work, reserving for each of the four mentioned areas one volume. Only three volumes were written, and all three deal with language. Hamann's preoccupation with the subject of language had influenced Herder. With Hamann he views literature and language from the perspective of historical development. What others, especially the French, but also Leibniz and Sulzer, had decried as primitive, and even as barbaric in German, he exalts as the poetic strength of the language. Like Hamann he views the early stages of a language as poetic, arguing that the more language becomes a suitable tool for expressing philosophical thought accurately, the more it will have lost its poetic beauty. Looking at his own time, Herder believes that German will develop into a purely scholarly language, unless authors emphasize the idiomatic aspects, and employ inverted word order. In that case it would move once again toward the strength it had possessed in a poetic age. We know that Goethe incorporated these ideas in his *Werther*, especially making use of the principle of inversion in such a way as to create the most beautiful rhythmical prose. Nor is it surprising that Herder has praise for Klopstock's *vers libre* or that he singles out Möser's and Hamann's writings as examples of poetic prose. Herder defines poetic languages as 'sinnlich-klar', and the philosophical language as 'logisch-deutlich', claiming that Latin had forced German to become a philosophical language and to suppress its poetic qualities. As a result the growth of a German literature had been prevented. Similarly, Herder calls for an end to the frequent use of ancient mythology in literary works. He prefers Nordic mythology. It is his historical perspective which causes him to warn against imitating the ancients. Constructive criticism of a literary work, Herder says, can be rendered only after the critic has sought first to understand the world of ideas in which the author lived and wrote. He demonstrates the method in a short work, written in memory of Thomas Abbt, a philosopher of history, who had died in 1766 at the age of twenty-eight, and whom Herder was to succeed in 1770 as preacher in Bückeburg: *Über Thomas Abbts Schriften: Der Torso zu einem Denkmal* (1768). Herder was not so much impressed with the depth or quality of Abbt's ideas as he was with his approach. Abbt, so Herder thought, took pains to relate a piece of writing to the intellectual climate of the period of its origin, and was thus able to appreciate the individual accomplishments of the author.

The publication of Lessing's *Laokoon* in 1776 more than anything else caused Herder not to continue with the *Fragmente*. Immediately, he wanted to write a critical discussion of Lessing's work, and began to plan a work called *Kritische Wälder*. The first volume appeared early in 1769, and consisted entirely of a critical commentary on *Laokoon*. In spite of his admiration for Lessing, Herder felt compelled to express his reservations, and to articulate his fundamental differences. Herder applauded Lessing's, Nicolai's, and Mendelssohn's efforts to direct German writers to Greek rather than Roman authors or French classicists who relied on the Romans in the first place. He was particularly impressed with Winckelmann's interpretations of Greek art, because he, Herder felt, paid attention to the historical conditions that existed when a particular work of art was created. Herder was unhappy with Lessing's criticism of Winckelmann because he attributed the opposing views to the different objectives these two critics pursued. Winckelmann was interested in the origin of the work and Lessing wanted to differentiate between art forms. Thus Herder's reservations about Lessing's *Laokoon* stemmed from Herder's emphasis on the historical approach in art criticism. To Lessing modes of artistic work remain the same, whereas Herder sees them change. While Homer was the greatest poet in Lessing's estimation, Herder sees him only as the greatest among the Greeks. The point is made again when Herder in the two remaining volumes of his *Kritische Wälder* attacks the Leipzig critic Christian Adolf Klotz (1738–1771) who had relegated Homer to a position below Horace. Herder calls upon the argument of historical relativity and claims that the eighteenth-century mind can neither understand weaknesses in Homer's work nor judge properly the dignity of his language. It is Herder's contention that there are no absolute literary standards and rules. Rather, he reads a work and allows himself to garner impressions from it, and only then does he seek to find out the particularities of a given author and discover why certain details impressed him.

In the spring of 1769 Herder began to feel restless in Riga. He had been treated well there, but some disputes had developed about his orthodoxy and about his sharp personal attacks on contemporary literary critics. In June he embarked on his most memorable voyage, one that would take him to Nantes. For five weeks he was the philosopher at sea, comparing his hovering between heaven and sea to his general feeling of insecurity and aimlessness. In Nantes he composed *Das Journal meiner Reise im Jahre 1769* which is not at all an ordinary type of diary, but a compilation of themes he felt he should investigate. There are repeated disavowels of further writings, suggestions for pedagogical reforms, strong condemnations of book learning – all in all, it is an informative introduction to the full range of interests that Herder wanted to pursue. He fervently argued that nature should only be studied in nature and not through books or laboratories, a view that is later shared by Goethe's Faust. He expressed his desire to become involved in political, social, and pedagogical projects. While writing the *Journal* he was also reading many French authors. Their names and ideas are mentioned in the *Journal* as well. The voyage produced just the effect he had hoped for because it forced him to view his own career critically from a distance. He went on to Paris, only to have his prejudices against French luxury and vanity confirmed. The acceptance of an offer to accompany the son of the prince of Lübeck-Eutin as tutor on an educational journey through Europe took him to Strasbourg in the summer of 1770. There he decided to give up that assignment in favor of an offer as court chaplain in Bückeburg.

In Strasbourg Herder and Goethe met, and Herder became the young poet's unrelenting critic. Goethe realized that he received from Herder most valuable criticism, and he therefore submitted gladly to Herder's arrogant way of dealing with him. Their relationship in Strasbourg can scarcely be called a friendship, but the significance of Herder's influence on Goethe cannot be overstated. Herder inspired Goethe to collect folk-songs in the Alsatian region, and urged him to read in Homer and Ossian, to study Shakespeare from the perspective according to which the balance achieved between form and content constitutes the value of a work of art. Before leaving Strasbourg in the spring of 1771, Herder finished one essay which was to bring him his first of many prizes.[6] The topic had been set by the Berlin Academy. It was the philosophical question about the origin of language, the much debated question whether language is a human invention or is of divine origin. Herder does not really discuss the problem of origin as such. Rather he deals with the nature of language and investigates language from a phonetic point of view at a time when everybody began with the written word. According to Herder language developed from sounds. Through his senses man reacts to the outside world. Man did not invent language, he merely developed it, for being man means having a language. Herder was eager to prove that the question of origins cannot really be answered in any significant way. However, after reading this essay one can only infer that Herder did indeed favor the theory of human origin, a view he altered later. But basically he was more fascinated by the psychology of language.

Count Wilhelm von Lippe-Schaumburg was able to attract as clergymen to his small realm some of the best young minds of Germany, first Thomas Abbt and now Herder. That was no mere accident. It was an indication that at this court new ideas were welcome. Born and raised in London, Count Wilhelm was educated in several European countries and travelled extensively in Switzerland, Germany, Italy and England. At the age of twenty-four he became the ruler of Lippe-Schaumburg and took up residence at Bückeburg where the court was located. He was an admirer of Frederick the Great and, accordingly, brought about substantive changes. Whereas his father had ruled as an absolute despot, using all his resources to demonstrate the usual Baroque splendor, Count Wilhelm did away with all that and strove to improve the military excellence of his realm. In 1762 he was chosen to command the United English and Portuguese army in a victorious war against the Spanish. Upon his return to Bückeburg, in 1763, he devoted all his energies to putting into practice the ideals of the Enlightenment period. Thomas Abbt had enjoyed an especially close relationship with the Count, mainly because Count Wilhelm appreciated Abbt's philosophical views. Herder, who had created a literary monument for Thomas Abbt, grew increasingly critical of many tenets of the Enlightenment. His sense of the historical put him at odds with the proponents of the German Enlightenment movement. His relationship with the Count was one of mutual respect, not one of cordiality. Yet the five years Herder spent in Bückeburg in Westphalia were unusually productive. The works he wrote there won him prizes and received national attention. In his Riga period he had often outlined his own position against other contemporary points of view. The time had come for Herder to speak more directly about particular issues of literature, to apply, as it were, the critical apparatus he had developed.

In a group of essays Herder addressed himself to MacPherson's Ossian songs, to Shakespeare, and to folk-songs. These essays must be counted among the most beautiful of Herder's writings. The attempt to understand folk-poetry as indigenous literature is probably the dominating thesis in all of them. His views on language and his historical studies had produced such a thesis. To him every language had its own literary spirit, and every culture its own basis for happiness: 'Jede Nation hat ihren Mittelpunkt der Glückseligkeit in sich wie jede Kugel ihren Schwerpunkt!'[7] The first essay in the series, *Auszug aus einem Briefwechsel über Ossian und die Lieder der alten Völker*, appeared in the collection *Von deutscher Art und Kunst. Einige fliegende Blätter* (1773). Herder considered Ossian to be on the same level as the great Greek poets. We must add, however, that Herder was merely the spokesman for an entire generation that took MacPherson's edition of alleged Ossian poems as authentic because these poems corresponded to what they were looking for in folk-poetry. They perceived folk-poetry as being most capable of true lyric expression.[8] Herder was well aware of questions about the genuineness of MacPherson's collection, but he and many others trusted their feelings and were not willing to investigate the matter. Herder's fictitious exchange of letters on Ossian dealt mainly with the problem of translation, a problem which Goethe had already faced through his decision to include several of the Ossian poems in his *Werther*. Many German authors tried their hands during the next few decades at producing German translations of MacPherson's Ossian poems. Without a doubt, the forceful and dynamic lyric of the *Sturm und Drang* developed its power of expression through these diverse attempts at rendering this kind of lyrical verse in German.

Herder himself knew that imitating Ossian was not what was needed most. He wanted to capitalize on the Ossian fever and to encourage others to collect samples of folk-poetry from many nations. Ossian to him was only the supreme example of unrefined, simple, but emotionally tense poetry. Much of medieval poetry had, in Herder's judgement, the qualities of folk-poetry. Seeing that the English were interested in collecting their medieval literature, Herder argued in his essay *Von der Ähnlichkeit der mittleren englischen und deutschen Dichtkunst* (1777) that the Germans should do the same. Gottsched and Bodmer had done just that, but Herder's reasons were different.

By pointing to the great medieval German literature, Herder challenged the assumption that more education and more refined and civilized culture also mean greater human or artistic achievements. A knowledge of medieval poetry could aid us in our understanding and proper evaluation of the culture of that period, possibly leading to a re-evaluation of the Middle Ages. The title of another prize essay, *Über die Wirkung der Dichtkunst auf die Sitten der Völker in alten und neuen Zeiten* (1781), is an indication of the strong feelings Herder had about the significance of the study of older literature, which he regarded largely as folk-poetry, and to which he attributed a far-reaching effect on a great number of people. (Only after he had written numerous essays to prepare the reading public for an appreciation of folk-songs did he publish his own collection in 1778–1779. The title, *Stimmen der Völker in Liedern*, was chosen by the editors of his works after his death.) The last essay to be mentioned in this group is simply entitled *Shakespeare*. It was also included in *Von deutscher Art und Kunst* (1773). In Herder's estimation Shakespeare was the greatest among the Northern poets, presenting us in his works with a true picture of his time and his nation. Shakespeare had a sense of the historical. And this seemed to Herder of the utmost importance, because he believed that history and literature are the two essential forces in explaining human existence. Thus Herder writes about Shakespeare: 'Hier ist kein Dichter, ist Schöpfer, ist die Geschichte der Welt.' Not that Herder was looking for historical accuracy in literature, or for the interpretation of certain historical events. He found in Shakespeare the totality of human life as viewed from a historical understanding of man and his position in the world.

Herder occupied himself increasingly with the study of history, more specifically with the problem of the philosophy of history, as the title of his treatise, *Auch eine Philosophie zur Geschichte der Bildung der Menschheit* (1774), another prize winning essay, bears out. Herder saw history more and more as a revelation of God's plan to mankind. He believed in process ('Progression'), but not in progress in an absolute sense. The treatise was, according to Herder, intended to heap glowing coals on the heads of his contemporaries, for in it he described the eighteenth century as an age of decadence. *Auch eine Philosophie* is the result of Herder's historical studies, which in turn reflect a renewed occupation with questions of faith and revelation. Studying history to Herder is the way by which to understand God's plan for mankind. In contrast to his contemporaries, Herder has praise for the middle-ages, preferring, as it were, even the 'darkness' of that epoch to

the mechanistic and wholly rationalistic approach of his own period,
for there were alive in medieval times such virtues as honor, freedom and
love. The Gothic cathedral with its twilight atmosphere to him is
symbolic of the spirit of the Middle Ages, a dark but firm period. It is
irony when Herder employs in *Auch eine Philosophie* the common
analogy of the stages in the life of man, i.e., childhood, youth, mature
manhood, old age, only to prove that the eighteenth century in the
history of mankind compares to the period of old age. The contemporary
philosopher Iselin had employed the same analogy and shown the
eighteenth century to be the stage of mature manhood. Herder's
different view of history is of course reflected in the title. He claims to
offer another point of view, different from that of Iselin and the
Enlightenment, which had little understanding for history.

In those Bückeburg years Herder's almost exclusive preoccupation
with historical themes is apparent in other treatises as well: *Wie die
deutschen Bischöfe Landstände wurden* (1774), and *Ursachen des
gesunckenen Geschmacks bei den verschiedenen Völkern da er
geblühet* (1775). But Herder also continued his work on Hebrew poetry,
publishing the *Älteste Urkunde des Menschengeschlechts* (1774–1776),
an interpretation of the first few chapters of the Bible. In this long work
the preacher Herder rejected the allegorical interpretation of the Bible
and maintained against the deists, the rationalistis, against Hume,·
Leibniz, Voltaire and Rousseau the dogma of original sin, not so much
as an orthodox dogma, but rather as an anthropological fact.

Herder left Bückeburg for Weimar in 1776 to join Goethe, who had
moved there the year before. At Wieland's suggestion Goethe had persuaded the young Duke Karl August of Weimar to extent an invitation
to Herder to accept a pastorate there. Herder agreed because he wanted
to be close to Goethe. After his arrival aesthetic questions in general
and literary criticism in particular seemed to take on new importance
for both men. At Goethe's urging, Herder published his folk-song
collections. On the whole, Goethe's and Herder's relationship was
strained more often than it was marked by periods of friendship. Yet
they always respected each other, and there would be times when
Herder's influence on Goethe was extremely significant, times when
one might actually speak of friendship.

II Young Goethe

Since the inception of specific studies in German literature as an
academic discipline — the first German university appointment in
German literature was made in 1873 — Goethe research has always

loomed very high. In fact, reading chronologically the huge list of major books that Goethe scholarship has produced will serve well as an introduction to the changing methods and ideas of the various schools of literary criticism as they developed during the past century.[9] Every generation has sought to cope with the phenomenon of Goethe anew. As a result, the number of Goethe biographies, editions, commentaries, dictionaries, yearbooks, bibliographies, and the huge number of special studies treating every imaginable aspect of his life and his work, defy all expectations. Besides, and partially as a consequence, we are unusually well-informed about details of Goethe's life, a fact which has tempted scholars again and again to seek parallels between his own life and the lives of many of the heroes of his dramas and novels. His personal experiences have been the cause of many a poetic or literary invention. But those experiences cannot explain either the form or the content of such inventions. We must understand Goethe's creative abilities as well as the period in which he lived and which he shaped so decisively, if we want to be able to appreciate the artistic accomplishments and qualities of his work and want to be able to grasp why his work was of such immense importance to the development of literature in eighteenth-century Germany.

There were other eighteenth-century poets and writers whose works had aroused nationwide acclaim and enthusiasm; Klopstock's *Der Messias* and Lessing's *Minna von Barnhelm* are examples. But the impact of the early works of Johann Wolfgang von Goethe (1749–1832) was quite different. His works appealed to the young in far vaster degree than those of other poets had, as he was able to give literary expression to his generation's feeling of frustration and to an intimacy with nature and people. He dared say what he felt and thought. That is why we know so much about him. He was open in letters, poems, speeches, but also in the very detailed and carefully composed poetic account of his life – his thoughts, his writings, his friendships, and the influences to which he was exposed – given in the famous autobiographical work *Aus meinem Leben. Dichtung und Wahrheit* (1812–1822). The opening paragraph is a beautiful example of how he presents the bare facts of his life through the veil of poetic imagination, be it to interpret these facts, or to minimize their importance by the use of irony:

Am 28sten August 1749, mittags mit dem Glockenschlage zwölf, kam ich in Frankfurt am Main auf die Welt. Die Konstellation war glücklich: die Sonne stand im Zeichen der Jungfrau und kulminierte für den Tag; Jupiter und Venus blickten sie freundlich

an, Merkur nicht widerwärtig, Saturn und Mars verhielten sich
gleichgültig; nur der Mond, der soeben voll ward, übte die Kraft
seines Gegenscheins um so mehr, als zugleich seine Planetenstunde
eingetreten war. Er widersetzte sich daher meiner Geburt, die
nicht eher erfolgen konnte, als bis diese Stunde vorübergegangen.

We see a poet as he points smilingly to the significance of his birth by
describing an imagined constellation which through its symbolism as
well as through its ironic tone achieves seriousness and, at the same
time, buoyancy.

Goethe was born into a wealthy family and was thus never to
experience financial worries at any time in his life. The origins of this
family are not without interest: his father, the grandson of a tailor
who had immigrated to Frankfort, had married the daughter of one
of the most influential ruling families in the city. His was a quiet life
which he devoted totally to his private interests. He held the title of
privy councilor without any political assignment, and therefore he had
time to look after his son's education, an education which emphasized
thorough knowledge of the Bible and of languages. Goethe's mother,
Katharina Elisabeth Textor, a young woman — twenty years younger
than her husband — who freely talked about herself, showed an
extraordinary interest in her son's literary development. Goethe·dis-
covered his talent very early. Even his earliest poems, such as 'Poetische
Gedanken über die Höllenfahrt Christi' (1765) testify to his marvelous
versatility in choosing poetic expressions. The treatment of such an
esoteric topic as Christ's descent to hell may well have been inspired
by Klopstock's *Messias*, which young Goethe and his sister Cornelia
had read enthusiastically, even though they had to keep it a secret
from their father who was unable to appreciate the unrhymed German
hexameter. The theme of the poem shows Goethe's complete
familiarity with the Bible. 'Die Höllenfahrt Christi' reflects the kind of
literary and religious influences to which he was exposed in Frankfort.
It offers a vision of Christ as hero and avenger, still very much in the
style of a Baroque hymn. By the time the poem appeared in print in a
Frankfort magazine in 1766, Goethe was enrolled as a student in
Leipzig, the center of Rococo literature.

Goethe soon became enthralled by Leipzig's elegance, and did everything to adapt to the Leipzig society, wearing fashions that were popular
in that town, and trying his hand at Rococo poetry. The poems, plays
and private letters he wrote during those three years in Leipzig are an
eloquent record of his playing the role of a Rococo man of letters. He

quickly developed full command of the forms and motifs of Rococo poetry, but also soon began expressing criticism of the Leipzig society in general and the Rococo ideals in particular. A group of nineteen poems in the style of the Anacreontics, entitled *Annette*, was written in Leipzig. These poems characteristically end with an unexpected epigrammatic twist that provides a witty and delightful comment on the amorous situation described. Also in Leipzig, in 1767, Goethe wrote a group of three poems, called *Oden an einen Freund*, in which he advises his friend Behrisch, who had lost his position as tutor, to flee Leipzig because of its artificiality and its moral dangers. There is nothing in these poems that reminds the reader any longer of Anacreontic motifs or themes. Goethe wanted to defend a friend. That required an individual handling of a real situation. Goethe's first published collection of poems, together with melodies, appeared in 1770: *Neue Lieder, in Melodien gesetzt von Bernhard Theodor Breitkopf*. Included in this collection were a number of poems he had presented in 1768 to Friederike Oeser, the daughter of his art professor in Leipzig. Probably the two most significant poems in this group are 'Die Nacht' and 'An den Mond'. The epigrammatic ending is done very successfully, but the expression of individual feelings and of personal views of nature point to a deeply felt criticism of Anacreontic poetry.

Also in Leipzig Goethe wrote his first play, a pastoral one act, *Die Laune des Verliebten* (1767), which is written in the traditional Alexandrine verse. The plot reminds the reader of Gellert's *Sylvia*. The similarities are unmistakable: two pairs of pastoral lovers, one in complete harmony, the other plagued by prudery and jealousy. The harmonious couple devises a scheme which consists of rational advice and a bit of trickery to help the other pair discover a state of harmonious love. Gellert was the most famous professor in Leipzig at that time, and Goethe imitated him for a while. Clearly, Goethe's writing a pastoral play was only a passing stage, proof that he was familiarizing himself with the existing forms and the conventional language of literature. He received different impulses from Lessing, whose *Minna von Barnhelm* Goethe saw produced in Leipzig, and from Shakespeare, whom he read with growing interest, although his image of Shakespeare would change radically within a few years. Goethe himself claimed Wieland's influence as significant, as well as Oeser's. This art teacher, whose drawing lessons Goethe enjoyed, introduced him to Winckelmann's ideas about Greek art, and urged the young poet to become more independent in his literary tastes and

judgements. The letters Goethe wrote in Leipzig speak most clearly of
a growing awareness that he would have to depend more and more on
his own impulses in his literary creativity, and less on literary models.
That he was indeed a poet really was no longer a question in his mind.
It is a rewarding task to read through his Leipzig literary productions and
list the verses and locutions of special beauty, lines such as 'Luna bricht
die Nacht der Eichen' from 'Die Nacht,' or the beginning of 'An den
Mond':

> Schwester von dem ersten Licht,
> Bild der Zärtlichkeit in Trauer,
> Nebel schwimmt mit Silberschauer
> Um dein reizendes Gesicht.
> Deines leisen Fusses Lauf
> Weckt aus langverschlossnen Höhlen
> Traurig abgeschiedne Seelen,
> Mich, und nächt'ge Vögel auf.

Illness eventually interrupted Goethe's studies and forced him to return
to Frankfort where he became intimately acquainted with the Pietists,
their songs and their religious experiences.[10] It was the circle around
prominent and beloved Susanna Katharina von Klettenberg (1723–
1774) which mainly attracted him to the Pietists. She was a friend and
distant relative of his mother's and also his friend, nourishing Goethe's
interest in alchemy. Her life story was to be included in the chapter
'Bekenntnisse einer schönen Seele' of Goethe's later novel *Wilhelm
Meister*. The circle of Pietists in Frankfort was not formally a branch
of Zinzendorf's 'Herrenhuter Gemeinde,' but all its members admired
Count Zinzendorf. Goethe's participation in this Pietism, which was
strongly oriented towards literature, lasted only a relatively short time,
but his friendship with several Pietists remained active for years.[11]

Goethe's own writings in these eighteen months in Frankfort include
the three act comedy *Die Mitschuldigen*. It has been stressed correctly
that *Die Mitschuldigen* makes very effective use of the stage – Goethe
himself performed it often in Weimar. Not a well-known play, its
importance lies in Goethe's having brought together elements from
several traditions, the *commedia dell'arte* with its grotesque elements,
and also the 'sächsische Typenkomödie' that was so popular in
Gottsched's and Gellert's Leipzig. Söller, the betrayed husband, may
be seen as a harlequin figure, the innkeeper as a representative of his
typically curious type, and Sophie as the unhappily married woman.

The second version of the play, completed in 1769, adds burlesque elements, and lends deeper emotional quality and sensitiveness to the main characters, Sophie and Alcest. Sophie's language in particular reflects the influence of Pietistic vocabulary. It is partly through this vocabulary that her character achieves depth:

> *Sophie:*   Das hindert meine Pein,
> Von Einem wenigstens, von dir beklagt zu sein.
> Alcest, bei dieser Hand, der teuern Hand, beschwöre
> Ich dich, behalte mir dein Herz gewogen!
> [. . .]
>   Dies Herz, das nur für dich gebrannt,
> Weiss keinen andern Trost, als den von deiner Hand.
>
>   [II, 4]

When Goethe left for Strasbourg, he was ready for new experiences. It was in Strasbourg that the movement commonly called *Sturm und Drang* was to be born. There he met Jacob Michael Reinhold Lenz, Heinrich Leopold Wagner, and Johann Heinrich Jung (-Stilling), all of whom would be known as 'Stürmer and Dränger'. Together they formed a circle of young aspiring authors, attracted others to join them, and experienced the most fruitful time during the months of Herder's stay in Strasbourg. The significance of Goethe's Strasbourg years is seen best in the *Sesenheimer Lieder*, a group of poems which grew out of his often retold love experience with Friederike Brion, the daughter of the country pastor in the Alsatian village of Sesenheim. The poems were written between the fall of 1770 and the summer of 1771, and most of them were published in 1775. Goethe sent them with his letters to Friederike to tell her of his love, of the feeling of total harmony between them, a harmony they shared with nature. The most famous of these poems, 'Kleine Blumen, kleine Blätter', 'Es schlug mein Herz', and 'Maifest', describe the full happiness of youthful love, but claim also the unconventionality of real love, and point to the influence of the folk-song. The lines

> O Lieb', o Liebe,
> So golden schön
> Wie Morgenwolken
> Auf jenen Höhn

from 'Maifest' tell of the reality of love experienced. Goethe's achievement is to have expressed his feelings in simple, convincing words, specifically rejecting the artificiality of the Anacreontic style. The *Sesenheimer Lieder* are unreflective and do not speak of the accepted or the norm, but of the individual and personal. Their fast rhythm and frequent short lines engagé the imagination of the reader.

Even before Goethe's first visit in Sesenheim in October 1770, Herder had arrived in Strasbourg. Herder not only pointed out the value of folk-poetry and explained his way of reading Shakespeare, but also valued Homer over Horace, and praised Ossian, the Gaelic bard. Goethe accepted Herder's views fully. Shakespeare became for him the greatest dramatist, Homer his favorite Greek author, and he welcomed the linguistic challenge of rendering Ossian in German. It was challenging because the literary German of the day did not provide the translator with readily available linguistic models for expressing the moods and feelings pertinent to death and loneliness which were so prevalent in the Ossian songs. Herder had pointed to the need for harmony between lyric content and poetic form. Thus Goethe himself chose rhythmical prose as the poetic form for his translation of the Ossian passages which he later included in *Werther*, and which in turn may have been the reason for his using rhythmical prose in other passages of the novel as well.

It was in the period between Strasbourg and Weimar, in the years 1771 to 1775, that Goethe produced his best *Sturm und Drang* works. For the most part he stayed during this time in Frankfort, but he also traveled, spending the memorable summer of 1772 in Wetzlar where he worked at the imperial court. Out of that experience grew *Werther*. Goethe was amazingly active and productive; he made friends, wrote numerous book reviews in which he surveyed the literature of the period, and took frequent hikes. Only a few weeks after his return from Strasbourg to Frankfort he celebrated Shakespeare's anniversary with a group of friends by reading his speech *Rede zum Schäkespears-tag*. In it he praised the artistic qualities of Shakespeare, especially his ability to portray true tragic experiences. During the last few weeks of 1771 Goethe wrote the play that made him known throughout Germany, the first version of his *Götz von Berlichingen*, a drama that intentionally and deliberately scorns the three unities, as is demon- strated by the enormously large number of scenes.

The *Sturm und Drang* characteristics in the play are fairly obvious: a language that prefers pithy expressions, an attempt to capture the manifold quality of human life and society through scenes only loosely related to the main action, and the unmistakable tendency to concentrate on the decadent features of contemporary society; in contrast the great man, the hero of the play, the untimely knight Götz von Berlichingen, is true to himself and assumes that he is also true to the ideals of the past. The theme of decadence is probably the most striking in the play. The hero warns repeatedly of the growing perverseness and corruption of the times. Specifically, Goethe shows decadence by portraying the mishandling of justice. Yet decadence is not limited to the topic of corrupt courts and judges, which is arbitrarily dropped after the second act. The fourth act introduces a totally new theme, the peasants' uprisings of the sixteenth century in Germany, historically an uprising against socially unjust oppression, to be sure. But the play dwells on the cruelty, dishonesty, and irresponsibility of the peasant leaders. The fifth act suggests that it is the structure of society itself which may bring about decadence, since it introduces a group of gypsies and portrays them as harmonious and unspoiled by contact with corrupting social influences. It is not the theme of justice that lends coherence to the drama, nor could this theme have become the dominant one since Goethe had chosen in Götz a hero whose concept of law was so individualistic that it could not possibly serve as a basis for social justice. Götz simply lacks the intellectual capability to be in the vanguard of any important ideas. Goethe had made Götz's fighter-personality the central figure, a national model of traditional uprightness in an age of strong, foreign, decadent influences. The plan to give coherence to the play by creating a powerful hero, rather than by concentrating on a single action, is a direct result of Goethe's Shakespeare studies. Just as Götz was feuding with all who tried to limit his individuality, so Goethe sought to carry on a feud with the art critics who put up limiting rules. Shakespeare inspired much of the language as well as the theme of *Götz*. Luther's translation of the Bible was another source, one which helped Goethe to create in *Götz* a drama of rich imagery and carefully chosen and consistently used motifs, giving the illusion of sixteenth-century speech patterns in a historical play that castigates the author's own time. These stylistic features must be regarded as Goethe's actual artistic achievement in *Götz*, and they have assured the play an important place in the development of German drama, in spite of its shortcomings.

A comparison of *Götz* with Goethe's next larger work, *Die Leiden des jungen Werthers*, the novel that brought him immediate international fame, calls attention to the author's great achievement: the rhythmic prose which conveyed so clearly the emotional disposition

of the hero, the consistent parallelism between Werther's inner thoughts
and the actual experiences of others in the novel, and the absolute con-
gruency of his own feelings with the typical changes from season to
season — all these established at once new stylistic and structural ideals
in German fictional literature. Goethe spent the summer months of
1772 in Wetzlar, where he received practical experience as a young
lawyer at the imperial court, which was located in this town, some
fifty miles north of Frankfort. During this short summer he met
Charlotte Buff, the Lotte of *Werther*. He also got to know Charlotte's
fiancé, the quiet Albert Kestner, who understandably was not
especially happy about Goethe's frequent visits to Charlotte. Among
Goethe's acquaintances in Wetzlar was a young man by the name of
Jerusalem. After Goethe's departure from Wetzlar in September of that
year he learned that this Jerusalem had committed suicide. The
Wetzlar experience quickly developed in his mind into a short novel,
the story of the aspiring young artist Werther and his deep love for
Lotte, who is already engaged to Albert. To escape the growing love
conflict Werther leaves town and takes a position elsewhere, only to
return a few months later, driven by the desire to be close to Lotte,
who is by now a married woman. Werther indulges in his own
melancholic feelings until he can think of no solution other than
suicide. In a matter of not quite four months, early in 1774, Goethe
wrote the novel, forging autobiographical details into a work of art
that expressed and described accurately the feelings and beliefs of the
Sturm und Drang generation.

The artist Werther discovers that he can draw best if he adheres
closely to the motifs which nature provides for him, and that he should
not worry about rules. He also discovers that he often is so caught up
in his emotions about a certain scene that it is impossible for him to
draw at all. As a member of the human race Werther deplores the lack
of humane concerns and values. He finds lawyers who judge according
to the letter of the law without awareness of what may have motivated
the criminal act. Similarly, he deplores the restrictive human attitudes
which he encounters, for example, when he has to leave a social
gathering because he is not of the noble class, or when he is forced to
write without any allowances for individual stylistic preferences.
Goethe found the ideal form for expressing these thoughts when he
decided that the novel would consist in its entirety of letters written by
Werther over an eighteen-month period. Others had written novels composed of letters but Goethe restricted his novel deliberately to only one
letterwriter because we are meant to see things from this admittedly

one-sided view. Because of this one-sidedness *Werther* became such a
best-seller in Europe that young men wore Werther clothes which were
made in bright blues and yellows. For all its subjectivity *Werther* as a
work of art expressed the true feelings of an entire generation
objectively:

> Wenn ich die Einschränkung ansehe, in welcher die tätigen und
> forschenden Kräfte des Menschen eingesperrt sind; wenn ich sehe,
> wie alle Wirksamkeit dahinaus läuft, sich die Befriedigung von
> Bedürfnissen zu verschaffen, die wieder keinen Zweck haben, als
> unsere arme Existenz zu verlängern, und dann, da alle Beruhigung
> über gewisse Punkte des Nachforschens nur eine träumende
> Resignation ist, da man sich die Wände, zwischen denen man
> gefangen sitzt, mit bunten Gestalten und lichten Aussichten bemalt
> — Das alles, Wilhelm, macht mich stumm. Ich kehre in mich selbst
> zurück, und finde eine Welt!
>
> [Book I, May 22, 1771]

Goethe intentionally created two levels in the story, the subjective and
the objective. He has the fictional editor of Werther's letters summarize
these two levels at the beginning of the work:

> Ihr könnt seinem Geist und seinem Charakter eure Bewunderung
> und Liebe, seinem Schicksale eure Tränen nicht versagen.
>
> Und du gute Seele, die du eben den Drang fühlst wie er, schöpfe
> Trost aus seinem Leiden, und lass das Büchlein deinen Freund
> sein, wenn du aus Geschick oder eigener Schuld keinen nähern
> finden kannst.

Werther himself knew the impact of literature on the reader, because he
had found his own subjective experiences mirrored in the pantheistic
feeling of oneness with nature, in the classical literary works, in the
simplicity and beauty of life that Homer depicts, or in the melancholy
and loneliness in the songs of Ossian.

During these years between Strasbourg and his move to Weimar
Goethe started a great number of works. He did not finish all of these,
and among those he did complete, *Werther* stands out as the single most
important in Goethe's personal literary development, and in the development of German literature as a whole. Still, Goethe was restless. He
played with numerous forms of literature: he wrote farces, satire, even

some theological prose. As *Werther* is autobiographical, so all of his works are reflections of his feelings and thoughts as a young artist. Nor was he so involved in his writing that he could not look humorously at himself, the genius he claimed to be. He does so in the hymn 'Wanderers Sturmlied' where the wanderer-poet, overtaken by a sudden storm, has to admit that the desire to reach the warm hut has more power than the supposed warmth of the poetic inspiration:

Wenn die Räder rasselten
Rad an Rad, rasch ums Ziel weg
Hoch flog
Siegdurchglühter
Jünglinge Peitschenknall,
Und sich Staub wälzt'
Wie vom Gebürg herab
Kieselwetter ins Tal,
Glühte deine Seel Gefahren, Pindar,
Mut. – Glühte. –
Armes Herz –
Dort auf dem Hügel,
Himmlische Macht,
Nur so viel Glut,
Dort meine Hütte,
Dort hin zu waten.

Goethe wrote a number of hymnal poems during these years, all of which are very different in their formal structure, but all of which deal with the figure of the genius, be it the religious founder in 'Mahomet', or be it the rebel who feels superior to the gods because he is the one who gives form and life to matter and creates people in 'Prometheus' – Goethe began to write dramas about both Mahomet and Prometheus without finishing them – or be it the youth whose longing for God is fulfilled as he experiences nature's spring in 'Ganymed'. There is even the self-confident traveller in a post-chaise, in 'An Schwager Kronos', for whom the grandiose view from the mountain ridge is like a glimpse of the totality of life's experiences in one big panorama, and who then, drunk with joy, asks to be driven directly into Orcus. The genius cult which Goethe was extolling in these works was evident everywhere in the *Sturm und Drang* and encompassed a number of diverse ideas. Only taken together may they be expected to yield an accurate definition of a genius. Herder once defined in a letter to his fiancée Caroline the genius as:

> Ein Licht, das, wenn wir darauf merkten und wenn wir es nicht
> durch Vernunftschlüsse und Gesellschaftsklugheit und
> wohlweisen bürgerlichen Verstand betäubten und auslöschten, ich
> sage, was uns denn eben auf dem dunkelsten Punkt der Scheidewege
> einen Stral, einen plötzlichen Blick vorwirft.[12]

At the heart of the *Sturm und Drang* movement is a concept of art that
defines artistic inspiration much in the way the religious enthusiasts
understood the inner light that guided them on the right path.
According to Herder a poet's genius does just that. Expressing inner
feelings freely on the one hand, and actively protesting against a purely
rationalistic understanding of life on the other, are the polar opposites
that generate much of the dynamic literature known as *Sturm und
Drang* and that imbue those poems of Goethe with special vitality.
During this period Goethe moved with ease in the circle of the so-called
enthusiastic sentimentalists in the city of Darmstadt. Johann Heinrich
Merck (1741—1791), the editor of the *Frankfurter Gelehrten Anzeigen*,[13]
who won Goethe as a regular contributor to the paper, had brought
together a group of sentimentalizing young people who enjoyed taking
extended walks in the countryside, loved small huts and were willing to
use a grave in their garden as a place for meditation and for arousing
their feelings. Goethe frequently visited this circle of friends, but he was
able to remain objective in this atmosphere, not least because he could
laugh about himself and satirize the excesses he saw around him as being
a modish exhibition of the cult of sad and lonely genius. Since he had
made the acquaintance of this group just before he went to Wetzlar, we
are probably not wrong in assuming that sentimentalism colored his
Wetzlar experiences and helped him create in the novel a highly
emotional atmosphere, one of which he would soon tire.

In 1773 and 1774 Goethe wrote several satirical works, employing
the 'Knittelvers', a German medieval doggerel which Merck had brought
to his attention, and which, with its four irregular stresses to each line
and its couplet rhyme pattern, creates a rather earthy atmosphere. The
titles of these farces bespeak the somewhat boisterous and exceedingly
self-confident frame of mind of Goethe and his friends during these
years: *Jahrmarktsfest zu Plundersweilern; Ein Fastnachtsspiel von
Pater Brey; Götter, Helden und Wieland* (this latter in prose); *Prolog
zu den neuesten Offenbarungen Gottes;* to name just a few. The most
significant is probably *Satyros oder der vergötterte Waldteufel* where

Goethe satirizes the genius cult — thus again smiling about himself — and the much-heralded call to return to nature. Satyros is seen in the dual role of gifted and persuasive singer and self-styled nature prophet, whose humanness becomes all the more apparent the more he is proclaimed as a god. In these farces the comic element is of a drastic and rather vulgar nature, a refutation of the polished comedy of the Enlightenment. Goethe went back to the Reformation period, to Hans Sachs, when he wrote this particular Shrovetide play.

In 1773 Goethe also entered into a correspondence with the successful Zürich pastor and poet Lavater, who had been most impressed with Goethe's quasi-theological essays, *Brief des Pastors zu *** an den Pastor zu **** and *Zwo wichtige bisher unerörterte biblische Fragen*. Goethe was equally impressed — for the time being — with Lavater's writings. Lavater's view of man as expounded in his preaching and his poetry appealed to Goethe. The Pietists had often enough been accused by the orthodox of treating the Divine too much on a human level. The humanness of Christ was what Goethe's *Brief des Pastors* extolled. Speculative theology was not Lavater's interest, and certainly not Goethe's. It is thus understandable that Goethe agreed to Lavater's plea for co-operation on the *Physiognomische Fragmente* because it afforded him an opportunity to formulate his view of man. For about a period of seven years the friendship with Lavater resulted in an active correspondence and joint travel experiences, such as the famous journey by boat on the Lahn and Rhine during the summer of 1774, together with the theologian Basedow, which prompted Goethe to call himself in the poem 'Diner zu Coblenz' 'das Weltkind in der Mitten'. The term 'Weltkind' may well imply that he felt there were strong differences between Lavater and himself. Yet their anthropocentric views brought them together since they both accepted and propagated the importance of feeling, specifically the dependence on feeling for the creative process.

We know that during their travels in 1774 Goethe wrote down two poems in dramatic form which define the role of the artist, *Künstlers Erdewallen*, where the muse appears to the artist, who is frustrated by critical, well-meaning but misunderstanding admirers and the duties of his daily life, and *Künstlers Vergötterung*, a short fragment depicting an art student who refuses to touch the paint brush again after he has recognized greatness in art for the first time. The need for feeling is taken up further in *Künstlers Abendlied*, where the artist asks nature to continue to grant him creative ability. It was Lavater who first published this poem, which treats the creative process. Goethe took up the theme of the artist in several other poems during this period, perhaps most importantly, however, in *Werther*. To discuss the artist and make him the subject of works of literature was something new. Most of these poems can hardly be counted among Goethe's greatest. Yet they signal clearly a new period as far as the concept of the artist is concerned. Goethe wanted to understand the creative process and presented in these poems the artist as dependent in his creativity on nature's favor. He was aware of the importance of and need for poetic inspiration. The fragment of the planned epic poem *Der ewige Jude* (1774) testifies to this:

> Um Mitternacht wohl fang' ich an,
> Spring aus dem Bette wie ein Toller;
> Nie war mein Busen seelenvoller,
> Zu singen den gereisten Mann,
> [. . .]
> Und hab' ich gleich die Gabe nicht
> Von wohlgeschliffenen leichten Reimen,
> So darf ich doch mich nicht versäumen;
> *Denn es ist Drang, und so ist's Pflicht.*

> [italics mine]

Of course, the poem was not just an improvisation. Goethe had given the subject considerable thought, as he tells us in *Dichtung und Wahrheit*. Had it been completed it would have been an epic treating the topic of the suffering Christ and His return to earth. The fragment makes it sufficiently clear how differently Goethe had conceived this topic than for instance Klopstock, who had written his *Messias* in hexameters. Goethe took the legend about Ahasver as the basis for the poem, and he employed the 'Knittelvers', thus achieving a folklore-like atmosphere which was regarded by some of his contemporaries as almost sacrilegious. The setting of Christ's return to earth is Germany, specifically the Protestant Germany of the seventeenth and early eighteenth centuries, which adds a note of stark realism to the poem. Even though Goethe did not finish the work he was convinced that folk-legends offered material for serious poetry. At the same time he was working on *Faust*. That of course also remained a fragment for the time being. However, his early *Faust* fragment, which has become known as *Urfaust*, may with considerable justification be read as Goethe's earliest *Faust* drama, rather than as a fragment of the later *Faust*. The fragment was first published in 1887 and its existence not known prior to that date.

Urfaust is less than one sixth as long as the completed version of the later *Faust I* and *II*. Yet the Gretchen tragedy is complete and remains practically unchanged in the later versions. The satirical treatment of university life and the longing for a study of nature in nature, the interest in alchemy and pansophism, are all elements that characterize the feelings, thoughts, and preoccupations of the young poets and critics around Goethe. To be sure, a number of the colorful details can be traced back to the Faust chapbooks from the late sixteenth century. They suggest a medieval setting, but the answers and ideas are those of the *Sturm und Drang* Goethe. The Gretchen tragedy, based on actual events of the early 1770s in Frankfort, represents Goethe's invention of a redemptive motif that would counterbalance the evil Mephistopheles. Because of the brevity of *Urfaust* the Gretchen scenes take on proportionately greater significance in this early version. Goethe had, through the representation of Gretchen, found a way to create a world of feelings and of wholeness and had been able to minimize the world of actions. The pact scene is not even included, and hence the question of salvation is left unsolved. Except for relatively minor changes the verse form of the lines in *Urfaust*, including the 'Knittelvers', the madrigal and the *vers libre*, remain the same in the later *Faust*. It was the *Sturm und Drang* Goethe who had claimed the Faust legend for poetic presentation, and he never needed to abandon the particular thematic direction nor the poetic form he had chosen, even though he was to continue working on this drama throughout his life.

Goethe's dramatic productivity during 1774–1775 includes two plays, *Clavigo* and *Stella*, which in form are much closer to what we might consider traditional drama. Using Beaumarchais's *Mémoires*, Goethe wrote *Clavigo* in an eight-day period in May 1774, only a few weeks after he had finished *Werther*. *Stella* (1775) has proved to be a much more puzzling drama than *Clavigo*, not only to Goethe's contemporaries but to the twentieth-century reader as well. The subtitle identifies it as a play for lovers. In no other play does Goethe make such extensive use of the language of the Pietists to express the happiness of fulfilled love as well as the torment of unfulfilled love through phrases that would in their religious context describe the contentment of a soul in union with God or the vexing suffering of being separated from God. Stella's vivid memory of their earlier love speaks of such contentment:

Stella. Ich brauche viel, viel, um dies Herz auszufüllen! — Viel?

Arme Stella? Viel? — Sonst, da er dich noch liebte, noch in deinem
Schosse lag, füllte sein Blick deine ganze Seele; ... Wenn ich von
seinen Küssen meine Augen zu dir hinauf wendete, mein Herz an
dem seinen glühte, und ich mit bebenden Lippen seine grosse Seele
in mich trank.

[Act II]

Fernando. Du fühlst nicht, was Himmelstau dem Dürstenden ist,
der aus der öden, sandigten Welt an deinen Busen zurückkehrt.

[Act III]

In this era of sentimentalism the characters in the play — by no means
young lovers, but middle-aged people of the upper social classes — react
predictably to certain Pietistic metaphorical phrases because they evoke
definite feelings in them. Fernando especially, the unfaithful, unstable,
and restless lover, is susceptible to the extremes of feelings, and yet in
spite of his unfaithfulness and unreliability is loved by both Stella and
Cäcilia, to the point that they are willing to live with him in a common
marriage of three. They are victims of the culture of feeling which they
themselves foster. In a later version (1816) Goethe offers an alternative
ending. The proposal for a marriage of three is ruled out when both
Stella and Fernando commit suicide.

III Fascination with the Stage

The enormous success of Goethe's *Götz* inspired other *Sturm und
Drang* authors to use their talents for the writing of drama. As the
active group moved from Strasbourg to Frankfort, drama became more
and more the central subject of their discussions. The admiration of the
Sturm und Drang writers for Shakespeare kindled their fascination with
the stage even more. Since in *Götz* Goethe had, in their opinion,
achieved the characterization of a powerful individual by following the
principles of Shakespeare's dramas, it seemed possible to write more
such plays for the German stage. Goethe himself was working on his
Faust drama, but was also soon making plans for his *Egmont*. In
addition, there was the influence that Heinrich Wilhelm von Gerstenberg
(1737–1823) exerted on the *Sturm und Drang*. In his *Briefe über
Merkwürdigkeiten der Literatur* (1766–1770) he had discussed
Shakespeare's dramas. His approach to the English playwright was not
different from Herder's, for Gerstenberg too wanted Shakespeare's work
to be judged by criteria that were particular to Shakespeare, and to the
times in which Shakespeare wrote. Unlike Herder, however, Gerstenberg

also sought to put into practice what he considered to be Shakespeare's greatness. Gerstenberg's *Ugolino* (1768) — the drama builds on the story of Count Ugolino Gherardesca in Dante's *Divine Comedy* — was intended to dramatize a great and morally strong character who maintains his own dignity in the face of death.

Ugolino was overthrown as ruler of Pisa and, together with his three sons, condemned to death by starvation in the tower of that Italian city. Their emotions and struggles in the face of death, but mainly Ugolino's successful fight against the temptation to take his own life, once he has watched his sons die, make up the plot of the drama. Gerstenberg's language gives full expression to Ugolino's range of feelings, from rage to despair to quiet composure. *Ugolino* was well received by Lessing who immediately following its publication summarized his impressions in a letter to Gerstenberg: 'Ihr *Ugolino* bleibt immer ein Werk von sehr grossen, ausserordentlichen Schönheiten ....'[14] But Lessing also had some questions which arose from his understanding of the nature of the medium of drama. How is it possible, he wonders, for Ugolino to refrain from taking his and his sons' lives if in fact their death is inevitable? Only uncertainty about their fate, Lessing argues, could keep Ugolino from hastening that end by his own intervention. That uncertainty does not exist, given the nature of the genre and the objective of the playwright. Gerstenberg replies a few months later with the observation that starvation was the topic of the drama, and that therefore it was necessary to show 'ob die Vorsehung den unglücklichen Menschen retten, ob er seinem Charakter gemäss ausdulden wird ....'[15]

In the meantime, the great and strong character that Gerstenberg had demanded of drama had been achieved by Goethe in his *Götz*. The *Sturm und Drang* authors took up the challenge and developed the new drama in various directions. Lenz, Klinger, Wagner, Maler Müller and Leisewitz all concentrated their efforts on creating for Germany plays that were no longer intended to teach but to portray real life.[16] In this they were successful, and most of them produced their work within a short time, between 1774 and 1778.

1 Lenz

Jakob Michael Reinhold Lenz (1751–1792), who was driven to insanity by the disparate forces of his personality, wrote within the span of some three years (1774–1776) several dramas which give expression to the period's belief in the complexity of human life, and which in form and language attest to the movement's protest against

the cult of wit and rationalism as well as against the existing social
system. Lenz's plays also show his unusual talent for achieving a life-
like portrayal of his times. His work therefore proved to be of singular
influence on other playwrights. The Romantic Tieck published Lenz's
work in three volumes in 1829. That edition was available to Büchner,
whose indebtedness to the *Sturm und Drang* dramatist has been convincingly shown. In our century Brecht prepared his own version of the
Lenz play *Der Hofmeister*, thus helping Lenz's play to a belated stage
success. Even more recent is a new adaptation of Lenz's *Die Soldaten*
by Heinar Kipphardt (1968), who considers the play to be of extraordinary importance in the history of German drama. There can be no
question that Lenz's contribution to the development of drama is
pivotal to its success during the *Sturm und Drang*. The leading literary
figures of his day recognized that fact when they corresponded with
him actively, especially following his debut as dramatist in 1774.
Hamann, Herder, Lavater, and especially Goethe acknowledged Lenz's
talent as shown in his successful techniques he uses for the portrayal
of social reality. Lenz's artistic accomplishments, however, must not
be overrated. There is not the parsimonious economy of language and
dramatic structure that is the hallmark of Büchner's *Woyzeck*, a play
that imitates and uses so effectively linguistic elements and poetic
inventions of *Die Soldaten*. Besides, Lenz's pervasive social and cultural
criticism lacks logical cohesiveness and thus the power to be convincing.
Nor are his plays dominated by the one overpowering character as is
the case in Goethe's *Götz*. The greatness of Lenz's dramas lies in the
telling use of highly idiomatic and vivid language, as well as in the
feeling of constant movement, achieved through the frequent change
in scenery, and the suggestion that a multiplicity of forces shapes the
life of an individual.

The son of a Pietistic minister and theologian, Lenz attended the
University of Königsberg as a student of theology. He became quite
familiar with the general cultural scene of rationalistic Germany, came
to admire Rousseau — who was read by all *Sturm und Drang* writers —
but probably also knew Hamann, who by this time had published his
major works. Lenz's first creative writings made use of the conventional
forms of Enlightenment literature, the philosophical poem and the
sentimental comedy. He was still in Königsberg when he began translating Shakespeare's *Love's Labour's Lost*. At the time of his arrival in
Strasbourg he was ready for the ideas and ideals of the emerging
Sturm und Drang. Lenz went there in 1771, accompanying two young
noblemen who were to receive army training near Strasbourg. Since

Lenz lived with them he experienced army life and became thoroughly familiar with the mentality of eighteenth-century military officers. The experience was to provide him with ample material for his drama *Die Soldaten.* The Strasbourg *Sturm und Drang* group was high-spirited at the time, and the impressionable and somewhat romantic Lenz was susceptible to the spirit of the genius cult and to its poetry. His review of Goethe's *Götz von Berlichingen* is a vivid testimony of his new literary ideals.[17] Arguing that action is at the center of all life and must be the central issue of literature, he holds up Goethe's *Götz* in its first version, widely considered impossible to perform, and proposes to prove its viability by mounting it himself: 'Lassen Sie mich für die Ausführung dieses Projekts sorgen, es soll gar so viel Schwürigkeiten nicht haben als Sie anfangs einbilden werden. Weder Theater noch Kulisse noch Dekoration—es kommt alles auf Handlung an.' The assertion that the abundance of scenes and frequent changes in the scenery make a staging of *Götz* almost impossible is countered by the opinion that intricate theatricals are not essential, whereas the portrayal of action is. He is willing to dispense with props and scenery altogether, is willing to indicate a change in locale by playing music that would function as a kind of identifying leitmotif, to create the impression of immediacy of action and of multifariousness of human life.

Lenz stayed in Strasbourg longer than the other *Sturm und Drang* writers and lingered on until 1776. It was the most fruitful period in his life. After Goethe left Strasbourg in 1771, Lenz initiated a correspondence with him. He idolized Goethe and relied on his relationship with him as a source of personal strength and encouragement, particularly since Goethe was willing to comment on Lenz's manuscripts. The first of these was *Der Hofmeister oder Vortheile der Privaterziehung* (1774) which treats the bitter lot of private tutors in houses of nobility, and demonstrates that the alleged advantages of private tutoring are in reality only disadvantages. It is dehumanizing to the tutor because it perverts his sensibilities, and is apt to turn the students into rash and reckless young people. Public education receives praise, and the public school teacher Wenzeslaus, who is not without his idiosyncrasies, plays the role of the honest and morally courageous man. A representative of the nobility, the privy councilor Berg is the outspoken advocate of public schools, who admonishes his son and his niece to live in the world of reality and not of fancy: ' . . . keine Romane spielen wollen, die nur in der ausschweifenden Einbildungskraft eines hungrigen Poeten ausgeheckt sind und von denen ihr in der heutigen Welt keinen Schatten der Wirklichkeit antrefft' [I, 6]. Indeed, his son shows himself

as having accepted this advice when he in turn seeks to instill a sense of
decency in a fellow student, the licentious Pätus: 'Wir sind in den
Jahren; wir sind auf der See, der Wind treibt uns, aber die Vernunft
muss immer am Steuerruder bleiben, sonst jagen wir auf die erste beste
Klippe und scheitern' [IV, 6]. Lenz uses here a characteristic *Sturm
und Drang* metaphor: the young sailor out on the stormy sea, in
danger of shipwreck on a cliff. Goethe liked this image as well because
it captured the feeling of uncertainty and the experience of adventure
that the genius cult welcomed.[18] Interestingly enough, Lenz appeals
in this context to reason and assigns to it the role of the pilot in a
person's life. The piteous tutor, the hero of the play, does not use
reason, running away from problems instead, as his name 'Läuffer'
suggests, he ruins his life when he castrates himself in a moment of
over-zealous striving for virtuousness, but subsequently has no
compunctions about marrying a young girl.

The awkwardness or even uncanniness of the situation is not uncommon with Lenz, who likes such stark and rude sketches of life.
They do have a certain comical effect, and the reader and viewer can
hardly accept them as serious. Nor are they intended to be taken
seriously, just as the play's subtitle was merely a ploy to get the
question about the advantages of private education into the open,
jokingly raising expectations that the author was not about to meet.
Lenz classified all his plays as comedies. It is probably more accurate
to call them tragi-comedies, as is commonly done. At any rate, un-
canny humor is part of all of Lenz's plays. Lenz distinguished between
tragedies and comedies by reserving portrayal of the development of
the individual character for the former, and treatment of a problem
for the latter. The distinction marks Lenz as a Shakespeare follower,
as might be expected of a *Sturm und Drang* playwright. For the
comedy, in particular, he claimed poetic subjectivity as a way of
underscoring the poet's freedom to deal with a given subject matter as
he pleases. Since all his plays are billed as comedies Lenz felt free to
include many episodes which do not bear on the hero's character or
personality, but which do elucidate the complexity of human life,
and to invent scenes of the stark comical nature found in *Der
Hofmeister*. Lenz's most important ideas on the theater are contained
in the lively critical treatise *Anmerkungen übers Theater* (1774), a
basic work for *Sturm und Drang* drama. His dominating interest in
drama is documented through his versions of five Plautus comedies, all
published in 1774.

The good reception of *Der Hofmeister* encouraged Lenz to continue with his approach to play-writing. In a short time followed *Der neue Menoza*, still in 1774, *Die Freunde machen den Philosophen* and *Die Soldaten*, both in 1776, and *Der Engländer, eine dramatische Phantasey* in 1777. A number of fragments of plays have also been preserved. Besides *Der Hofmeister*, the plays *Die Soldaten* and *Der neue Menoza* have contributed most to the development of drama. The latter play with the subtitle *Geschichte des kumbanischen Prinzen Tandi* treats the problem of decadence in European culture. The name 'Menoza' was taken from a contemporary Danish novel by Erik Pontoppidan. The 'Menoza' of the novel is an Asian prince who had traveled to enlightened Europe in search of true Christians. Lenz did not retain the name 'Menoza', except in the title. He calls his hero Tandi and declares him an African prince, actually a European by birth, who expects to find in Europe a society of enlightened people adhering to a rigid code of moral and ethical behavior. In that expectation he is disappointed. There is a good deal of Rousseauism in *Der neue Menoza*, as when the morally impeccable prince from Africa uses harsh language to castigate the Europeans:

> In Eurem Morast ersticke ich . . . . Das der aufgeklärte Weltteil! Allenthalben wo man hinriecht, Lässigkeit, faule ohnmächtige Begier, lalender Tod für Feuer und Leben, Geschwätz für Handlung. . . . Was ihr Empfindung nennt, ist Schmincke, womit ihr Brutalität bestreicht.
>
> [IV, 4]

This sort of cultural criticism reminds one of Herder's attacks on contemporary European culture in his *Auch eine Philosophie*. *Der neue Menoza* is an all-encompassing denunciation of society in Germany. The narrow thought pattern of the middle class is depicted in the representative Biederling, for he is 'bieder' in his views and activities. The prophet of doom, Beza, embodies the self-righteous Pietist-theologian who counterbalances the optimistic world view of the Enlightenment. Zierau serves as an example of the arrogant young pedantic man who has returned home from the university and now attempts to put into practice the ideas of the rationalistic age which he has not even understood. In contrast, his father, the unschooled but level-headed mayor, employs common sense in all areas of life, even in aesthetic matters. As a result he is able to enjoy the escapades of a harlequin on stage and naively looks for entertainment in a theatrical performance, and not for the strict observance of the dramatic unities, as does his son. The world of nobility is captured in Count Camäleon, who, true to his name, possesses many personalities, but tries to hide his true identity. His wife, the alleged Spanish countess Donna Diana, a fury of jealousy, eventually turns out to be Biederling's daughter, for she had been exchanged as a baby. Concurrently the romantic middle-class Wilhelmine, who in the play is Biederling's daughter, turns out to be a countess. The fact frees her from the guilt of incest because the African prince to whom she has become married has in the meantime been identified as Biederling's missing son. Confusion throughout the drama is great. Lenz causes it because he employs two such extreme plot elements as the exchange of babies and the unexpected return of a long lost son. Lenz's liking for the uncommon and unbelievable again comes to the surface here. The more the African prince becomes entangled with European society the less he can fulfill his active and outspoken role as cultural critic. Yet his reaction to what he believes to be his participation in incest is vastly different from that of all others. While he seeks to do penance, the others merely try to explain it away. The theologian Beza looks for ways to justify it after all, and Biederling for excuses to avoid embarrassment. Thus it is precisely the prince's relationship to Wilhemine and the ensuing confusion that broadens the portrait of eighteenth-century society in Germany, a society that lives by artificial standards. The prince, a learned but humble man, is at odds with this society because he uses common sense. That is the point Lenz wants to drive home, and is apparently the reason why the play ends with a scene that exemplifies once more the dichotomy between the artificial rule-consciousness of an alleged age of reason and the positive existence that is possible where common sense rules.

Die Soldaten emerges not only as Lenz's strongest stricture against existing social conditions, but also as his best play because it goes beyond mere social accusations. It is a moving document of human frailty in the unrelenting clutches of temptation. Both the middle-class dealer in jewelry and other fancy goods, Wesener, and his daughter, Marie, are blinded by glitter. Glitter is the stuff of Wesener's business, and the glitter of the military as evidenced in the uniform and free life of the high officers, all of them representatives of the nobility, captures Marie's fancy. Neither can withstand the strong pull of this temptation, and in the penultimate scene of the play father Wesener finds his daughter begging in the streets. Upon mutual recognition they fall into each other's arms and to the ground. 'Beide wälzen sich halb tot auf der Erde,' reads the stage direction at this point. Their final fate remains uncertain, allowing the playwright once more to return to the topic of social improvement in the final scene.

The plan for improvement is advanced by a high military officer who is shocked over the plight that has befallen the Wesener family. His proposal recognizes the custom that military men were not permitted to marry, a fact which he views as the root of many social and moral problems. Realizing the ineffectuality of suggesting that the king should permit marriage, he envisions a group of women in the employ of the king sacrificing, as it were, their honor and their concept of love and marriage, and by their sacrifice guaranteeing the moral safety of young girls from middle-class families. The totally unrealistic and even grotesque plan is typical for Lenz, who wants to arouse the reader's reaction by describing such stark, inhuman courses of action. The officer's plan is not advanced as a possible solution. Rather it calls attention to the fundamental unacceptability of the existing situation better than any real improvement plan could do. The fact that Lenz did make a similar proposal in a separate essay does not alter the function of the plan within the context of the play.[19] Indeed, the presentation of the self-centered life and the contemptible world of thought of army officers was a daring denunciation of the military, certainly at a time when soldiery in Prussia was admired.

At no time did Lenz consider literature a means of changing the world, but he certainly thought it a means of branding its wrongs. Lenz did not choose the form of the idyl to describe a world free from present social evils because he was afraid that readers might confuse a literary fictive reality with actual reality. Thus he has the Countess La Roche, who presents Lenz's own views in *Die Soldaten*, warn Marie not to read the idyl in Richardson's *Pamela* in terms of social reality in which a marriage between members of different social classes is possible. Marie's happiness, which would have been assured in a marriage with Stolzius, the middle-class dealer in cloth, is destroyed because she responds to Baron Desportes' flirtings. Her weakness for glitter makes it easy for her to brush aside the occasional pangs of conscience she feels about the way she has been treating Stolzius, whose mental torment and psychological anguish are caused by Marie's unfaithfulness, and even more by the contemptuous manner in which the officers who take delight in his suffering inform him of Desportes's escapades with Marie. These officers find pleasure in sadistic pranks. Their military existence has subverted their humanity completely. The creation of Stolzius is one of the great literary accomplishments of Lenz's work. Büchner would draw on this figure when he created the character Woyzeck for his well-known play by that name. Lenz's careful observance of speech patterns and dialect peculiarities constitutes the basic device used to lend this figure an aura of general hauntedness and insecurity. His worry about Marie leads to stages of mental depression which cause his seemingly absentminded remarks. The ominous seriousness of his responses to the jocular comments of the officers testifies how badly he feels hurt by them. Yet they do not perceive that their pranks and jokes threaten his very existence, and drive him toward madness and revenge.

More and more Lenz's plays began to reflect the author's growing alienation from society. This is strongly the case with his prose works, especially with the novel fragment, *Der Waldbruder*, written in 1776, and published in Schiller's influential journal *Die Horen* in 1797. The novel's hero is given the name Herz, thereby reaffirming the period's faith in the right of an individual to trust his own feelings. Herz speaks of this dimension of personal freedom when he writes: 'Nur Freiheit will ich haben, zu lieben was ich will und so stark und dauerhaft, als es mir gefällt.'[20] It is unrequited love, love for a countess whom he has never even seen, that drove Herz to become a hermit. The novel consists of letters from Herz to his friend Rothe, as well as those written by Rothe and others who discuss the hermit's motives and views. The work is a semi-autobiographical account, including the aspects of love for a woman he had never met and the plan to go to America and fight in the Revolutionary War. Lenz wrote this work at the beginning of his estrangement from Goethe. In 1775 Goethe had visited Lenz in Strasbourg, and Lenz put his enthusiastic admiration and veneration for Goethe into words in his *Pandemonium germanicum*. The critical work ridicules outright all contemporary German literary works which will not bear comparison with those of Goethe. Written in 1775, it was not published until 1819. But when the Goethe admirer showed up in Weimar in the spring of 1776, disagreements developed quickly, leading by the year's end to an almost formal expulsion from Weimar. Lenz returned to the Strasbourg region. There he experienced prolonged periods of depression and madness. He sought help from Pastor Oberlin, who lived in an Alsatian village. Oberlin's carefully kept diary of his encounters with Lenz would serve later as the basis for Büchner's novella *Lenz*. The illness eventually forced the young author to return to his home in Riga. His mental health improved for a time, and he went to St Petersburg and to Moscow where he did some teaching. In 1792 he was found dead in a street in Moscow.

2 *Klinger*

The dramatic work of Friedrich Maximilian Klinger (1752–1831),
which in many ways offers the most characteristic *Sturm und Drang*
writing, does not simply glorify the titanic person or heap praise on
the unbridled challenger of all human order. Goethe had moved from
portraying the powerful individual Götz, who felt so sure about his
principles that he was willing to battle even the emperor, to describing
the life of the emotion-filled Werther, who could not cope with the
strength of his feeling. Lenz, meanwhile, showed preference for the
individual who is destroyed by unjust social realities, and Klinger
constructed his dramas around the egocentric person of unusual
strength, who is given to rage and acts of violence and madness, and
who is totally unrestrained and unrestrainable in his passionate outbreaks of anger. For that very reason his work has been cited whenever
someone wanted to point to the boisterousness of *Sturm und Drang*
personalities and utterances. Yet the question has been asked
correctly whether the obstreperous, frenzied and boastful heroes of
Klinger's plays are to be taken as positive representatives of the age,
or whether the author criticized his own age for producing such self-
styled 'geniuses'.

Klinger, like Goethe a native of Frankfort, found in the circle of
Sturm und Drang authors what his searching mind needed. He was
only nineteen in 1771 when Goethe returned home from his
university studies in Strasbourg. Meeting Goethe and other like-minded
adherents of the movement influenced Klinger decisively. Goethe took
a liking to the aspiring writer who came from a humble background. He
even supported his studies at the university, and Klinger followed in
Goethe's footsteps by choosing law, although play-writing was Klinger's
major activity at the university. Given that Goethe had written his
Götz late in 1771, and that this work was to be discussed and admired
most by the young authors and intellectuals involved in the new
literary movement, it will not come as a surprise to discover that
Klinger's first drama, *Otto* (1775), was another example of the
increasingly popular type that sought to glorify the age of knighthood.
Klinger completed four plays during the two years at the university
between 1774 and 1776, *Das leidende Weib* (1775), *Die Zwillinge*
(1776), *Die neue Arria* (1776), and *Simsone Grisaldo* (1776). Being
separated from his friends in Frankfort, for he studied in Giessen,
Klinger felt a strong need to express himself in writing. The plays he
wrote there deal with the battle an individual may experience within
himself, as well as the problems such an individual may encounter in

his relationships to others. The play that gave the period its name, *Sturm und Drang* (1776), he wrote after he had demonstrated his opposition to the existing cultural and educational institutions by leaving the university. Yet only a very short time later Klinger would reach the conscious decision to change his writing style and disassociate himself from the *Sturm und Drang* movement. While he did not return to a university to complete his studies formally, embarking rather on the successful career of a military officer, he did later on play an important role in university life as the curator of the University of Dorpat in Russia.

When he left Giessen, he was at the height of his involvement with the ideas and ideals of the movement, and he was in inner turmoil. That probably was the reason for his going to Weimar to be close to Goethe once again. Yet Goethe's interests had shifted away from the subjective *Sturm und Drang* life. He was a high public official in Weimar by now, no longer experiencing individual emotional turmoil and tensions, if indeed he ever had identified in reality, and not merely in imagination, with the extreme *Sturm und Drang* position. As a result, Goethe had little appreciation of Lenz's and Klinger's plight when they showed up in Weimar in 1776. Lenz took revenge for Goethe's coldness by creating the figure of Rothe in the novel fragment *Der Waldbruder*, who is accused by the novel's hero Herz of having compromised his convictions when he joined the court society. Klinger also felt alienated by Goethe, and he too rejected the comfortable life at the Weimar court. His inner turmoil became even more intense. Klinger left Weimar in the early fall of 1776, for almost two years associating with a traveling theater troupe, and then choosing for himself the military life which proved to be satisfying to him, and which was to bring him many honors, take him to Russia, and eventually make him an influential person at the Russian court. That fact is important because it tells us that in Klinger's case being a high officer in the Russian military afforded the kind of intellectual challenge that he needed. He remained extremely active as a writer, turning his attention primarily to the novel, treating topics of concern to the general climate of the period, and doing so in a fashion that holds the fascination even of today's reader, especially his treatment of Faust. Klinger's biography exemplifies why the life story of a *Sturm und Drang* author is of interest. Klinger admittedly used writing as a way of contending with his own passionate feelings, just as being a soldier was to him a way of maintaining strength of character.

Recent analyses of Klinger's dramatic *Sturm und Drang* work have called attention to a recurring motif that throws an interesting light on the author's view of the literary movement of which he was a part. The characters he creates, these titanic, boisterous, screaming, God-and-world-accusing, self-centered, raging heroes let themselves be guided exclusively by uncontrolled urges and exaggerated outbursts of feeling. They are, to be sure, representatives of the *Sturm und Drang* generation. Yet their Promethean defiance stems from childish stubbornness, and is not the result of a reasoned protest against the world. Klinger's portrayal of his characters as childlike heroes is the recurring motif which reflects his critical view of the *Sturm und Drang* rebel.[21] His sympathies lie not simply with these powerful characters for whom life has become a game in which outbreaks of passion determine the nature of each move. Klinger's plays show the sufferings of these passionate characters who are unable to control themselves. The author views this kind of inner turmoil as a result of the *Sturm und Drang* cult of genius in which feeling and passion reign supreme, and he warns against it.

In *Das leidende Weib* Brand — his name is suggestive of the consuming desire he feels for the ambassador's wife — strikes us as a person totally without any self-control. This impression of him is vividly portrayed in the fifth scene of the first act: 'Soll ich hingehen? soll ich? du trinkst mehr Gift. Soll ich? will ich? Da liegt's. Ich will, will immer, weil meine Sinne trunken sind.' His inability to even want to resist the desire of being with the ambassador's wife corresponds to her feeling as well, when she confesses to be weeping over her sin: 'Über meine Sünde, Brand! Und in meiner Brust brennt's — o fühl's, ich bin bereit, neue zu begehen' [I, 7]. While the ambassador's wife is torn between her love for her husband and the desire to be with Brand, the latter's uncontrolled passion for her is matched by Count Louis's desire to possess her. He feels betrayed by Brand and is eager to prove that Brand enjoys an illicit relationship with the ambassador's wife. Klinger's masterful presentation of feelings and jealousies, of sufferings and passion, which lead to the destruction of these characters, provided the most important literary source for Büchner's *Woyzeck*.[22]

Die Zwillinge exposes the reader to a kind of literature which has often been regarded as a portrayal of the extreme rule of emotions and passions. Guelfo is outraged against his twin brother Ferdinando, who is the first-born, and who has won the Countess Camilla, whom he, Guelfo, loves. This plot permits Klinger to develop the themes of the prodigal son and of fratricide — themes which are prominent in *Sturm und Drang* literature. Klinger bases the hero's denunciation of his father, and his murder of his brother, solely on Guelfo's inability to deal with his own emotions and feelings in a rational way. His is not a case of rebellion against apparent injustice. Neither father nor brother have tried to deceive him, although he makes the unfounded and unsubstantiated charge that he was the first-born and not Ferdinando. His pathological condition is betrayed in his own words with which the first scene closes.[23] He sees his own senseless raging as building castles in the air:

> Was hilft das nun all, wenn ich mir mit geballter Faust vor die Stirne schlag und mit den Winden heule — droh und lärme, und bei alledem nur Luftschlösser, Kartenhäuser baue! . . . Nichts lautet närrischer, als wenn ich mir selbst rufe. Guelfo!
>
> [I, 1]

Guelfo withdraws again and again from his family to be by himself. He can never be completely by himself, for Grimaldo is always with him. However, since Grimaldo is merely the symbolic personification of Guelfo's raging self, this technique works to remind the reader and viewer of Guelfo's schizophrenic existence. Those around Guelfo treat him as a sick person and demonstrate love and even patience for the tormented member of the family. Still, their kindness does not bring healing to him, but rather increases Guelfo's anger. He is the irrational hero *par excellence*, and the play a characteristic example of *Sturm und Drang* drama. That does not mean, however, that it should be read as an endorsement of the autonomy of feeling.

Nor is Klinger concerned with outward social reality, although he has often been featured as a social critic. His dramas are peculiarly devoid of impressive settings or particular events. The reader may be told that a certain play takes place in Italy or in America, but nothing further in the drama will reinforce this piece of information. What is described could happen anywhere and is not tied to any special locale. The major place of action is in the minds of the heroes. Klinger writes about the worlds his heroes create in themselves. What Drullo in *Die neue Arria* says of the play's hero, Julio, can be said of Klinger: 'Das ist ein überspannter Mensch von einem Poeten, wie ich immer sagte, der neue Welten in sich schafft, und die würklichen vergisst' [II, 5]. The entire play revolves around the question whether Julio can escape the normality of life and achieve the greatness which would correspond to the greatness of his feelings and win him the respect and love of the power-hungry Solina.

The great person is also the theme of *Simsone Grisaldo*. General Grisaldo's accomplishments on the battlefield are enhanced by his humane actions and wise decisions. Grisaldo has found harmony within himself and has adjusted to political reality. Although it may appear that Klinger created more mature heroes after *Die Zwillinge*, such an impression is certainly not appropriate in view of his play *Sturm und Drang* — initially given the title *Wirrwarr* — which he wrote after *Simsone Grisaldo*. Klinger assigns the telling name 'Wild' to the play's hero, and indicates its setting as America, which may simply underscore the idea of wildness, for there is nothing else in particular that would remind the reader of being in the midst of the Revolutionary War in America. A feud between two English families is settled in America after much confusion about the identity of persons. Before the outbreak of hatred between the families the children had been promised each other in marriage. Now Lord Bushy's son Wild finds Lord Berkley's daughter Jenny Caroline in America, and the appearance of Lord Bushy, who had been presumed dead, ends plans for revenge and brings about reconciliation. To be sure, Klinger borrowed from Shakespeare names and plot details. But the emphasis here is on finding harmony and inner peace. Several sub-plots serve as a foil to Wild's and Jenny Caroline's love experience. In contrast to their strong love the courtship of the minor characters ridicules forms of love which are not based on mutual attraction and consuming feeling. Wild's impetuousness is soothed by Jenny Caroline's unswerving love for him. He confesses that only his love for her has sustained him, that he has been searching for her all over the world, and has come to America to seek death in battle: 'Ja, Miss! nur die Liebe hat diese Maschine zusammengehalten, die durch ewigen, innern Krieg ihrer Zerstörung jede Stunde so nah war.' [II, 4] Even though Wild's words in the first scene speak of restlessness, of the happiness of taking part in a war and of blaming himself for his misfortunes, the language of the entire play conveys a much calmer mental attitude than was the case in *Die Zwillinge*. The playwright Klinger had reached a point in his life when he was more interested in dealing with philosophical issues of human existence. He was no longer the *Sturm und Drang* author who was seeking to portray the turbulence and confusion of uncontrolled feeling. This is documented outwardly when he employs the novel as a carrier of his ideas, although he does not abandon the dramatic form.

His novels in particular — he planned a cycle of ten and executed nine — testify to his sharp analytical mind. In them he deals with diverse topics as he intended to portray human society in all its forms of existence. *Fausts Leben, Taten und Höllenfahrt* (1791) is an example of the philosophical novel that seemed to correspond to his own interests. The work captured the imagination of the public, partly because the Faust theme had become so timely by 1791, but mainly because Klinger's treatment, with its satirical overtones, is a fascinating and highly intellectual commentary on human nature. That intellectualism imbues the novel with a sense of timelessness which holds the interest of today's reader as well. In the novel *Der Weltmann und der Dichter* (1798) Klinger addressed the problem of the relationship between the artist and society. He provided an early example of a historical novel in *Geschichte Raphael des Aquillas* (1793), and touches on basic questions of the period in *Geschichte eines Teutschen der neuesten Zeit* (1796/98). It is the story of the liberal, political reformer, Ernst von Falkenburg, whose idealism is in irreconcilable conflict with the system as it represents itself in his uncle. Ernst's tutor, spurred on by Rousseau's *Emil*, has awakened in him a desire to be human rather than a nobleman, and to distinguish between true virtue and mere rule observance. Accordingly, the uncle dismisses the tutor who achieves one of Klinger's own dreams when he goes to America. The new tutor is willing to teach a moral system that knows only the criterion of usefulness and allows for sensuality without the restrictions of virtue. Ernst knows, and that is the point of the novel, that the two philosophies exclude each other. He must choose one or the other. The choice is, of course, not difficult since he represents a generation that is influenced by Rousseau. The theme of the generation conflict reminds us of the *Sturm und Drang* period in general, and of Klinger's early plays in particular. It is just as noteworthy that in some aspects Ernst removes himself from Rousseau's ideas for he does not necessarily advocate a return to nature.

3 *Wagner*

The *Sturm und Drang* writers were not oblivious to technical requirements of the stage even though they often were writing for a reading public. Heinrich Leopold Wagner (1747–1779) became more involved in stage production than the other *Sturm und Drang* playwrights, and his plays were especially successful as theater pieces. In that respect he is similar to Lenz, with whom he shares also the desire to display on the stage a realistic social milieu. Wagner was the oldest of the *Sturm und Drang* writers who were attached in some way to the circle around Goethe. Yet he was one of the last to join, and his name is connected mainly with only one play, *Die Kindermörderin*. The title indicates that the play treats a topic similar to that of the Gretchen episode in Goethe's *Urfaust*. Goethe even accused Wagner of plagiarism. That charge was unfounded, for Wagner had made radically different use of the motif of an unwed mother murdering her child out of fear and desperation than had Goethe.[24] It was not until 1775 that Wagner came to know Goethe in Frankfort, even though Wagner, who was born in Strasbourg, had been there when Goethe pursued his studies in the Alsatian town. Wagner's early interest in literature was along traditional lines, and he continued to write Anacreontics even after he had made the acquaintance of Lenz in Strasbourg and had become a member of the circle around Josef Daniel Salzmann, Goethe's mentor during his Strasbourg stay. He did not seem to become convinced of the value of the new literary ideals until he spent two years as a tutor in Saarbrücken. There he came into contact with the life of the lower classes, an experience which appeared to make him more sensitive to the aims of the *Sturm und Drang*, and which influenced his views of society. When he met Goethe and other *Sturm und Drang* authors in Frankfort in 1775, he began writing dramas almost immediately. *Der wohltätige Unbekannte*, a one act play, appeared in 1775, as did *Die Reue nach der Tat*. His successful *Die Kindermörderin* was published in 1776. After that he broke with Goethe and returned to Strasbourg to complete his studies. His old friends there gave strong approval to *Die Kindermörderin*

As soon as he received his doctorate and was licensed as a lawyer in the fall of 1776, Wagner devoted his energies entirely to the theater. He worked with the then famous Seyler troupe, translating for them, directing at times, and adapting plays for them to perform. In this capacity he prepared Shakespeare's *Macbeth*, which he published in 1779. His active interest in the theater led him also to translate Mercier's *Du théâtre ou nouvel essai sur l'art dramatique* (1773). The *Sturm und Drang* authors were attracted to Mercier's views whose insistence on genius rather than rules appealed to them, especially because he, too, had praise for Shakespeare. Wagner applied Mercier's dramatic precepts when he attempted life-like portrayal in his dramas. He also made considerable use of dialect language in his writings and created characters who were representatives of the lowest classes.

Both *Die Reue nach der Tat* and *Die Kindermörderin* have six acts, a demonstration of Wagner's freedom from the usual dramatic rules. Madam Langen in *Die Reue nach der Tat* thwarts a marriage between her son and the daughter of the coachman Walz. When the unrebellious girl becomes seriously ill over her fate Madam Langen is willing to give in. Her consent comes too late to save the life of either the girl or her son. Wagner did not create convincing characters in this play, but he was successful in evoking a sense of reality by paying attention to details. If the play reminds the reader of nineteenth-century realism and naturalism this is even more true of *Die Kindermörderin*. It evokes impressions one gains from reading Friedrich Hebbel's *Maria Magdalene*, which treats a similar subject. Hebbel's famous Meister Anton has his precursor in the butcher Martin Humbrecht. Their moral and ethical views, their dealings with their children, their treatment of legal officials and their inability to compromise are features which they share. Wagner had to defend the realism of the play because the seduction scene in the first act had been attacked and eliminated by Lessing's brother, who had prepared an edition of the play. When the poet himself published an edition for the stage he, too, cut the first act and added a happy ending. He did so maintaining that the original play had been written to be read, not played. Wagner refused to take out, however, what was to him an extremely important dramatic device, the theft of a silver snuff-box which brought the legal officers to the house of the self-righteous butcher where they revealed that the butcher's wife and daughter had been to a brothel, albeit unknowingly. The snuff-box links Madam Humbrecht's vanity, which permits her daughter's seduction to happen, with the butcher's assertive self-righteousness, which forces his daughter to flee from home and kill her child. Wagner does not employ the frequent scene changes so popular with other *Sturm und Drang* playwrights. While the first act takes place in a brothel-inn and the sixth act in a poor washerwoman's hut, the remaining four acts are all set in Humbrecht's house, the place which is ruled solely by Humbrecht's moralizing views and questionable actions. Our knowledge of this house can explain why it was possible for a virtuous girl to become the victim of a seducer, and why a tragic ending was inescapable.

4 *Maler Müller*

Maler Müller and Leisewitz are two writers whose contributions to *Sturm und Drang* drama deserve mention because of the choice of subject matter and the form of treatment. Müller's seizing upon the Faust theme, and his independence and originality in treating it, and Leisewitz's subdued yet thoughtful and almost traditional presentation of the *Sturm und Drang* fratricide motif have preserved for both of them a place in literary history. Friedrich Müller (1749–1825) chose for himself the name Maler Müller because he was a painter and etcher before he also became a poet. Apart from his interest in dramatic idyls, which goes back to his admiration for the writer and painter Salomon

Gessner, Maler Müller was only loosely connected with the Strasbourg circle, even though he came from the nearby Palatinate. It was not until 1775 that he met Goethe, and not until 1776 that he became acquainted with Lenz, Klinger and Wagner. Before that time he felt a literary kinship with Klopstock and the 'Göttinger Hainbund', which may account for his interest in writing idyls. As the *Sturm und Drang* group broke up, Maler Müller began laying plans for an extended stay in Rome. He left in 1778 and was never to return to Germany. Neither was he ever to complete his literary presentation of Faust, although he continued working on the theme for many years.

Maler Müller was fascinated by the popular moralizing presentations of the Siegfried and the Faust legends. The first he formed into the drama *Golo und Genoveva*, and the second into *Fausts Leben*. Only the first part of the five part *Faust* drama was published in 1778, written mainly between 1776 and 1778. He continued reworking the other four parts in Rome. Goethe's publication of *Faust I* in 1806 gave him the impetus to rewrite the *Faust* drama in verse but he never finished it. We have already noted that Lessing, Goethe and Klinger were drawn to the Faust topic. Contrary to the popular portrayal of a smallish, deceiving Faust, the *Sturm und Drang* writers saw in him the strong person. Maler Müller claims in the preface to the drama that he desired to defend Faust because of his striving 'ganz zu sein, was man fühlt, dass man sein könnte.' In Müller's *Faust* the metaphysical realm does not take on importance. Scenes depicting the spirits in hell are much like those in the familiar puppet play. Faust's goals are simply to live independently, to scorn conventions, to enjoy gambling and to gain honor. He is the kind of person Mephistopheles can admire because he dares to live without restraints. Faust's yearning to rise above the lowness of life remains unfulfilled. Yet the forcefulness and richness of the language, as well as the poet's ability to create the impression of real life scenes, mark Müller's *Faust* fragment as an important event. The play *Golo und Genoveva*, which was written during the second half of the seventies, treats the change of the desperate lover Golo into a violent person when Genoveva, Siegfried's faithful wife, rejects his advances. The passion and singlemindedness of Golo's love force the change upon him. In this drama, too, the author is unduly preoccupied with the colorful and realistic detail, which provides poetic quality, but which often detracts from the dramatic tension.

5 *Leisewitz*

Johann Anton Leisewitz (1752–1806) is the only dramatist of the period who had no connection with any members of the Strasbourg circle. He studied in Göttingen and joined the 'Göttinger Hainbund' in 1774. In the fall of that year he returned to his native Hanover, practicing law and, for a few years, devoting much time to writing. Besides a few short poetic dialogues the play *Julius von Tarent* (1776) is his only extant literary work. The short but poignant dialogue *Die Pfändung* betrays the convictions which he shared with the other members of the 'Hainbund'. A peasant and his wife philosophize about the personal and spiritual freedom they will retain even though they know that their unjust immoral prince will take from them the very bed in which they are lying. Schiller was attracted to the deep religious feeling and the belief in final justice that are manifested in Leisewitz's work. As in Klinger's *Die Zwillinge* and later in Schiller's *Die Räuber*, so we find in *Julius von Tarent* two brothers, sons of a nobleman, who are in love with the same girl. But only in Leisewitz's play is love itself described as the one force in human experience that is not subject to reason. Guido's greed for honor and Julius's love for Blanca constitute the conflict. It would please Guido's honor to possess Blanca, and satisfy Julius's innermost longing for Blanca, if she could be his. Julius would gladly not become prince, although he knows that running away with Blanca would put his brother Guido, a tyrant, on the throne. The father's solution is to make Blanca a nun. Yet cloister walls cannot shut out the force of love. The conflict ends when Guido stabs his brother. Blanca is seized by madness when she sees the dead Julius. But it is the father who establishes justice when he kills Guido, not in a moment of rage, but rather deliberately and after having rejected the easier solution of suicide. The play is characterized by such deliberate actions and by reasoned discussions about the tension between personal freedom and social responsibility. This deliberateness is paralleled by a tight and well-balanced plot, a fact which may well betray Leisewitz's admiration for Lessing.

IV Drawn to Nature: the 'Göttinger Hain'

'Göttinger Hain' was the name a number of authors, predominantly lyrical poets, chose for the group which they formed in 1772. Leisewitz was the only dramatist in the 'Göttinger Hain,' whose aims were otherwise focused exclusively on furthering lyric poetry. However, Leisewitz's drama, *Julius von Tarent*, champions the ideals which the members of the 'Hain' held in common: a longing for individual freedom, a firm belief in the lasting reality of personal love, strong anti-feudalistic feelings, and a patriotic devotion to praise simple forms of human existence. Their unbounded enthusiasm for Klopstock and the desire to gain his approval tended to encourage poetic forms which were more representative of the rationalistic and sentimental poetry of the age than of *Sturm und Drang*. Where they found their own style and showed independence from Klopstock — for example, Hölty's development of the ballad and his individualistic handling of the ode — the 'Hain' had its greatest impact. The group's single most lasting and effective contribution was its annual publication of the *Göttinger Musenalmanach*, which followed the tradition of the Parisian *Almanach des Muses*. The first volume, *Musenalmanach für das Jahr 1770*, which offers a good selection of German poetry, was written in the years just prior to 1769 and prepared by two friends, Christian Heinrich Boie (1744–1806) and Friedrich Wilhelm Gotter (1746–1797). Their successful collaboration in this venture provided the immediate impulse from which the 'Göttinger Hain' grew and took form. Established poets, such as Gleim, Klopstock and Gerstenberg lent their names to this publication venture, and unknown poets such as Bürger, Claudius, and Voss were brought to the attention of Germany's reading public. It was so successful that poetic almanacs were to become a permanent feature of the German literary scene for the next hundred years.

The history of the 'Göttinger Hain' is a vivid testimony to the enthusiastic friendship cult of the eighteenth century. These friends and poets spent their evenings criticizing and correcting each other's poetic attempts and discussing technical aspects of poetry in general. The formal founding of the 'Göttinger Hain' came at the end of an evening which these friends had spent together outside of Göttingen. It was a sudden plan to formalize their friendship. They conducted a friendship-swearing ceremony in an oak grove under a moonlit sky. Klopstock's poetry had inspired them to use the word 'Hain' or grove as a designation for their group, and individually to choose Teutonic names, which they borrowed from Klopstock's writings. Their patriotism had its roots in Klopstock's glorification of everything Teutonic. Klopstock was the spiritual father whom they honored and to whom they presented a handwritten book of their poems in 1773.[25] His approval, his promise to prepare detailed criticism of individual poems, and his eventual official request that he be received as a member into the 'Göttinger Hain' brought elation to the young poets. Klopstock was officially made a member in 1774. At that time he occupied the chair which the young poets in their enthusiasm had from the very beginning reserved for the master at their meetings. Unfortunately, Klopstock's active participation also encouraged them to turn even more inward and isolate themselves from other movements. Their denunciation of Wieland became more pronounced because of it, although it is true that most *Sturm und Drang* authors felt negatively toward Wieland. The 'Göttinger Hain' saw in Wieland the destroyer of those virtues which they held in high esteem: religion, morality, patriotism and friendship. Klopstock joined the group just at a time when criticism of his own work was beginning to be voiced more audibly; and so the 'Göttinger Hain' poets could hardly expect to escape criticism of themselves as well. The brilliant aphorist Lichtenberg, also a resident of Göttingen after 1770, did not spare them his ironic chastisement, although he recognized the genius of Hölty. But the young poets also received support, certainly when Goethe contributed to the *Musenalmanach*, or when the 1774 edition of the almanac was awarded the high praise it deserved. In particular the anthology for 1774 was a representative example of the amazing development of German poetry in the early seventies. The 'Göttinger Hain's' almost exclusive devotion to lyrical poetry, and their *Sturm und Drang* insistence on folklorishness and on the experience of real nature as opposed to idealized nature – Maler Müller's realistic idyls have their origin here – combined to imbue their literary creations with lasting beauty.

Besides those who were actually members of the 'Hain,' there were poets who for various reasons stayed away from the organization, but who in their poetry pursued similar aims, such as Bürger, Claudius, and Schubart. We must refer to their works to understand the broader contribution of the 'Göttinger Hain' to the development of poetry in the *Sturm und Drang* period. The leading poets of the narrowly defined 'Göttinger Hain' besides Hölty were Friedrich Leopold Stolberg (1750–1819) and Heinrich Johann Voss (1751–1826). Stolberg and his brother Christian Günther Stolberg brought prestige to the 'Hain' because of their position as imperial counts. Their friendship with Voss, the grandson of a freed bondsman, signaled the social awareness underlying their writing. Both Stolberg and Voss were primarily active during their Göttingen years as translators of Homer's works.

1 *Hölty*

It is Ludwig Christoph Heinrich Hölty (1748–1776) who dominates in any anthology that brings together the poetic works of the members of the 'Göttinger Hain'. The son of a minister, Hölty – he died of tuberculosis at the age of twenty-eight – achieved a natural tone in his

odes that has endeared them to many a reader. While the genre reminds
one of Klopstock, the easy flow of words makes the reader forget its
sophisticated meter, and the complete lack of pathos allows the poet to
allude to death in most of his poems without creating a sense of
melancholy. Sadness does run through his work, but the poet is never
overcome either by the experience of unfulfilled love or by the
knowledge of impending death. There are some Anacreontic lines in
his poetry, overtones of a smiling observer of life, but usually Hölty
praises forthrightly simple forms of life. He prefers the hut to the
palace, the maid to the lady of high birth. His folk-like

> Üb immer Treu und Redlichkeit,
> Bis an dein kühles Grab;
> Und weiche keinen Finger breit
> Von Gottes Wegen ab. . . [26]

is an expression of how Hölty equates simplicity with virtue. Where lack
of virtue or unfaithfulness is evident it is usually in representatives of
the aristocracy. In his ballad 'Die Nonne', a knight first awakens love in
a young nun. This causes in her a spiritual battle. But her love for the
knight grows, and she realizes only too late that his love had been mere
play and amusement. She resorts to a devilish and cruel revenge which is
dictated by the immensity of her suffering. The folk-like ballad is to
Hölty a vehicle for pointing up that evil has one of its roots in unjust
social conditions. It is also a form which helps make his poetry
immediate.

2 *Bürger*

Gottfried August Bürger (1747–1794) was well acquainted with the
poets of the 'Hain', who had introduced him to the ideals of *Sturm und
Drang* poetry by pointing him to Herder and Ossian. Herder's folk
poetry and Ossian's ghost-like scenes inspired Bürger to develop the folk
ballad for artistic expression. He achieved unusual dramatic sound
effects and created chilling scenes in which horror and fear, ghosts and
apparitions dominate. His well-known ballad 'Lenore' (1773, published
in the famous *Göttinger Musenalmanach* in 1774) brought immediate
success and urged him to continue with this almost naturalistic, highly
passionate form of poetry. To him popular success was decisive in
determining the quality of the work. Bürger's fame reached a climax
in 1778 when an entire collection of his poems appeared in print. Still,
'Lenore' remained his best ballad. Lenore in desperation denounces

God for not letting Wilhelm return from war. She scoffs at the prospect of eternal bliss if Wilhelm cannot be with her on earth now. In response to her blasphemies the dead Wilhelm appears during the night, inviting her to their wedding. The heavenly bridegroom becomes the apocalyptic rider who reveals his true identity when he offers his grave as their bed for the wedding. Allusions to Biblical phrases and Protestant hymns serve to convey the meaning of the poem.[27] In typical folklore tradition, the ballad ends with a forceful moral teaching:

Nun tanzten wohl bei Mondenglanz,
Rundum herum im Kreise,
Die Geister einen Kettentanz
Und heulten diese Weise:
Geduld! Geduld! Wenn's Herz auch bricht!
Mit Gott im Himmel hadre nicht!
Des Leibes bist du ledig;
Gott sei der Seele gnädig!

Through repetition of phrases and sounds, through dialogue, and through the imagination of a galloping ride, Bürger has created the impression of breath-taking action, but also of terrifying events that paralyze feelings and responses. Bürger found material for subsequent ballads in Percy's *Reliques of Ancient Poetry*, but also in local folklore as it was told by the peasants with whom the poet dealt in his role as civil servant. His ability to retell these stories in realistic and idiomatic language spurred him on to further creation.

In 1786 and again in 1788 he translated and retold the tall tales of Baron Münchhausen. Bürger had found these in an English edition that had been prepared by the fugitive German author Rudolf Erich Raspe (1737–1794). Bürger's *Wunderbare Reisen zu Wasser und Lande, Feldzüge und lustige Abenteuer des Freiherrn von Münchhausen* testify to the author's interest in popular literature, even though Bürger wrote them under the pressure of financial need. The poet's lack of personal discipline shows up in his tempestuous love life, the unsavory nature of which was ultimately to isolate him from all his friends. Just as destructive to Bürger was Schiller's sharp criticism (1791) of his concept of popular folk-poetry. The young Schiller had admired Bürger; the mature Schiller judged by the ideals of German classicism. It was Bürger's tragedy that he never outgrew his *Sturm und Drang* period.

3   *Claudius*

Independence of thought is the hallmark of the poetry of Matthias
Claudius (1740–1815). The strong desire to remain independent
prevented him from any association with the 'Göttinger Hain',
although ties of close friendship existed between him and Voss.
Claudius's independence stemmed from his strong Christian faith,
which inspired him to be confident in adverse situations and which
constituted the spiritual basis for his opposition to the intellectual
autonomy of Enlightenment. It also prompted him to assume a
journalistic role, which enabled him to address himself to such
diverse topics as art and politics. Writing poetry to him was more a
natural means of expressing himself than it was a conscious artistic
pursuit. In fact, his talent was such that in all of his journalistic
writings the poet Claudius holds a stronger appeal than the pedagogically
oriented popular philosopher. His fame rests entirely on his poetry
which is characterized by simplicity and originality. His humorous
treatment of everyday events and problems in folk-like fashion, his
defense of virtue and honesty and his many anti-feudalistic statements
all support the aims of the 'Göttinger Hain', and they contribute to
Claudius's popularity.

Claudius gave up the formal study of theology soon after he had enrolled at the University of Jena and took up law and wrote Anacreontic
poetry. He left Jena and returned to his native Reinbek near Hamburg in
1763, without having earned an academic degree. The rest of his life he
spent in and around Hamburg, mostly in Wandsbek, a village outside of
Hamburg's city limits. Twice he accepted positions elsewhere, only to
discover that the life of an official was not for him. In 1764–1765 he
was secretary to the Count of Holstein in Copenhagen where he got to
know Klopstock and his circle of friends; and in 1776 he moved to
accept a position in the provincial government of Hesse-Darmstadt, and
to serve as editor of the *Hessen-Darmstädtische Landzeitung.* Again he
returned home within a year. Claudius never enjoyed the glamorous
life at court. He needed family and friends to find satisfaction. Whenever he wrote articles it was as though he were engaged in a dialogue
with a friend, and his poems frequently seem to be written about
smallish events of everyday family life. He began his journalistic career
in 1768 in Hamburg. From 1771 to 1775 he was the editor of the
Wandsbecker Bote, a name which has been used ever since as an
appropriate designation for Claudius himself; for he was the voice of
common sense and criticism in the name of decency,and honesty. He
wrote about the poetry of the *Sturm und Drang*, about politics,

religion, music and philosophy. His fame spread quickly, and many
Sturm und Drang authors were among those who published in the
Wandsbecker Bote. When the paper ceased publication in 1775,
Claudius collected his poems and articles under the title *Asmus omnia
sua secum portans oder Sämtliche Werke des Wandsbecker Boten.*
Indeed, all man needs to carry with him in his pilgrimage are his con-
victions and beliefs.

There is social criticism in Claudius's poetry, when he has the black
slave bemoan his fate in 'Der Schwarze in der Zuckerplantage', or when
in his 'Kriegslied' he says that no crown could comfort his conscience if
he were responsible for war:

> Was hülf mir Kron und Land und Gold und Ehre?
> Die könnten mich nicht freun.
> 's ist leider Krieg, – und ich begehre
> Nicht schuld daran zu sein.

The questions that are dealt with most often in various ways are those
that seek answers to such basic experiences as joy and suffering, life and
death. The individual experience of death takes on general significance
when Claudius combines Biblical imagery with solemn meter in the
poem 'An –, als ihm die – starb.'

> Der Säemann säet den Samen,
>   Die Erd empfängt ihn, und über ein kleines
>   Keimet die Blume herauf -

> Du liebtest sie. Was auch dies Leben
>   sonst für Gewinn hat, war dir klein geachtet,
>   und sie entschlummerte dir.

> Was weinest du neben dem Grabe
>   Und hebst die Hände zur Wolke des Todes
>   Und der Verwesung empor?

> Wie Gras auf dem Felde sind Menschen
>   Dahin, wie Blätter. Nur wenige Tage
>   Gehn wir verkleidet einher.

> Der Adler besucht die Erde,
>   Doch säumt nicht, schüttelt vom Flügel den Staub, und

> Kehret zur Sonne zurück.

Usually, however, Claudius chose simple verse forms and drew on man's everyday surroundings for illustrations. As a result his poetry speaks directly to the reader and his lasting impact, especially through such well-known creations as 'Abendlied', 'Ein Lied, hinterm Ofen zu singen', and 'Der Tod und das Mädchen'.

4 *Schubart*

The most direct criticism of unjust social conditions, and especially of absolutistic rulers by whose whims and capricious acts innocent citizens felt threatened, is found in the work of Christian Friedrich Daniel Schubart (1739–1791). Unlike Claudius, but like Bürger and so many *Sturm und Drang* writers, he led a highly unstable and unquiet life. He too found his challenge and satisfaction in journalistic writing as editor of *Die Deutsche Chronik* (1774–1777). In that role he resembles Claudius. The impact of his writing was heightened by the fact that he spent ten years (1777–1787) imprisoned, without trial and without verdict, in the famous Hohenasperg fortress. Duke Karl Eugen of Württemberg whose monstrous tyranny was to cause Schiller to flee his realm in later years, had ordered the imprisonment as a move to quiet the discomforting voice of Schubart. Earlier the poet had been expelled from Württemberg because of his openly immoral ways at court. He wrote much of his poetry on the Hohenasperg, which in the poem 'Die Aussicht' he calls the 'mount of tears'. His poetry speaks of his deep faith in God, which enables him to endure his sufferings patiently. His most famous poem, written during the imprisonment, he entitled 'Die Fürstengruft'. In it he attacks tyrannical lords. He imagines looking at the decaying bodies of dead princes in their burial vault, and he remembers the inhumanity of many a proud ruler. Seemingly, he is speaking of his own fate when he claims that outspokenness has often led to incarceration:

> Nun ist die Hand herabgefault zum Knochen,
>   Die oft mit kaltem Federzug
> Den Weisen, der am Thron zu laut gesprochen,
>   In harte Fesseln schlug.

Schubart's work made a definite impression on the youthful Schiller, who was inspired to his first drama, *Die Räuber* (1781), by a story from Schubart's pen.

V A Critical Look at the Period: Lichtenberg

Sturm und Drang as a movement in German literary history was as
effective as it was short-lived. Like most intellectual movements it had
its formidable critics, mostly among the older generation, understandably so because *Sturm und Drang* was a youthful movement. One
critic, Georg Christoph Lichtenberg (1742–1799), was of the same age
as the majority of the *Sturm und Drang* authors. Since he lived and
taught in Göttingen, the members of the 'Göttinger Hain' proved to be
convenient objects for his attacks. Nor did he spare Lavater's
physiognomic writings. In many ways Lichtenberg continued the
tradition of the German Enlightenment with its rationalistic and deistic
assumptions. Yet he did not subscribe to the optimism that characterized the 1730s and 1740s. Essentially, he saw his mission as that of
branding all kinds of foolishness and subjectivism in literature. His
sharp wit, his humorous style, his devotion to the ideals of intellectual
enlightenment have earned him a place of considerable respect. His
ideas summarize, as it were, the major achievements and developments
of the eighteenth century. They do not anticipate the age of classicism
in German literature, undoubtedly because he was not concerned
whether literary movements or trends were forward-looking, but
rather whether the individual work of literature exemplified the
standards of clarity and objectivity which he demanded. Thus, this
contemporary of the *Sturm und Drang* writers has come to be
considered a representative of the age of rationalism. Chronologically
it is only appropriate that a discussion of Lichtenberg should conclude
this account of the development of literature in the eighteenth century.
It is just as appropriate in view of the intellectual contribution which he
made.

If there was any model that Lichtenberg desired to emulate it was
the British way of life as he had encountered it during his several visits
to London. He enjoyed the cosmopolitan outlook on life that he found
there. Being a professor at Göttingen he was of course teaching at a
university that was conscious of its ties to England, and Lichtenberg
felt greatly honored when, in 1788, the British court conferred on him
the title of royal councilor. Like Haller, Lichtenberg was a scientist
whose literary writing has become his major legacy, and like so many
eighteenth century men of letters he, too, was the son of a minister. A
childhood accident left him a hunchback, a fact which has often been
cited to explain his satirical tone, a very questionable explanation.
Lichtenberg was part of an age which loved satire as a means of
strengthening a rationalistic critical interpretation of life. No other

motivation for the writing of satire is needed. He began his studies of
mathematics at Göttingen in 1763 and, except for his travels to
England, he remained there and became known for his lectures on
experimental physics.

In 1776 Lichtenberg published his important essay on Garrick whose
acting had fascinated him in London. He had spent part of 1774 and all
of 1775 in London, invited by Lord Boston whose son he had tutored
in Göttingen. From then on he considered England his intellectual
home. His many scathing remarks about conditions in Germany were
prompted in part by his admiration for England. Two years later he
became the editor of the *Göttinger Taschenkalender*, a periodical with
scientific-popular essays, and in 1780 he founded, together with
Forster, the *Göttingensche Magazin*, a periodical intended more for the
scholar. Franz Mautner correctly declares that Lichtenberg's most
central concern was his thinking about man.[28] He had a great love for
people, and that love prompted his fight against all human foolishness.
The loving observations of small, everyday details turn into maxims,
sometimes formal aphorisms, as soon as Lichtenberg examines those
details with his critical mind. Mautner appropriately states: 'Verstand
ist die Signatur seiner Schriften, Herz immer wieder die seines
Handelns.'[29]

'Sudelbücher' — a word from the language of merchants designating
the immediate recording of sales and actions — was the term he used
for his diary-like account of his thoughts, experiences, readings,
mathematical calculations, collections of quotations, and even
meterological observations.[30] In fact he chose the word 'Sudelbuch' as
the translation for 'Waste book':

Die Kaufleute haben ihr Waste book (Sudelbuch, Klitterbuch
glaube ich im Deutschen), darin tragen sie von Tag zu Tag alles
ein was sie verkaufen und kaufen, alles durcheinander ohne
Ordnung .... Dieses verdient von den Gelehrten nachgeahmt
zu werden.[31]

These diaries indicate how well he knew himself and knew his love for
people:

Bei mir liegt das Herz dem Kopf wenigstens um einen ganzen
Schuh näher als bei den übrigen Menschen, daher meine grosse
Billigkeit. Die Entschlüsse können noch warm ratifiziert
werden.[32]

His view of comedy and satire reflect a modified rationalistic stance when he argues that they do not improve human behavior, merely enlarge our horizons:

> Die Komödie bessert nicht unmittelbar, vielleicht auch die Satyre nicht, ich meine man legt die Laster nicht, die sie lächerlich macht. Aber das können sie tun, sie vergrössern unsern Gesichtskreis, vermehren die Anzahl der festen Punkte aus denen wir uns in allen Vorfällen des Lebens geschwinder orientieren können.[33]

The 'Sudelbücher' abound with critical remarks about Lavater whose physiognomic studies he rejects, especially the thesis that physical beauty is a sign of virtue or inner beauty. The books document Lichtenberg's contempt for contemporary literature, Goethe's *Götz* and *Werther*, Klopstock's *Messias*, and the many Ossian translations. Lichtenberg's favorite poets were Haller and Hagedorn. The many notes and aphoristic statements of the 'Sudelbücher' provided the material which Lichtenberg often enough used for writing those successful essays which he published. Those to be mentioned here must include his *Über die Physiognomik; Wider die Physiognomen* (1778), and *Briefe aus England. An Heinrich Christian Boie* (1775). Famous in his own time were his lengthy and detailed *Ausführliche Erklärung der Hogarthschen Kupferstiche* (1794–99). His reliable knowledge of England made it possible for him to explain Hogarth's engravings with penetrating and delightful analyses, highlighting the satirical intent of the artist. Lichtenberg had discovered in Hogarth a mind and a view of society with which he agreed. The explanations were also proof that Lichtenberg was not at all part of the literary developments in Germany, the classicistic approach of Goethe and Schiller, but rather continued to think and write in the spirit of eighteenth-century rationalism.

Notes

1. Chapter 73, entitled 'Die Ehre nach dem Tode'.
2. In the section 'Aesthetica in Nuce. Eine Rhapsodie in kabbalistischer Prose'.
3. From *Fünf Hirtenbriefe das Schuldrama betreffend* (1763).
4. For a detailed analysis see S. P. Atkins, 'J. C. Lavater and Goethe: Problems of Psychology and Theology in *Die Leiden des jungen Werthers*,' *PMLA*, 63 (1948), 520–576.
5. *Ausgewählte Schriften*, 3rd edn. (Zurich, 1859), p. 73.
6. *Abhandlung über den Ursprung der Sprache* (1772).

7.   From chapter one of *Auch eine Philosophie zur Geschichte der Bildung der Menschheit* (1774). Herder's understanding of history was rooted in his views of language and literature. F. Meinecke, *Entstehung des Historismus*, II, 385–386, speaks of Herder's 'grossartiger und einziger Fähigkeit, geschichtliches Leben "ästhetisch" zu erfühlen,' and of the fact that this ability made him 'zum genialen Entdecker neuer Provinzen des geschichtlichen Lebens überhaupt und zum Schöpfer einer neuen Methode der "Einfühlung" – dies von ihm selbst geschaffene Wort. . . '

8.   In 1765 James MacPherson had published a group of poems with the claim that he had discovered Ossian's manuscripts and translated the Old Gaelic verses into modern English. Doubts about the veracity of MacPherson's claims were soon voiced, because MacPherson failed to produce the Old Gaelic texts when he was asked to do so. In time it was confirmed that these poems were actually MacPherson's own. The impact of Ossian's poetry, however, was in no way affected by the impropriety of the translator's action.

9.   For a full treatment of this question see W. Leppmann, *The German Image of Goethe* (Oxford, 1961).

10.   Even before leaving Leipzig, Goethe had become acquainted with Ernst Theodor Langer, whom he now makes the confidant of his religious experiences and thoughts. The correspondence with Langer is valuable because it gives evidence of the fact that Goethe was intimately familiar with the vocabulary of the Pietists, their songs and practices.

11.   Goethe reports to Langer about meetings of Pietists in his parents' house. His mother participated in the circle. Besides, she was a distant relative of the canoness Susanna Katharina von Klettenberg.

12.   Letter of 1 November, 1770. *Herders Briefwechsel mit Caroline Flachsland*, ed. H. Schauer, *Schriften der Goethe Gesellschaft* XXXIX (Weimar, 1926), p. 126.

13.   In some ways the *Frankfurter Gelehrten Anzeigen* became the 'official' journal of the *Sturm und Drang* circle around Goethe. During 1772 and 1773 Goethe and his friends published in it numerous reviews of literary or general cultural works of the period. They used this forum successfully to formulate and propagate their views about literature.

14.   Letter to Gerstenberg of 25 February, 1768.

15.   Letter to Lessing of May/June, 1768.

16.   For a full presentation of *Sturm und Drang* drama see Mark O. Kistler, *Drama of the Storm and Stress* (New York, 1969); Roy Pascal, *The German Sturm und Drang* (Oxford, 1953).

17.   Lenz's 'Über *Götz von Berlichingen*' was probably written shortly after the publication of Goethe's play. Lenz's review was prepared as a lecture delivered to the 'Société de philosophie et des belles lettres' in Strasbourg.

18.   Cf. especially Goethe's poem 'Seefahrt' (1777).

19.   His essay *Über die Soldatenehen* (not published until 1914) shows how concerned Lenz was with the problem. The essay is different from the play in that Lenz assumes marriage for soldiers, when he argues that they would fight much better if they fought for wife and children.

20.   Part I, letter 8.

21.   Two recent articles, which appeared almost simultaneously, deal with the problem: J. Snapper, 'The Solitary Player in Klinger's Early Dramas,' *GR* XLV (1970), 83–93; K. S. Guthke, 'F. M. Klingers *Zwillinge*: Höhepunkt und Krise des Sturm und Drang,' *GQ* XLIII (1970), 703–714.

22.   The play *Das leidende Weib* was included in Tieck's three volume edition of Lenz's works, as Tieck had mistakenly identified it as one of Lenz's plays. Thus Büchner, who used the Tieck edition to immerse himself in Lenz's dramas at the time when he was writing his Woyzeck, read *Das leidende Weib* and took it to be by Lenz. The plot and the expressive language mark the play readily as being

written by Klinger.

23. Cf. K. S. Guthke, 'F. M. Klingers *Die Zwillinge*,' p. 709.

24. The motif of the unwed mother was common in *Sturm und Drang* literature, not least because it related literature to social reality. Cf. L. G. Seeger, '*The Unwed Mother*' *as a Symbol of Social Consciousness in the Writings of J. G. Schlosser, Justus Möser, and J. H. Pestalozzi* (Bern, 1970). Schlosser (1739–1799) was a minor *Sturm und Drang* author, also Goethe's brother-in-law. Pestalozzi (1746–1827) wrote his famous *Lienhard und Gertrud* toward the end of the *Sturm und Drang*. The first volume was published in 1779.

25. The book into which the members of the 'Hain' had written their poems, after the group had given its approval in each case, was found in 1950 and edited by A. Lübbering in 1957.

26. From the song 'Der alte Landmann an seinen Sohn'.

27. See A. Schöne, 'Bürger-*Lenore*', in B. v. Wiese (ed.), *Die deutsche Lyrik – Form und Gedichte* (Düsseldorf, 1964), pp. 190–210.

28. Franz H. Mautner, *Lichtenberg. Geschichte seines Geistes* (Berlin, 1968), p. 8.

29. Ibid., p. 41.

30. Only recently have these 'Sudelbücher' been published in their totality. See Wolfgang Promies (ed.), *Georg Christoph Lichtenberg. Schriften und Briefe* (München, 1968 ff). On the 'Sudelbücher' see the editor's notes in I, 950–52.

31. Ibid., I, 352.

32. Ibid., I, 159.

33. Ibid., I, 243.

BIBLIOGRAPHY

The purpose of this bibliography is to provide hints for a further study of the period and its authors. The selection of the items in the bibliography is in part determined by the knowledge that a fairly extensive and highly useful bibliographical guide to the literature of the eighteenth and nineteenth centuries is available to the English reader in E. L. Stahl and W. E. Yuill, *German Literature of the Eighteenth and Nineteenth Centuries* (New York, 1970).

I. General Background: Historical, Cultural, Philosophical

Balet, Leo and Gerhard, E.: *Die Verbürgerlichung der deutschen Kunst, Literatur und Musik im 18. Jahrhundert*, ed. G. Mattenklott, Frankfurt, Berlin, Wien, 1973.

Beloff, M.: *The Age of Absolutism 1660–1815*, London, 1954.

Bergmann, Ernst: *Die Begründung der deutschen Ästhetik durch A. G. Baumgarten und G. F. Meier*, Leipzig, 1911.

Biedermann, Karl: *Deutschland im 18. Jahrhundert*, 4 vols., Leipzig, 1867–80; repr. 1969.

Bithell, Jethro: *Germany, a Companion to German Studies*, rev. edn. by M. Pasley, London, 1972.

Boeschenstein, Hermann: *Deutsche Gefühlskultur. Studien zu ihrer dichterischen Gestaltung*, vol. I: *Die Grundlagen. 1770–1830*, Bern, 1954.

Bruford, W. H.: *Germany in the Eighteenth Century: The Social Background of the Literary Revival*, Cambridge, 1935.

Cassirer, Ernst: *Die Philosophie der Aufklärung*, Tübingen, 1932; Engl. trans., 1951.

Ermatinger, Emil: *Deutsche Kultur im Zeitalter der Aufklärung*, ed. Eugen Thurnher and Paul Stapf, Frankfurt, 1969. [Handbuch der Kulturgeschichte]

Flenley, Ralph and Spencer, Robert: *Modern German History*, 4th rev. edn., London, 1968.

Gay, Peter: *The Enlightenment: An Interpretation*, 2 vols., New York, 1966–1969.

Gebhardt, Bruno: *Handbuch der deutschen Geschichte*, ed. H. Grundmann, 4 vols., 8th edn., Stuttgart, 1954–1960.

Hinske, Norbert (ed.): *Was ist Aufklärung?* Darmstadt, 1973.

Holborn, Hajo: *A History of Modern Germany*, vol. II, 1648—1840, New York, 1964.

Kahn, Ludwig W.: *Social Ideals in German Literature, 1770—1830*, New York, 1938.

Kaiser, Gerhard: *Pietismus und Patriotismus im literarischen Deutschland*, Wiesbaden, 1961; 2nd edn. 1964.

Langen, August: *Der Wortschatz des deutschen Pietismus*, Tübingen, 1954; 2nd edn. 1968.

Martens, Wolfgang: *Die Botschaft der Tugend. Die Aufklärung im Spiegel der deutschen moralischen Wochenschriften*, Stuttgart, 1968.

Mollenauer, Robert (ed.): *Introduction to Modernity: A Symposium on Eighteenth-Century Thought*, Austin, 1965.

Mönch, Walter: *Deutsche Kultur von der Aufklärung bis zur Gegenwart*, München, 1962; 2nd edn. 1971.

Prudhoe, John: *The Theatre of Goethe and Schiller*, Totowa, New Jersey, 1973.

Randall, John Herman, Jr.: *The Career of Philosophy*. Vol. II. *From the German Enlightenment to the Age of Darwin*, New York and London, 1965.

Ritschl, Albrecht: *Geschichte des Pietismus*, 3 vols., Bonn, 1880—86.

Saine, Thomas P.: 'Was ist Aufklärung? Kulturgeschichtliche Überlegungen zu neuer Beschäftigung mit der deutschen Aufklärung,' *ZDP*, XCIII (1974), 522—45.

Schöffler, Herbert: *Deutscher Geist im 18. Jahrhundert. Essays zur Geistes- und Religionsgeschichte*, 2nd edn., Göttingen, 1967.

Schöne, Albrecht: *Säkularisation als sprachbildende Kraft. Studien zur Dichtung deutscher Pfarrersöhne*, Göttingen, 1958. [Palaestra no. 226]

Schumann, Detlev W.: 'The Latecomer. The Rise of German Literature in the Eighteenth Century,' *GQ*, XXXIX (1966), 417—49.

Vierhaus, Rudolf: 'Deutschland im 18. Jahrhundert. Soziales Gefüge, politische Verfassung, geistige Bewegung,' in *Lessing und die Zeit der Aufklärung*, Göttingen, 1968.

Viëtor, Karl: *Deutsches Denken von der Aufklärung bis zum Realismus*, 3rd edn., Berlin, 1958.

Wellesz, E. and Sternfeld, F. (eds.): *The Age of Enlightenment 1745—1790*, New York and Toronto, 1973. [The New Oxford History of Music, vol. VII]

Wolff, H. M.: *Die Weltanschauung der deutschen Aufklärung in geschichtlicher Entwicklung*, 2nd edn., Bern und München, 1963.

188   *Bibliography*

II. Criticism, Movements, Genres

Anger, Alfred: *Literarisches Rokoko*, Stuttgart, 1962. [Sammlung Metzler no. 25]

Arntzen, Helmut: *Die ernste Komödie. Das deutsche Lustspiel von Lessing bis Kleist*, München, 1968.

Beaujean, Marion: *Der Trivialroman in der zweiten Hälfte des 18. Jahrhunderts. Die Ursprünge des modernen Unterhaltungsromans*, Bonn, 1964.

Blackall, Eric A.: *The Emergence of German as a Literary Language 1700–1775*, Cambridge, 1959.

Bodi, Leslie: 'Enlightened Despotism and the Literature of Enlightenment,' *GLL*, XXII (1969), 324–33.

Böschenstein-Schäfer, Renate: *Idylle*, Stuttgart, 1967. [Sammlung Metzler no. 63]

Brüggemann, Diethelm: *Die Sächsische Komödie: Studien zum Sprachstil*, Köln und Wien, 1970.

Daunicht, Richard: *Die Entstehung des bürgerlichen Trauerspiels in Deutschland*, Berlin, 1963.

Garland, H. B.: *Storm and Stress*, London, 1952.

Guthke, Karl S.: *Das bürgerliche Trauerspiel*, Stuttgart, 1972.

Guthke, Karl S.: *Literarisches Leben im achtzehnten Jahrhundert in Deutschland und in der Schweiz*, Bern and München, 1975.

Haller, Rudolf: *Geschichte der deutschen Lyrik vom Ausgang des Mittelalters bis zu Goethes Tod*, Bern, 1967.

Heitner, Robert R.: *German Tragedy in the Age of Enlightenment: A Study in the Development of Original Tragedies*, 1724–1768, Berkeley and Los Angeles, 1963.

———: 'Real Life or Spectacle? A Conflict in Eighteenth-Century German Drama,' *PMLA*, LXXXII (1967), 485–97.

Hinck, Walter: *Das deutsche Lustspiel des 17. und 18. Jahrhunderts und die italienische Commedia dell' arte und Theatre italien*, Stuttgart, 1965.

Kaiser, Gerhard: *Geschichte der deutschen Literatur von der Aufklärung bis zum Sturm und Drang 1730–1785*, Gütersloh, 1966.

Kimpel, Dieter: *Der Roman der Aufklärung*, Stuttgart, 1967. [Sammlung Metzler no. 68]

Kistler, Mark O.: *Drama of the Storm and Stress*, New York, 1969. [Twayne Author Series]

Kurth, Liselotte,E.: *Die zweite Wirklichkeit: Studien zum Roman des 18. Jahrhunderts*, Chapel Hill, 1969.

Leibfried, Erwin: *Fabel*, Stuttgart, 1967. [Sammlung Metzler no. 66]

McInnes, Edward: 'The Sturm und Drang and the Development of Social Drama' *DVLG*, XLVI (1972), 61–81.

Martini, Fritz: 'Die Poetik des Dramas im Sturm und Drang,' in *Deutsche Dramentheorien*, (1971), 123–66.

Mason, Gabriel R.: *From Gottsched to Hebbel*, London, 1961.

Michelson, Peter: *Lawrence Sterne und der deutsche Roman des 18. Jahrhunderts*, Göttingen, 1962.

Miller, Norbert: *Der empfindsame Erzähler. Untersuchungen an Romananfängen des 18. Jahrhunderts*, München, 1968.

Neumann, Alfred R.: 'The Changing Concept of the *Singspiel* in the Eighteenth Century,' *Studies in German Literature* (1963).

Pascal, Roy: *The German Sturm und Drang*, Manchester 1953.

Purdie, Edna: *Studies in German Literature of the Eighteenth Century*, London, 1965.

Ritchie, J. M. (ed.): *Periods in German Literature*, London, 1966.

Sander, Gerhard: *Empfindsamkeit*, vol. I. *Voraussetzungen und Elemente*, Stuttgart, 1974.

Scherpe, K. R.: *Gattungspoetik im 18. Jahrhundert. Entwicklung von Gottsched bis Herder*, Stuttgart, 1968.

Schönert, Jörg: *Roman und Satire im 18. Jahrhundert. Ein Beitrag zur Poetik*, Stuttgart, 1969.

Sengle, Friedrich: *Das historische Drama in Deutschland*, 2nd edn., Stuttgart, 1969.

Steinmetz, Horst: *Die Komödie der Aufklärung*, Stuttgart, 1966. [Sammlung Metzler no. 47]

Wicke, Günter: *Die Struktur des deutschen Lustspiels der Aufklärung*, Bonn, 1965; 2nd ed., 1968.

Wierlacher, Alois: *Das bürgerliche Drama und seine theoretische Begründung im 18. Jahrhundert*, München, 1968.

Wiese, Benno von (ed.): *Der deutsche Roman. Vom Barock bis zur Gegenwart. Struktur und Geschichte*, 2 vols., Düsseldorf, 1963; 2nd ed., 1965.

—— (ed.): *Das deutsche Drama*, 2 vols., Düsseldorf, 1958.

—— (ed.): *Die deutsche Lyrik*, 2 vols., Düsseldorf, 1956.

—— : *Die deutsche Tragödie von Lessing bis Hebbel*, Hamburg, 1964.

Zeman, Herbert: *Die deutsche anakreontische Dichtung. Ein Versuch zur Erfassung ihrer ästhetischen und literarisch historischen Erscheinungsformen im 18. Jahrhundert*, Stuttgart, 1972.

III. Specific Authors

Bodmer & Breitinger

Bender, Wolfgang: *Johann Jakob Bodmer und Johann Jakob Breitinger*, Stuttgart, 1973. [Sammlung Metzler no. 113]

Bender, Wolfgang: 'J. J. Bodmer und J. Miltons *Verlorenes Paradies*,' in *Jahrbuch der deutschen Schillergesellschaft*, XI (1967), 225–67.

Bräker, Jakob: *Der erzieherische Gehalt in J. J. Breitingers 'Critische Dichtkunst'*, St. Gallen, 1950.

Brown, Francis A.: 'John Locke's Essay and Bodmer and Breitinger,' *MLQ*, X (1949), 16–32.

Grotegut, E. K.: 'Bodmer contra Gellert,' *MLQ*, XXIII (1962), 383–96.

Brockes

Böckmann, Paul: 'Anfänge der Naturlyrik bei Brockes, Haller und Günther,' in *Literatur und Geistesgeschichte: Festgabe für Heinz Otto Burger*, ed. R. Grimm and C. Wiedemann, Berlin, 1969.

Jantz, Harold: 'Brockes' Poetic Apprenticeship,' *MLN*, LXXVII (1962), 42–43.

Mainland, W. F.: 'Brockes and the Limitations of Imitation,' in *Reality and Creative Vision in German Lyrical Poetry*, ed. A. Closs, London, 1963.

Pfund, Harry W.: *Studien zu Wort und Stil bei Brockes*, New York, 1935.

Wolff, Hans M.: 'Brockes Religion.' *PMLA*, LXII (1947), 1124–1158.

Bürger

Jolles, Evelyn B.: *Gottfried August Bürgers Ballade "Lenore" in England*, Regensburg, 1974.

Jung, Paul: 'Strukturtypen der Komik. Ein Beitrag zur formalen Analyse der "lustigen Geschichten" (z. B. Münchhausen),' *DU*, XXV (1973), H. I, 44–66.

Rossel, Sven H.: 'Bürgers Gedichte,' *Nerthus* III (1972), 73–100.

Schöffler, H.: 'Bürgers "Lenore",' in H. Schöffler, *Deutscher Geist im 18. Jahrhundert*, Göttingen, 1956.

Schöne, Albrecht: 'Bürgers "Lenore",' *DVLG*, XXVIII (1954), 324–44.

Claudius

Hesselbacher, K.: *Der Wandsbecker Bote. Leben und Schaffen von Matthias Claudius*, Hamburg, 1948.

Kranefuss, Annelen: *Die Gedichte des Wandsbecker Boten*, (with
English summary), Göttingen, 1973. [Palaestra, no. 260]
Rüttenauer, I.: *Die Botschaft. Versuche über Matthias Claudius*,
München, 1947; rev. edn. under title *Matthias Claudius. Die
Botschaft des Dichters an unsere Zeit*, 1952.

Gellert

Abbé, Derek M. van: 'Some Unspoken Assumptions in Gellert's
Schwedische Gräfin,' *Orbis Litterarum*, XXVIII (1973), 113–23.
Grotegut, E. K.: 'Gellert: Wit or Sentimentalist?' *Monatshefte*, LIV
(1962), 117–22.
Martens, Wolfgang: 'Lektüre bei Gellert,' in *Festschrift fur Richard
Alewyn*, Kölne, 1967.
Russel, K.: '*Das Leben der schwedischen Gräfin von G . . .* : A Critical
Discussion,' *Monatschefte*, XL (1948), 328–36.
Schlingmann, Carsten: *Gellert. Eine literar-historische Revision*, Bad
Homburg, Berlin, Zürich, 1967.
Spaethling, Robert H.: 'Die Schranken der Vernunft in Gellerts *Leben
der Schwedischen Gräfin von G . . . .* Ein Beitrag zur Geistesgeschichte
der Aufklärung,' *PMLA*, LXXXI (1966), 224–35.
Stamm, I. S.: 'Gellert: Religion and Rationalism,' *GR*, XXVIII (1953),
195–203.

Gerstenberg

Stein, Gerd: 'Genialität als Resignation bei Gerstenberg,' in *Literatur
der bürgerlichen Emanzipation im 18. Jahrhundert*, ed. G.
Mattenklott und K. R. Scherpe, Kronberg, 1973.

Gessner

Hibberd, John: 'Gessner in England,' *Revue de Littérature Comparée*,
XLVII (1973), 296–306.
Hibberd, John: 'Salomon Gessner's Idylls as Prose Poems,' *MLR*,
LXVIII (1973), 569–76.
Hoffmeister, Gerhart: 'Gessners *Daphnis* – das Ende des europäischen
Schäferromans,' *Studia Neophilologica*, XLIV (1972), 127–41.
Leemann-van Elck, Paul: *Salomon Gessner, sein Lebensbild mit
beschreibenden Verzeichnissen seiner literarischen und künstlerischen
Werke*, Zürich und Leipzig, 1930.

Young Goethe

Barner, Hans: *Zwei "theologische Schriften" Goethes. Ein Beitrag zur*

Religiosität des jungen Goethe, Gräfenhainichen, 1930.

Bragg, Marvin: 'Goethe's Conquest of the Enlightenment Through Reevaluation of the Nature of Poetry,' *South Central Bulletin,* XXXI (1971), 171–75.

Castle, Eduard: '*Stella. Ein Schauspiel für Liebende,*' in E.C., *In Goethes Geist,* Wien, 1926.

Flitner, Wilhelm: 'Die religiöse Wandlung Goethes in den Jahren 1772 bis 1774,' in *Vom Geist der Dichtung,* ed. F. Martini, Hamburg, 1949.

Gish, Theodore G.: 'The Evolution of the Goethean Theme of the "Wanderer" and the "Cottage",' *Seminar,* IX (1973), 15–27.

Graham, Ilse: *Goethe and Lessing: The Wellsprings of Creation,* New York, 1973.

Grosser, A.: 'Le jeune Goethe et le pietisme,' *Etudes Germaniques,* IV (1949), 213–226.

Henel, Heinrich: 'Der Wanderer in der Not: Goethes "Wanderers Sturmlied" und "Harzreise im Winter",' *DVLG,* XLVII (1973), 69–94.

Leppmann, Wolfgang: *The German Image of Goethe,* Oxford, 1961.

Loewen, Harry: 'Goethe's Pietism as Seen in His Letters and *Dichtung und Wahrheit,*' in *Deutung und Bedeutung: Studies in German and Comparative Literature Presented to Karl Werner Maurer,* ed. B. Schludermann and E. Firchow, The Hague, 1973.

Martini, Fritz: 'Goethes *Götz von Berlichingen*: Charakterdrama und Gesellschaftsdrama,' in *Dichter und Leser: Studien zur Literatur,* ed. F. v. Ingen, *et al.,* Groningen, 1972.

Meessen, H. J.: '*Clavigo and Stella* in Goethe's Personal and Dramatic Development,' in *Goethe Bicentennial Studies,* ed. H. J. Meessen, Bloomington, Indiana, 1950. [Indiana University Publications. Humanities Series no. 22]

Mignon, Heinrich: *Goethe in Wetzlar. Kleine Chronik aus dem Sommer 1772,* Wetzlar, 1972.

Redslob, Edwin, '*Die Leiden des jungen Werther* 200 Jahre,' *Neue Deutsche Hefte,* CXXXIV (1972), 41–57.

Reuter, Hans-Heinrich: 'Goethes Lyrik 1771–1775,' *Weimarer Beiträge,* XVII (1971), 72–94.

Sahn, Peter: 'Werther and the Sensibility of Estrangement,' *GQ,* XLVI (1973), 47–55.

Schöffler, Herbert: '*Die Leiden des jungen Werther. Ihr geistesgeschichtlicher Hintergrund,*' in H. Schöffler, *Deutscher Geist im 18. Jahrhundert,* Göttingen, 1956.

Silz, Walter: 'Werther and Lotte at the Well,' in *Traditions and Transitions: Studies in Honor of Harold Jantz*, ed. L. Kurth, Wm. McClain, H. Homann, München, 1972.

Staiger, Emil: *Goethe*, vol. I. *1749–1786*, Zürich, 1952.

Steinhauer, Harry: 'Goethe's *Werther* after two Centuries,' *University of Toronto Quarterly*, XLIV (1974/75), 1–13.

Johann Christoph Gottsched

Birke, Joachim: 'Gottscheds Neuorientierung der deutschen Poetik an der Philosophie Wolffs,' *ZDP*, LXXXV (1966), 560–75.

Freier, Hans: *Kritische Poetik: Legitimation und Kritik der Poesie in Gottscheds Dichtkunst*, Stuttgart, 1973.

Heitner, Robert R.: 'A Gottschedian Reply to Lessing's 17th "Literaturbrief",' *Studies in Germanic Languages and Literatures* (1963), pp. 43–58.

Heydebrand, Renate von: 'Johann Christoph Gottscheds Trauerspiel *Der sterbende Cato* und die Kritik: Analyse eines Krätespiels,' in *Festschrift für Günther Weydt*, ed. W. Rasch, H. Geulen, K. Haberkamm, Bern, 1972.

Klinger, Uwe R.: 'Gottsched und *Die Belustigungen des Verstandes und des Witzes*,' *LY*, III (1971), 214–25.

Rieck, Werner: *Johann Christoph Gottsched: Eine kritische Würdigung seines Werkes*, Berlin, 1972.

Luise Adelgund Gottsched

Richel, Veronica C.: *Luise Gottsched. A Reconsideration*, Bern, Frankfurt, 1973.

———— : 'An Enlightened Jest. Luise Gottsched's *Horatii*,' *Germanic Notes*, IV (1973), 50–52.

Hagedorn

Coffman, B. R.: 'Friedrich von Hagedorn's Version of "Philemon und Baucis",' *MLR*, XLVIII (1953), 186–89.

Grotegut, E. K.: 'Hagedorn's "Seifensieder" and Freedom,' *Monatschefte*, LII (1960), 113–20.

———— : 'The Popularity of F. v. Hagedorn's "Johann der Seifensieder",' *Neophilologus*, XLIV (1960), 189–95.

Guthke, Karl S.: 'F. v. Hagedorn und das literarische Leben seiner Zeit im Lichte unveröffentlichter Briefe an J. J. Bodmer,' in *Jahrbuch des Freien deutschen Hochstifts*, (1966), 1–108.

Stix, Gottfried: *Friedrich von Hagedorn, Menschenbild und Dichtungs-*

auffassung, Roma, 1961.

Haller

Guthke, Karl S.: 'Hallers "Unvollkommene Ode über die Ewigkeit".
Veranlassung und Entstehung,' *DVLG*, XLVIII (1974), 522–45.
—— : *Albrecht von Haller und die Literatur*, Göttingen, 1962.
—— : 'Edle Wilde mit Zahnausfall. Albrecht von Hallers Indianerbild,'
in *Amerika in der deutschen Literatur*, ed. S. Bauschinger, H. Denkler,
W. Malsch, Stuttgart, 1976.
—— (ed.): *Hallers Literaturkritik*, Tübingen, 1970.
Helbling, Josef: *Albrecht von Haller als Dichter*, Bern, 1970.
Hirzel, Ludwig (ed.): *Albrecht von Hallers Gedichte*, Frauenfeld, 1882.
Menhennet, A.: 'Haller's "Gedanken über Vernunft, Aberglauben und
Unglauben": Structure and Mood,' *Forum for Modern Language
Studies*, VIII (1972), 95–106.
—— : 'Order and Freedom in Haller's "Lehrgedichte": On the
Limitations and Achievements of Strict Rationalism Within the
"Aufklärung",' *Neophilologus*, LVI (1972), 181–87.
Siegrist, C.: *Albrecht von Haller*, Stuttgart, 1967. [Sammlung Metzler
no. 57]
Stäuble, Eduard: *Albrecht von Hallers "Über den Ursprung des übels,"*
Zürich, 1953. [Züricher Beiträge zur deutschen Literatur- und·
Geistesgeschichte no. 3]
Toellner, Richard: *Albrecht von Haller: Uber die Einheit im Denken
des letzten Universalgelehrten*, Wiesbaden, 1971.

Hamann

Herde, Heinz: *Johann Georg Hamann: Zur Theologie der Sprache*,
Bonn, 1971.
Lumpp, Hans-Martin: '*Philologia Crucis*'. *Zu J. G. Hamanns Auffassung
von der Dichtkunst*, Tübingen, 1970.
Metzke, Erwin: *J. G. Hamanns Stellung in der Philosophie des 18.
Jahrhunderts*, Halle, 1934. [Schriften der Köngsberger Gelehrten
Gesellschaft]
Nadler, Josef: *Johann Georg Hamann 1730–1788. Der Zeuge des
Corpus Mysticum*, Salzburg, 1949.
Nebel, Gerhard: *Hamann*, Stuttgart, 1973.
O'Flaherty, James C.: 'Hamann's Concept of the Whole Man,' *GQ*,
XLV (1972), 253–69.
Smith, Ronald Gregor: *J. G. Hamann 1730–1788. A Study in
Christian Existence*, New York, 1960.

Unger, Richard: *Hamann und die Aufklärung. Studien zur Vorgeschichte des romantischen Geistes im 18. Jahrhundert*, 2 vols., Jena, 1911.

Herder

Blackall, Eric A.: 'The imprint of Herder's Linguistic Theory on His Early Prose Style,' *PMLA*, LXXVI (1961), 512–18.

Clark, Robert T. Jr.: *Herder, His Life and Thought*, Berkeley, 1955.

Dobbek, Wilhelm: *Herders Humanitätsidee als Ausdruck seines Weltbildes und seiner Persönlichkeit*, Braunschweig, 1949.

—— : *Johann Gottfried Herders Jugendzeit in Mohrungen und Königsberg. 1744–1765*, Würzburg, 1961. [Marburger Ostforschungen, no. 16]

Gillies, Alexander: '*Auch eine Philosophie der Geschichte zur Bildung der Menschheit*,' in *The Era of Goethe*, Oxford, 1959.

—— : *Herder*, Oxford, 1945. [Modern Language Studies]

Haym, Rudolf: *Herder nach seinem Leben und seinen Werken*, 2 vols., Berlin, 1880–1885. [Reprinted in 1954]

Maillard, Claude: 'Pour une nouvelle approche de Herder: Esquisse d'une analyse typologique,' *Recherches Germaniques*, I (1971), 3–39.

Maltusch, Johann G. (ed.): *Bückeburger Gespräche über Johann Gottfried Herder 1971*, Bückeburg, 1973.

Salmony, Hansjörg A.: *Die Philosophie des jungen Herder*, Zürich, 1949.

Sommerhalder, Hugo: *Herder in Bückeburg als Deuter der Geschichte*, Frauenfeld-Leipzig, 1945. [Wege zur Dichtung. Zürcher Schriften zur Literaturwissenschaft no. 46]

Staiger, Emil: 'Der neue Geist in Herders Frühwerk,' in E. Staiger, *Stilwandel. Studien zur Vorgeschichte der Goethezeit*, Zürich, 1963.

Wells, G. A.: 'Herder's Two Philosophies of History,' *Journal of the History of Ideas*, XXI (1960), 527–37.

Wolff, Hans M.: 'Der junge Herder und die Entwicklungsidee Rousseaus,' *PMLA*, LVII (1942), 735–819.

E. v. Kleist

Guggenbühl, Hans: *Ewald von Kleist. Weltschmerz als Schicksal*, Erlenbach-Zürich, 1948.

Klinger

Geerdts, H. J.: 'F. M. Klingers Faust-Roman,' *Zeitschrift für deutsche Literaturgeschichte*, VI (1960), 58–75.

Guthke, Karl S.: 'F. M. Klingers *Zwillinge*: Höhepunkt und Krise des

Sturm und Drang,' *GQ*, XLIII (1970), 703–714.

Hering, C.: *F. M. Klinger. Der Weltmann als Dichter*, Berlin, 1966.

Kaiser, Gerhard: 'F. M. Klingers Schauspiel *Sturm und Drang*,' in *Untersuchungen zur Literatur als Geschichte: Festschrift für Benno von Wiese*, ed. V. J. Günther, H. Koopmann, *et. al.*, Berlin, 1973.

Martini, Fritz: 'Die feindlichen Brüder: Zum Problem des gesellschaftskritischen Dramas von J. A. Leisewitz, F. M. Klinger und F. Schiller,' in *Jahrbuch der deutschen Schillergesellschaft*, XVI (1972), 208–65.

Smoljan, Olga: *F. M. Klinger. Leben und Werk* (transl. from Russian), Weimar, 1962.

Snapper, J.: 'The Solitary Player in Klinger's Early Dramas,' *GR*, XLV (1970), 83–93.

Klopstock

Grimm, Reinhold: 'Marginalien zu Klopstocks *Messias*,' *GRM*, XLII (1961), 274–95.

Hellmuth, Hans-Heinrich: *Metrische Erfindungen und metrische Theorie bei Klopstock*, München, 1973.

Hohler, August E.: *Das Heilige in der Dichtung*, Zürich, 1954. [Zürcher Beiträge zur deutschen Literatur- und Geistesgeschichte no. 10]

Kaiser, Gerhart: *Klopstock. Religion und Dichtung*, Gütersloh, 1963.

Murat, J.: *Klopstock. Les thèmes principaux de son oeuvre*, 1959.

Schneider, Karl Ludwig: *Klopstock und die Erneuerung der deutschen Muttersprache im 18. Jahrhundert*, Heidelberg, 1960.

——— : 'Klopstock: Sein Werk und seine Wirkung,' in *Texte und Kontexte: Studien zur deutschen und vergleichenden Literaturwissenschaft. Festschrift für Norbert Fuerst*, ed. M. Durzak, E. Reichmann, U. Weisstein, Bern, 1973.

Thayer, Terence K.: 'Klopstock's Occasional Poetry,' *LY*, II (1970), 181–212.

Lavater

Atkins, Stuart Pratt: 'J. C. Lavater and Goethe: Problems of Psychology and Theology in *Die Leiden des jungen Werthers*,' *PMLA*, LXIII (1948), 520–76.

Graham, J.: 'Lavater's Physiognomy in England,' *Journal of History of Ideas*, XXII (1961), 561–72.

Guinaudeau, O.: 'Les rapports de Goethe et de Lavater,' *Etudes Germaniques*, IV (1949).

Holl, Oskar: 'Von steifer Halbwürde, horchendem Argwohn und

anderen Physiognomien: Unbekannte Chodowiecki-Figuren aus
Lavaters Sammlung,' *LY*, IV (1972), 7–26.
Huppert, O.: *Humanismus und Christentum; Goethe und Lavater, die
Tragik einer Freundschaft*, Meiringen, Loepthien, 1949.
Radwan, Kamal: *Die Sprache Lavaters im Spiegel der Geistesgeschichte*,
Göppingen, 1972. [Göppinger Arbeiten zur Germanistik no. 75]

Leisewitz

Kühlhorn, Walter: *J. A. Leisewitzens 'Julius von Tarent'*, Halle, 1912,
repr. 1973.
Martini, Fritz: 'Die feindlichen Brüder: Zeum Problem des
gesellschaftskritischen Dramas von J. A. Leisewitz, F. M. Klinger und
F. Schiller,' in *Jahrbuch der deutschen Schillergesellschaft*, XVI
(1972), 208–65.
Menhennet, A.: 'Drama Between Two Stools: Leisewitz's *Julius von
Tarent* and von Gemminingen's *Der deutsche Hausvater*,' *Oxford
German Studies*, VI (1971), 33–49.

Lenz

Blunden, Allan: *J. M. R. Lenz*, in *German Men of Letters*, VI (1972),
207–40.
Girard, René: 'Die Umwertung des Tragischen in Lenzens Dramaturgie,'
in *Dialog: Literatur und Literaturwissenschaft im Zeichen deutsch-
französischer Begegnung. Festgabe für Josef Kunz*, ed. R. Schönhaar,
Berlin, 1973.
Harris, Edward P.: 'Structural Unity in J. M. R. Lenz's *Der Hofmeister*:
A Revaluation,' *Seminar*, VIII (1972), 77–87.
Kindermann, H.: *J. M. R. Lenz und die deutsche Romantik*, Wien und
Leipzig, 1925.
Osborne, John: 'From Pygmalion to Dibutade: Introversion in the Prose
Writings of J. M. R. Lenz,' in *Oxford German Studies*, VIII (1973),
23–46.
Parkes, Ford B.: *Epische Elemente in Jakob Michael Reinhold Lenzens
Drama 'Der Hofmeister'*, Göppingen, 1973. [Göppinger Arbeiten zur
Germanistik]

Lessing

Allison, Henry E.: *Lessing and the Enlightenment: His Philosophy of
Religion and its Relation to Eighteenth-Century Thought*, Ann
Arbor, 1966.
Altmann, Alexander: 'Lessing und Jacobi: Das Gespräch über den

Spinozismus,' *LY*, III (1971), 25–70.

Bauer, Gerhard and Sibylle (eds.): *Gotthold Ephraim Lessing*, Darmstadt, 1968. [Wege der Forschung no. 211]

Briegleb, Klaus: *Lessings Anfänge 1742–1746: Zur Grundlegung kritischer Sprachdemokratie*, Frankfort, 1971.

Brown, Andrew F.: *Gotthold Ephraim Lessing*, New York, 1971. [Twayne Author Series]

Garland, H. B.: *Lessing: The Founder of Modern German Literature*, London, 1937; 3rd edn. 1962.

Heitner, Robert R.: '*Emilia Galotti*: An indictment of Bourgeois Passivity,' *JEGP*, LII (1953), 480–90.

Mann, Otto: *Lessing: Sein und Leistung*, 2nd edn., Hamburg, 1961.

Meyer, Reinhart: '*Hamburgische Dramaturgie' und 'Emilia Galotti': Studie zu einer Methodik des wissenschaftlichen Zitierens entwickelt am Problem des Verhältnisses von Dramentheorie und Trauerspielpraxis bei Lessing*, Frankfort, 1973.

Pelters, Wilm: *Lessings Standort: Sinndeutung der Geschichte als Kern seines Denkens*, Heidelberg, 1972.

Politzer, Heinz: 'Lessings Parabel von den drei Ringen,' *GQ*, XXXI (1958), 161–77.

Ritzel, Wolfgang: *Gotthold Ephraim Lessing*, Stuttgart, Köln, Mainz, 1966.

Rudowski, Victor A.: *Lessing's Aesthetica in Nuce: An Analysis of the May 26, 1769, Letter to Nicolai*, Chapel Hill, 1971. [University of North Carolina Studies in Germanic Languages and Literatures no. 69]

Ryder, Frank, G.: '*Emilia Galotti*,' *GQ*, XLV (1973), 329–47.

Schneider, H. Guthke, Karl S.: *G. E. Lessing*, Stuttgart, 1967; Guthke, Karl S.: *G. E. Lessing*, 2nd edn., Stuttgart, 1973. [Sammlung Metzler no. 65]

Schröder, Jürgen: *Gotthold Ephraim Lessing: Sprache und Drama*, München, 1972.

——— : '*Minna von Barnhelm*: Ästhetische Struktur und "Sprache des Herzens",' *LY*, III (1971), 84–107.

Schultz, H. S.: '*Emilia-Druckvorlage*,' *Modern Philology*, XLVII (1949), 88–97.

Siebert, Donald T., Jr.: 'Laokoon and *Polymetis*: Lessing's Treatment of Joseph Spence,' *LY*, III (1971), 71–83.

Thielicke, Helmut: *Offenbarung, Vernunft und Existenz. Studien zur Religionsphilosophie Lessings*, 4th edn., Gütersloh, 1957.

Wiese, Benno von: *Lessing: Dichtung, Aesthetik, Philosophie. Das wissenschaftliche Weltbild*, Leipzig, 1931.

Wölfel, K. (ed.): *Lessings Leben und Werk in Daten und Bildern*, Frankfurt, 1967.

Lichtenberg

Boyle, Nicholas: *Georg Christoph Lichtenberg*, in *German Men of Letters*, VI (1972), 169–206.

Brinitzer, C.: *Lichtenberg. Die Geschichte eines gescheiten Mannes*, Tübingen, 1956; transl. B. Smith, *A Reasonable Rebel: G. C. Lichtenberg*, New York, 1960.

Gockel, Heinz: *Individualisiertes Sprechen: Lichtenbergs Bemerkungen im Zusammenhang von Erkenntnistheorie und Sprachkritik*, Berlin, 1973. [Quellen und Forschungen zur Sprach-und Kulturgeschichte der Germanischen Völker, N. F. no. 52]

Marshall, Alan: 'Lichtenberg as an Interpreter of Hogarth,' *Publications of the English Goethe Society*, XXXVI (1966), 83–110.

Mautner, Franz: *Lichtenberg. Geschichte seines Geistes*. Berlin, 1968.

Pütz, Peter: 'Lichtenberg und der Pietismus,' in *Deutsche Beiträge zur geistigen Überlieferung*, VII (9172), 110–21.

Liscow

Jacobs, J.: 'Zur Satire der frühen Aufklärung: Rabener und Liscow.' *GRM*, XLIX (1968), 1–13.

Saine, Thomas P.: 'Christian Ludwig Lizcow: The First German Swift,' *LY*, IV (1972), 122–56.

Möser

Bäte, Ludwig: *Justus Möser. Advocatus patriae*, Frankfurt, Bonn, 1961.

Flaherty, Marie G.: 'Justus Möser. Pre-Romantic Literary Historian, Critic, and Theorist,' in *Traditions and Transitions: Studies in Honor of Harold Jantz*, ed. L. Kurth, Wm. McClain, H. Homann, München, 1972, 87–104.

Sheldon, William F.: *The Intellectual Development of Justus Möser. The Growth of a German Patriot*, Osnabrück, 1970.

Nicolai

Sichelschmidt, Gustav: *Friedrich Nicolai: Geschichte seines Lebens*, Herford, 1971.

Pyra and Lange

Hanson, W. P.: 'Lange, Pyra and "Anacreontische Tändeleien",' *GLL*, XVIII (1964/5), 81–90.

Rabener

Jacobs, J.: 'Zur Satire der frühen Aufklärung: Rabener und Liscow,' *GRM*, XLIX (1968), 1–13.

Wyder, Hansuli: *Gottlieb Wilhelm Rabener. Poet, Welt und Realität*, Zürich, 1953.

J. E. Schlegel

Martini, Fritz: 'J. E. Schlegels *Die stumme Schönheit*,' *DU*, XV (1963), 7–32.

May, Kurt.: 'J. E. Schlegels *Canut*,' *Trivium*, VII (1949), 257–85.

Steffen, H.: 'Die Form des Lustspiels bei J. E. Schlegel. Ein Beitrag zur Lustspielform der deutschen Frühaufklärung,' *GRM*, XLII (1961), 413–31.

Wilkinson, Elizabeth: *J. E. Schlegel: A German Pioneer in Aesthetics*, Oxford, 1945; repr. Darmstadt, 1973.

Schnabel

Haas, R.: 'Die Landschaft auf der Insel Felsenburg,' *ZfdA*, XCI (1961), 63–84.

Lamport, F. J.: 'Utopia and "Robinsonade". Schnabel's *Insel Felsenburg* and Bachstorm's *Land der Inquiraner*,' Oxford, 1965. [Oxford German Studies no. 1]

Mayer, H.: 'Schnabels Romane,' in H. M., *Studien zur deutschen Literaturgeschichte*, Berlin, 1954; 2nd edn., 1955.

Steffen, H.: 'J. G. Schnabels *Insel Felsenburg* und ihre form-geschichtliche Einordnung,' *GRM*, XLII (1961), 51–61.

Vosskamp, Wilhelm: 'Theorie und Praxis der literarischen Fiktion in J. G. Schnabels Roman *Die Insel Felsenburg*,' *GRM*, XLIX (1968), 131–52.

Uz

Khaeser, Peter: *Johann Peter Uz. Ein Lebensbild*, Erlangen, 1973.

Weisse

Hurrelmann, Bettina: *Jugendliteratur und Bürgerlichkeit. Soziale Erziehung in der Jugendliteratur der Aufklärung am Beispiel von C. F. Weisses 'Kinderfreund,' 1776–1782*, Paderborn, 1974.

Wieland

Abbée, Derek Maurice van: *C. M. Wieland. A Literary Biography*, London, 1961.

Bäppler, Klaus: *Der philosophische Wieland. Stufen und Prägungen seines Denkens*, Bern, München, 1974.

Boa, Elizabeth: 'Wieland's Musarion and the Rococo Verse Narrative' in *Periods in German Literature*, ed. J. M. Ritchie, II, 23—41.

Craig, Charlotte: 'From Folk Legend to Travesty. An Example of Wieland's Artistic Adaptations,' *GQ*, XLI (1968), 369—76.

Dreger, Johannes-Heinrich: *Wielands 'Geschichte der Abderiten': Eine historisch-kritische Untersuchung*, Göppingen, 1973. [Göppinger Arbeiten zur Germanistik no. 103]

Jacobs, Jürgen: *Wielands Romane*, Bern, 1969.

McCarthy, John: *Fantasy and Reality. An Epistomological Approach to Wieland*, Bern, Frankfurt, 1974.

McNeely, James A.: 'Historical Relativism in Wieland's Concept of the Ideal State,' *MLQ*, XXII (1961), 269—82.

Martini, Fritz: 'Christoph Martin Wieland. Zu seiner Stellung in der deutschen Dichtungsgeschichte im 18. Jahrhundert,' *DU*, VIII, 5 (1956), 87—112.

Miller, Steven R.: *Die Figur des Erzählers in Wielands Romanen*, Göppingen, 1970.

Müller-Solger, Hermann: *Der Dichtertraum. Studien zur Entwicklung der dichterischen Phantasie im Werk Christoph Martin Wielands*, Göppingen, 1970.

Parker, John L.: 'Wieland's *Lady John Gray*, das erste deutsche Blankversdrama,' *GQ*, XXXIV (1961), 409—421.

Preisendanz, Wolfgang: 'Wieland und die Verserzählung des 18. Jahrhunderts,' *GRM*, N. F., XII (1962), 5—47.

Ratz, Alfred E.: 'C. M. Wieland: Toleranz, Kompromiss und Inkonsequenz. Eine kritische Betrachtung,' *DVLG*, XLII (1968), 493—514.

Reichert, Herbert W.: 'The Philosophy of Archytas in Wieland's *Agathon*,' *GR*, XXIV (1949), 8—17.

Seiffert, Hans-Werner: 'Die Idee der Aufklärung bei C. M. Wieland,' *Wissenschaftliche Annalen*, II (1953), 678—689.

Sengle, Friedrich: *Wieland*, Stuttgart, 1949.

Sommer, Cornelius: *Christoph Martin Wieland*, Stuttgart, 1971. [Sammlung Metzler no. 95]

Staiger, Emil: 'Wielands Musarion,' in E. S., *Die Kunst der Interpretation*, Zürich, 1955.

Stamm, Israel S.: 'Wieland and Skeptical Rationalism,' *GR*, XXXIII (1958), 15—29.

Teesing, H. P. H.: 'Wieland als Dichter van het Rococo,' *Neophilologus*, XXX (1946), 166—71.

Weyergraf, Bernd: *Der skeptische Bürger: Wielands Schriften zur französischen Revolution*, Stuttgart, 1972.
Yuill, W. E.: 'Abderitis and Abderitism' in *Essays in German Literature*, ed. F. Norman, (1965), 72–91.

INDEX

Titles are listed under author's name, except that English and French authors are found under their respective countries. 'Latin' and 'Greek' are the entries for authors of antiquity. Page numbers in italic type indicate the more important references.

Abbt, Thomas 135, 137
American War of Independence 95, 118, 163, 168–9
Anacreontic 33, 70, 72, 74–8, 79, 96, 97, 98, 108, 143, 146
Anna Amalia, duchess of Weimar 103
Arnd, Johann 27
Absolutism 22

Bach, Johann Sebastian 44
Baroque 17, 19, 20, 22, 24, 25, 35, 39, 45, 61, 104, 127, 137
Basedow, Johann Bernhard 152
Basel 34
Behrisch, Ernst Wolfgang, 143
Berlin 12, 16, 19, 21, 22, 44, 63, 72, 81, 98, 108, 110–11, 114, 117, 137 (Berlin Academy)
Bern 35, 37, 98
Bernstorff, Count von 95
Biberach 97, 98, 99
Blackall, Eric 77, 96
Blanckenburg, Christian Friedrich, 38, 101; Versuch über den Roman 101
Bodmer, Johann Jacob 15, 35, 41, 50–4, 67, 73, 81, 90, 93–4, 98, 138; Critische Abhandlung von dem Wunderbaren 52; Critische Betrachtungen über die poetischen Gemälde der Dichter 53; Der Noah 54; Die Discourse der Mahlern 15, 51; Die Synd-Flut 54; Jacob und Joseph 54; Jacob und Rachel 54; Noah ein Helden-gedicht 54; Von dem Einfluss und dem Gebrauch der Einbildungskraft 52
Boie, Christian Heinrich 174, 183
Brecht, Bertold 157
Breitinger, Johann Jakob 15, 41, 50–4, 67, 73; Critische Abhandlung von der Natur, den Absichten und dem Gebrauch der Gleichnisse 53; Critische Dichtkunst 52; Die Discourse der Mahlern 15, 51; Von dem Einfluss und dem Gebrauch der Einbildungskraft 52;
'Bremer Beiträger' 66–9, 85, 90; Neue Beiträge zum Vergnügen des Verstandes und Witzes 67
Breslau 115, 117, 123
Brion, Friederike 145
Brockes, Barthold Heinrich 11, 12, 15, 24–9, 32, 34, 38, 50, 54, 72, 78, 80, 81, 82, 111, 116; Der für die Sünden der Welt gemarterte und sterbende Jesu 25; 'Der Goldkäfer' 26; Der Patriot 15, 29, 51; 'Die auf ein starkes Ungewitter erfolgte Stille' 28; Irdisches Vergnügen in Gott 11, 25–8, 32; 'Kirschblüte bei der Nacht' 28; Verdeutschter Bethlemitischer Kindermord 24
Büchner, Georg, 157, 162–3, 166; Lenz 163; Woyzeck 157, 163, 166
Bückeburg (see also Wilhelm, count of Lippe-Schaumburg) 137
Bürger, Gottfried August 174, 176–7; 'Lenore' 176–7; Wunderbare Reisen... Münchhausen 177
'Bürgerliches Trauerspiel' ('bourgeois tragedy', domestic tragedy) 72, 98, 112–13

Canitz, Friedrich Rudolf Ludwig von 78
Catholic, Catholicism 14, 50

Claudius, Matthias 174, *178–80*; 'An-, als ihm die - starb' 179; 'Kriegslied' 179; *Wandsbecker Bote* 178–9
Comedy 43, 46, 57, 61, *64–5, 69–70*, 83, 108, 144, 152, 159, 181
Commedia dell'arte 144
Copenhagen 24, 57, 68, 94–5, 178
Cramer, Johann Andreas 67–8; *Der Nordische Aufseher* 68

Denmark, Danish influences 31, 57, 68, 79, 93, 94–5, 160
Descartes, René 17
Drollinger, Karl Friedrich 34–5

East Prussia 12, 44, 133
Ebert, Johann Arnold 68
England, English influences 14, 31, 41, 47, 50, 51, 52, 68, 78, 81, 91, 96, 101, 111, 112, 114, 133, 181–2; Addison 50, 51, 52, 91; Coffey 71; Fielding 101; Garrick 182; Glover 68, 91; Goldsmith 134; Hume 133, 140; Lillo 112; Locke 16; Milton 29, 50, 54, 91, 133; Moore 113; Percy 177; Pope 29, 41, 91, 112; Richardson 65, 162; Rowe 91, 98; Shadwell 113; Shaftesbury 34, 97; Shakespeare 55, 58, 72, 99, 117, 123, 133, 136, 139, 143, *146– 7*, 155, 157, 159, 170; *The Spectator* 15, 50–1; Spence 117; Swift 85; *The Tatler* 15; Thomson 29, 80, 81; Young 68, 91
Enlightenment *11–22*, 24, 27, 29, 34, 35, 38, 44, 50, 61, 68, 72, 83, 88, 96–7, 111, 123, 126, 127, 137, 160, 178, 181
Erfurt 99, 103
Ernst August, duke of Brunswick 117, 121

Fable 31–2, 42–3, 61–2
France, French influences 16, 21, 22, 24, 32, 41, 46, 47, 51, 55, 58, 68, 78, 81, 84, 90, 96, 103, 114, 117, 136; *Almanach de Muses* 174; Batteux 68; Bayle 84; Boileau 84; Corneille 58; Diderot 81; Mercier 170; *Mercure de France* 103; Montaigne 84, 140; Racine 58; Rousseau 81–2;

Voltaire 21, 133, 140, 160, 169
Francke, August Hermann 11, 16
Frankfort 22, 44, 127, 142, 144, 155, 164, 170
Frederick the Great 19, *21–2*, 71, 76, 79, 80, 90, 117, 137
Frederick William I 19, 21
Fuchs, Gottlieb 68

Gärtner, Karl Christian 67
Gellert, Christian Fürchtegott 12, 35, *60–6*, 69, 85, 126, 132, 143; *Das Band* 62; *Das Leben der schwedischen Gräfin* 62, 65–6; *Das Loos in der Lotterie* 64; 'Der Zeisig' 61; *Die Betschwester* 62–3; *Die zärtlichen Schwestern* 64–5; *Geistliche Oden* 66; *Pro comoedia commovente* 65; *Sylvia* 62, 143
Genius 129, 131, 150, 164
Gerstenberg, Heinrich Wilhelm *155–6*, 174; *Briefe über Merkwürdigkeiten der Literatur* 155; *Ugolino* 155–6
Gessner, Salomon 78, *81–3*, 116; 'Amyntas' 82; *Daphnis* 81; *Der erste Schiffer* 83; *Der Tod Abels* 83
Giessen 164–5
Giseke, Nikolaus Dietrich 68
Gleim, Johann Wilhelm Ludwig 68, *74–8*, 79, 80, 127, 132, 174; *Lieder fur das Volk* 76; *Preussische Kriegslieder von einem Grenadier* 76–7; *Versuch in scherzhaften Liedern* 76; 'Zefir' 76
Gluck, Willibald 104
Goethe, Cornelia 142
Goethe, Johann Wolfgang von 21, 44, 78, 81, 97, 107, 132, *140–55*, 157, 159, 163–5, 172; 'An den Mond' 143–4; 'An Schwager Kronos' 150; *Annette* 143; *Brief des Pastors* 152; *Clavigo* 154; *Der ewige Jude* 153; *Dichtung und Wahrheit* 133–4, 141–2, 153; *Die Laune des Verliebten* 143; *Die Mitschuldigen* 144–5; 'Die Nacht' 143–4; *Faust* 37, 136, 172; *Götter, Helden und Wieland* 104; 'Ganymed' 150; *Götz von Berlichingen* 146–7, 155, 157–8,

164, 183; 'Künstlers Abendlied' 152; 'Künstlers Erde- wallen' 152; 'Künstlers Vergötterung' 152; 'Mahomet' 150; 'Maifest' 145; *Neue Lieder* 143; *Oden an einen Freund* 143; 'Poetische Gedanken über die Höllenfahrt Christi' 142; 'Prometheus' 150; *Rede zum Schäkespearstag* 146; *Satyros oder der vergötterte Waldteufel* 151–2; *Sesenheimer Lieder* (Strassburger Lieder) 128, 145–6; *Stella* 154–5; *Urfaust* 153–4, 169–70; 'Wanderes Sturmlied' 150; *Werther* 88, 131, 134, 138, 146, *147–50*, 153, 183; *Wilhelm Meister* 144

Goeze, Melchior 120–1
Gotter, Friedrich Wilhelm 174
Göttingen 22, 37, 173, 181–2
Göttinger Gelehrten Anzeigen 37
Göttinger Hain 89, 95, 104, 127, 172, *173–80*, 181; *Göttinger Musenalmanach* 174, 176
Gottsched, Johann Christoph 22, *41–7, 50–4*, 55, 57, 60, 66, 67, 68, 69–70, 73, 74, 84, 90, 91, 108, 123, 126, 130, 138; *Beiträge zur Historie der deutschen Sprache* 46; *Der Biedermann* 45; *Der sterbende Cato* 45–6; *Deutsche Schaubühne* 46–7, 58; *Deutsche Sprachkunst* 46–7; *Die vernünftigen Tadlerinnen* 45, 51; *Versuch einer kritischen Dichtkunst vor die Deutschen* 41–3, 52, 55, 64, 67
Gottsched, Luise Adelgunde Victorie 46, 69; *Die Pietisterei im Fischbeinrock* 46
Götz, Johann Nikolaus 74–8; *Die Oden Anakreons in reimlosen Versen* 75
Greek Literature; Aristotle 117–18; Homer 135–6, 146, 149, 175
Gronegk, Johann Friedrich 68
Günther, Johann 24
Gutermann, Sophie (*see* La Roche, Sophie) 97

Hagedorn, Friedrich 25, *29–34*, 38, 50, 61, 67, 72, *74*, 78, 97; 'An die Dichtkunst' 33, 34; 'An die Freude' 30; 'Anacreon' 74;

'Johann der Seifensieder' 31; *Oden und Lieder* 32; *Sammlung neuer Oden* 32; *Sammlung neuer Oden und Lieder* 30; *Versuch einiger Gedichte* 30; *Versuch in poetischen Fabeln* 31
Halle 11, 13, 16, 19, 24, 72, 76
Haller, Albrecht 12, *34–8*, 54, 67, 72, 78, 80, 82, 111, 181; *Alfred, König der Angelsachsen* 37–8; 'Die Alpen' 35; *Fabius und Cato* 37–8; *Tagebuch religiöser Empfindungen* 36–7; *Usong* 37–8; *Versuch Schweizerischer Gedichte* 35; 'Vom Ursprung des Uebels' 36
Hamann, Johann Georg *128–30*, 132, 133–4, 157; *Gedanken über meinen Lebenslauf* 129; *Kreuzzüge eines Philologen* 129; *Sokratische Denkwürdigkeiten* 129
Hamburg 15, 19, 22, 24–5, 29, 30, 31, 44, 50, 95, 117, 120, 178
Hamel Richard 90
Handel, George Frederick 25
Hanover 17, 173
Hebbel, Friedrich 171; *Maria Magdalene* 171
Herder, Caroline 150
Herder, Johann Gottfried 81, 91–2, 97, 116, 128, *132–40*, 150–1, 157, 177; *Älteste Urkunde* 140; *Auch eine Philosophie* 139–40, 160; *Briefwechsel über Ossian* 138; *Das Journal meiner Reise* 136; *Fragmente über die neuere deutsche Literatur* 92, 133–4; *Kritische Wälder* 115, 135; *Shakespeare* 139; *Stimmen der Völker* 139; *Über Thomas Abbts Schriften* 135; *Von der Ähnlichkeit der mittleren englischen und deutschen Literatur* 138
Herrenhuter Brudergemeinde (*see also* Moravian Brethren; Zinzendorf) 11, 144
Hesse-Darmstadt 178; *Hessen-Darmstädtische Landzeitung* 178
Hohenasperg 180
Hölderlin, Friedrich 96
Hölty, Ludwig Christoph Heinrich 174, *175–6*; 'Die Nonne' 176; 'Üb immer Treu und Redlichkeit' 176

Idyl 81–3
Imitation of nature 42–3, 53, 57
Italy, Italian influences 24, 51;
    Boccaccio 122; Dante 156

Jacobi, Friedrich Heinrich 123
Jena 85, 178
Jung- (Stilling), Johann Heinrich
    145

Kant, Immanuel 12, 133
Karl August, prince of Weimar 103,
    140
Karl Eugen, duke of Württemberg
    180
Kipphardt, Heinar 157
Kleist, Ewald von 37, *78–81*, 82,
    90, 114; 'An Wilhelminen' 79–80;
    Cissides und Paches 80; *Der
    Frühling* 80, 90, 114; 'Sehnsucht
    nach Ruhe' 80; *Seneca* 80
Klettenberg, Susanna Katharina von
    144
Klinger, Friedrich Maximilian 156,
    164–9, 172–3; *Das leidende
    Weib* 164, *166*; *Der Weltmann
    und der Dichter* 169; *Die neue
    Arria* 164; *Die Zwillinge* 164, *166*,
    173; *Fausts Leben, Taten und
    Höllenfahrt* 168–9; *Geschichte
    eines Teutschen der neuesten
    Zeit* 169; *Otto* 164; *Simsone
    Grisaldo* 164, 167–8; *Sturm und
    Drang (Wirrwarr)* 165, *168*
Klopstock, Friedrich Gottlieb 37, 54,
    67, 68, 73, 80, 81, *88–96*, 127,
    128, 132, 134, 172, *173–5*; *David*
    95; *Der Messias* 54, 67, 81, 88,
    89–93, 112, 141, 142, 153, 183;
    Der Tod Adams 83, 95; 'Der
    Zürchersee' 93, *94*; *Die deutsche
    Gelehrtenrepublik* 96; *Hermann*
    (trilogy) 95; *Salomo* 95
Klotz, Christian Adolf 135
Knittelvers 151, 153
König, Eva 118
Königsberg 12, 22, 44, 79, 133, 157
Konstantin, prince of Weimar 103
Krüger, Johann Christian 70; *Die
    Candidaten* 70; *Die Geistlichen
    auf dem Lande* 70

La Roche, Sophie (*see* Gutermann,
    Sophie) 97, 99

Lange, Samuel Gotthold *72–3*, 75,
    112; *Thirsis und Damons
    freundschaftliche Lieder* 73
Latin Literature; Horace 106, 135,
    146; Plautus 159
Lavater, Johann Kaspar *131–2*, 152,
    157, 181; *Physiognomische
    Fragmente* 131–2, 152
Leibniz, Gottfried Wilhelm, 13, *17–
    18*, 36, 42, 72, 78, 140; *Essais de
    Theodicee* 18
Leipzig 11, 12, 16, 21, 22, 44, 45, 50,
    55, 56, 57, 62, *66*, 67, 68, 71,
    85, 108, 114, 142–4
Leisewitz, Johann Anton *173*; *Die
    Pfändung* 173; *Julius von Tarent*
    173
Lenz, Jakob Michael Reinhold 128,
    145, *156–63*, 164, 165, 169,
    172; *Anmerkungen übers
    Theater* 159; *Der Engländer* 160;
    Der Hofmeister 157, *158–9*, 160;
    Der neue Menoza 160–1; *Der
    Waldbruder* 163, 165; *Die Freunde
    machen den Philosophen* 160;
    Die Soldaten 157, 158, 160, 161;
    Pandemonium Germanicum 163
Lessing, Gotthold Ephraim 11, 12,
    37, 46, 55, 60, 69–70, 78, 88,
    91–2, 98, 101, *106–23*, 126, 135,
    173; *Beiträge zur Historie und
    Aufnahme des Theaters* 110; *Der
    Freigeist* 110; *Der junge Gelehrte*
    108–9; *Die Juden* 109–10; *Die
    Religion* 91, 111–2; *Ein
    Vademecum* 112; *Emilia Galotti
    118–20*; *Ernst und Falk* 122;
    *Erziehung des Menschengesch-
    lechts* 122–3; *Fragmente eines
    Ungenannten* 120–1; *Hamburgische
    Dramaturgie 117–18*, 120;
    Laokoon 116–17, 135; *Literatur-
    briefe* 98, 114; *Minna von
    Barnhelm* 70, 107, *115–16*, 141,
    143; *Miss Sara Sampson* 112,
    113–14; *Nathan der Weise 121–2*;
    Philotas 114; *Samuel Henzi* 113;
    Vossische Zeitung (Berlinische
    Zeitung) 110–11
Leyden 24, 34
Lichtenberg, Georg Christoph 175,
    181–3; *Ausführliche Erklärung
    der Hogarthschen Kupferstiche*
    183; *Briefe aus England* 183;

Göttingensche Magazin 182;
Göttinger Taschenkalender 182;
Sudelbücher 182–3; *Über die
Physiognomik; Wider die
Physiognomen* 183
Liscow, Christian Ludwig *83–4; Die
Vortrefflichkeit und Notwen-
digkeit der elenden Skribenten* 84;
*Sammlung satirischer und
ernsthafter Schriften* 83–4
London (*see also* England) 31, 129,
181–2
Lutheranism see Orthodoxy

MacPherson, James 138
Mannheim 19
Maria Theresa 22, 90
Martens, Wolfgang 15
Mattheson, Johann 15; *Der
Vernünftler* 15
Mautner, Franz 182
Meissen 44, 108
Mendelssohn, Moses 35, 111, 123,
135
Merck, Johann Heinrich 151;
Frankfurter Gelehrten Anzeigen
151
Middle High German literature 52
Miller, Johann Martin 89; *Siegwart*
89
Moralische Wochenschriften 14–15,
51, 113; *Der Biedermann* 45; *Der
Fremde* 58; *Der Patriot* 15, 29,
51; *Der Teutsche Sokrates* 20;
Der Vernünftler 15; *Der
Zuschauer* 63; *Die Discourse der
Mahlern* 15, 51; *Die vernünftigen
Tadlerinnen* 45, 51
Moravian Brethren (*see also*
Herrenhuter Brüdergemeinde;
Zinzendorf) 11
Moscow 163
Möser, Justus 126–7, *130*, 134;
Osnabrückische Geschichte 130;
Patriotische Phantasien 127, 130
Müller, Friedrich (Maler Muller) 156
171–2; Fausts Leben 172; *Golo
und Genoveva* 172
Mylius, Christlob 110; *Berlinische
Zeitung* (Vossische Zeitung) 110–
11; *Der Naturforscher* 110

Neuber, Friederike Caroline and
Johann 45, 55

Nicolai, Friedrich 12, 20, 21, 40,
111, 113, 114, 135; *Das Leben
und die Meinungen des Herrn
Magister Sebaldus Nothanker* 12,
20
Novel 15, 38, 41

Oeser, Adam Friedrich 143
Opera 20, 22, 42
Opitz, Martin 78
Orthodoxy and orthodox positions
(German Lutheran and Swiss
Reformed) 12, 20, 46, 50, 51,
108, 120, 121
Osnabrück 130
Ossian (*see also* MacPherson) 136,
138, *146*, 149, 176, 183

Peursen, C.A. van 17
Pietism/Pietists (*see also* Francke;
Herrenhuter; Brüdergemeinde;
Moravian Brethren; Spener;
Zinzendorf) *11–13*, 16, 19, 20,
25, 46, 72–3, 88, 97, 113, 128,
129, *131* (impact on *Sturm und
Drang* literature) 132, 133, 144–
5, 152, 154–5, 157
Protestant (*see also* Orthodoxy) 11,
14, 22, 44
Prussia (*see also* East Prussia) 16, 19,
21, 22, 44, 71, 76, 79, 90, 115,
162
Pyra, Jakob Immanuel 72–3, 75,
126; 'Der Tempel der wahren
Dichtkunst' 73; *Erweis, dass die
G*ttsch*dianische Sekte* 73;
*Thirsis und Damons freund-
schaftliche Lieder* 73

Quedlinburg 68, 89

Rabener, Gottlieb Wilhelm 68, 83,
84–5; 'Kleider machen Leute'
84–5; *Sammlung satirischer
Schriften* 84; *Sendschreiben von
der Zuverlässigkeit der Satire* 85;
*Versuch eines deutschen
Wörterbuchs* 85
Ramler, Karl Wilhelm 111, 132
Raspe, Rudolf Erich 177
Rationalism (*see also* Enlightenment)
11, 12, *17*, 88, 126
Riga 133–4, 136, 163
Rilke, Rainer Maria 96

Rococo 32, 33–4, 61, 70, 72, 79, 81–2, 88, 96–7, 98, 99, 105, 142–3

Sachs, Hans 152
St Petersburg 163
Salzmann, Josef Daniel 170
Satire 68, *83–5*, 181
Saxony 71, 76, 108
Schiller, Friedrich von 81, 97, 120, 128, 163, 173, 177, 180; *Die Horen* 163; *Die Räuber* 120, 173, 178
Schlegel, August Wilhelm 97
Schlegel, Johann Adolf 68; *Vom Natürlichen in Schäfergedichten* 68
Schlegel, Johann Elias *54–60*, 66, 68, 69, 78, 95, 126; *Canut 58–60*; *Der Fremde* 58; *Der geschäftige Müssiggänger* 57; *Dido* 56; *Die drei Philosophen* 57; *Die entführte Dose* 56; *Die Langeweile* 58; *Die Pracht zu Landheim* 57; *Die stumme Schönheit* 60; *Die Trojanerinnen* 56; *Gedanken zur Aufnahme des dänischen Theaters* 58; *Herman* 58, 95; *Orest und Pylades* 55–6; *Schreiben an den Herrn N. N. über die Comödie in Versen* 57; *Triumph der guten Frauen* 60; *Vergleichung Shakespears und Gryphs* 58
Schnabel, Johann Gottfried *38–41*; *Der im Irr-Garten der Liebe herumtaumelnde Cavaljer* 40; *Insel Felsenburg* 39–40; *Stollbergische Sammlung neuer und merkwürdiger Weltgeschichte* 39
Schools; Pforta (Saxony) 55, 89; St Afra 108
Schubart, Christian Friedrich Daniel 127, 180; *Die Deutsche Chronik* 180; 'Die Fürstengruft' 180
Schwabe, Johann Joachim 67; *Belustigungen des Verstandes und Witzes* 67
Schweitzer, Anton 104
Sengle, Friedrich 71
Sesenheim 145–6
Seven Years War 20, 71, 76–7, 80, 114
'Singspiel' 70–1, 104
Spener, Philip Jakob 11
Spinoza, Baruch 123
Stolberg, Christian Günther 175
Stolberg, Friedrich Leopold 175
Strasbourg 22, 127, 133–4, 136–7, 145–6, 157, 163, 173
Sturm und Drang, 22, 51, 88, 89, 92, 97, 104–5, 116, 123, *126–40*, 146–55, 155–73 (drama); *Von deutscher Art und Kunst* 130, 138, 139
Sulzer, Johann Georg 111; *Kritische Nachrichten aus dem Reiche der Gelehrsamkeit* 111
Swabia 127
Switzerland, Swiss influences (*see also* Bodmer, Breitinger) 12, 14, 22, 34, 35, 41, 57, 70

Telemann, Georg Philip 25, 29
Textor, Katharina Elizabeth 142
Theatre 15, 19, 45, 69; Berlin 19; Copenhagen 58; Hamburg 19, 51, 117; Leipzig (Neuber troupe) 45, 55, 57, 69; Mannheim 19; Seyler troupe 170; Zurich 51
Theodicy 17, 36, 77
Thieck, Ludwig 97, 157
Thomasius, Christian 11, 12, *16–17*, 19, 24; *Monatsgespräche* 16
Trescho, Sebastian Friedrich 133
Tübingen 34, 97

Universities 16; Erfurt 99; Göttingen 22, 37; Halle 16, 72; Jena 85, 178; Königsberg 79, 133, 157; Leipzig 44, 56, 62, 68, 108
Uz, Johann Peter *74–8*, 98; *Die Oden Anakreons in reimlosen Versen* 75; *Lyrische Gedichte* 77; *Poetische Briefe* 78; *Sieg des Liebesgottes* 78; 'Theodices' 78

Voss, Heinrich Johann 174–5, 178

Wagner, Heinrich Leopold 145, 156, *169–71*, 172; *Die Kindermörderin* 169–71; *Die Reue nach der Tat* 169
Weimar 103, 105, 140, 163
Weisse, Christian Felix 68, *70–2*, 132; *Alter hilft für Thorheit nicht*

70; *Die Befreiung von Theben* 71;
Die Jagd 71; *Eduard II* 71; *Die
Liebe auf dem Lande* 71; *Poeten
nach der Mode* 70; *List über List*
70; *Lottchen am Hofe* 71; *Richard
III* 71
Wetzlar, 146, 148, 151
Wieland, Christoph Martin 11, 12, 88,
96–106, 140, 143, 175;
Agathodämon 106; *Agathon* 96,
100–2; *Alceste* 104; *Comische
Erzahlungen* 100; *Der geprüfte
Abraham* 98; *Der goldene
Spiegel* 103; *Der Teutsche
Merkur* 103, 104; *Die Abderiten*
105; 'Die Natur der Dinge' 97;
Die Wahl des Herkules 104; *Don
Sylvio* 99–100; *Empfindungen
eines Christen* 98; *Erzählungen*
98; *Idris* 102, 104; *Lady Johanna
Gray* 98; *Musarion* 102; *Oberon*
105; *Rosamund* 104; *Socrates
Mainomenos* 103
Wilhelm, count of Lippe-Schaumburg
137
Winckelmann, Johann Joachim 105,
135, 143
Wittenberg 108, 110, 112
Wolfenbüttel 118, 121
Wolff, Christian 11, 13, 16, *18–19*,
42; *Vernünftige Gedanken von
Gott, der Welt und der Seele des
Menschen* 19

Zachariae, Just Friedrich Wilhelm 68,
83, *85*; *Der Renommist* 85
Zernitz, Christian Friedrich 68
Zinzendorf, Count Nikolaus von 11,
13, 20, 128, 144; *Der Teutsche
Sokrates* 20
Zurich 15, 22, 50, 51, 81, 94, 98,
132